New Vistas in Psychology

An Anthropsophical Contribution

Stewart C. Easton

Rudolf Steiner Press
LONDON
1985

ISBN 0 85440 454 6

Rudolf Steiner Press
London

Printed in Great Britain by
Whitstable Litho Ltd., Whitstable, Kent

Contents

Introduction

THIS BOOK was written in its present form for a specific and definite reason. Many introductory books on anthroposophy have been written, including several by the present author. But it is difficult to use any of these, or indeed the books and lectures of Rudolf Steiner himself, to extract the kind of information given in this book, which is intended to help those whose interest it is to give counsel to their fellow men and women and to help them understand their lives. The anthroposophy* that forms the content of the work of Rudolf Steiner is so wide ranging and far reaching that there is scarcely any realm of life or activity to which it has not something pertinent to contribute; and the field of psychology is certainly no exception. What anthroposophy has to say about the invisible worlds of spirit is truly unique in our time, no one else having developed both the necessary ability to perceive in these worlds and then put the knowledge thus acquired into earthly language.

Steiner's spiritual teachings underlie all that is said in this book, making it necessary for readers to lay aside any scepticism and accept as a minimum *the possibility* that what he taught is true. Nevertheless, I have made an effort not to introduce more of this kind of knowledge than is essential for the fullest possible understanding of human life on earth.

*It is surely significant that a recently published encyclopedia (Macmillans Encyclopedia) should have included a brief definition of anthroposophy in which it is described as a 'philosophy propounded by Rudolf Steiner', thus pre-empting for the movement he inaugurated a word that was in occasional use long before he began his work. For this reason we may be able in future to dispense with the inexact translations of the German word *Geisteswissenschaft,* variously rendered as spiritual science and science of the spirit, still to be found in most English anthroposophical works, and simply use the word anthroposophy for the knowledge conveyed to mankind by Steiner.

The first chapter, for example, discusses some of the scientific evidence for the spiritual nature of man, showing why the Darwinian theory of evolution and the materialism that follows from it cannot be true. The second chapter endeavours to show why psychoanalytic theory in particular is inadequate to explain the soul life of human beings, suggesting at the same time how Steiner's teachings can contribute to this understanding.

The book then takes up what may be thought of as the central theme of anthroposophical psychology, the seven-year rhythms in human life. Three chapters are devoted to this subject in order to show how the development of soul and spirit proceeds throughout an entire lifetime. Some modern psychologists have noted how certain human qualities and capacities mature only at certain ages, but most of them confine their study to the years of childhood and adolescence. Anthroposophy has much very precise information to contribute to this subject; the curriculum and educational practices of the Waldorf Schools owe everything to Steiner's insights in just this realm. But it is not so widely known what a significant inner change takes place in all of us at the age of 21 when we 'come of age'. Further changes of a similar nature occur around 27 to 28, and again at 35 when we embark on the second half of our lives. It seems to me that all of us, teachers and parents, psychologists and simply friends need to be aware of the inner changes taking place in those around us (because of the age they have reached), and it is the purpose of these three chapters to outline these changes.

Rudolf Steiner often spoke of the 'human conscience', explaining what it is, when it originated, how it has evolved, and the role it is now required to play in human life. In the process he emphasized how different it is from the 'superego' posited by Freud. Linked necessarily to conscience are our feelings of guilt. These cause such ravages in the human soul that psychologists are constantly called upon for help in overcoming them. Chapter six is devoted to this subject, which, it seems to me, is greatly illuminated by insights drawn from anthroposophy. Lastly, Steiner's teachings on reincarnation and karma, while they do not have any obvious direct relevance to the work of the consultant and counsellor, may be considered as an indispensable background that should always be taken into account when advice is given. This particular topic is virtually inexhaustible, and no attempt is made here to do more than offer a brief sketch of the essentials of Steiner's teachings in so far as they may prove helpful to a counsellor.

The writer is not a professional psychologist, but a former university professor of history. My interest in formal psychology was aroused soon after the last war when I was in contact with a highly gifted Austrian psychologist of the Adlerian school who became one of my best friends. I helped put some of her insights into a book which in effect I wrote for her. A few years later while still in contact with her I wrote the first draft of the present book, but, though she approved of it as far as it went, we decided that my own experience and knowledge were insufficient to warrant making the effort to publish it. Over the years since then that draft has been read by friends and even by professional consultants interested in anthroposophy, some of whom urged me to bring it up to date, using the knowledge of anthroposophy acquired in the last decades, as well as the valuable first hand experience of having known and advised personally many students, some of whose problems I may have helped to solve. The footnotes are mostly for the guidance of the non-specialist; those initialled SC have been added by the editor, otherwise they are by the author.

The limitations of the book, including the failure to discuss more than a few aspects even of Steiner's contributions to the study of human psychology, may be accounted for by my wish to touch only those subjects on which I feel myself to be reasonably well informed. Such as it is, I hope this short book will be found to be of some value, perhaps even introducing Steiner and his work to students of psychology who have hitherto had no knowledge of them.

Before closing this brief introduction I wish to pay tribute to the valuable work done by Simon Crosby on the manuscript of this book. It had always been Simon's intention to publish the book himself, through his own publishing house, but unforeseen circumstances prevented him from doing this, even though the book had already been set in type. Not only are the footnotes signed SC by him, but on almost every page he contributed his editorial expertise as well as his knowledge of the subject. I can truly say that without Simon's dedicated work the book would be greatly inferior to what it now is, and I freely acknowledge the magnitude of this debt.

Kinsale, Republic of Ireland, 1985 STEWART C. EASTON

Chapter One

The gradual undermining of Darwinism

UNTIL very recent times the dominant scientific theory concerning the origin of man held that he has developed from much lower forms of life, each higher form having resulted from chance mutations of the genetic heritage of the lower form. It was of course recognized that most mutations are detrimental and therefore have no survival value. But once in a very long while a beneficial mutation has occurred, and as a result the new organism is able to survive and pass on its new and improved heritage to its offspring. The latter is now better equipped for survival in the struggle for existence, and in due course the earlier less well equipped organisms are eliminated. Through this process there has been a continuous evolution upward, while numerous less successful organisms have died out, even though in some instances they were able to persist for millions of years. According to this theory a purely random element – chance – was ultimately responsible for all evolution, though once the mutant had come into existence the environment into which it inserted itself took over the task of selecting that organism best fitted to survive. The fact that it did survive meant that it was able to pass on its new and improved genes to its successors.

Against this theory (promulgated by Charles Darwin in the nineteenth century and greatly refined by his twentieth century successors) the so-called 'creationists', relying mainly on the accounts given in the Bible – dismissed by most scientists as unscientific and unverifiable myths – could only say that they preferred to believe what the Bible taught. Namely that God had created each species in succession, culminating in man, and there could be no question of attributing either creation or the evolution of man to mere chance. Some who continued to accept the Bible but who did not wish to take a position against the scientific trend of the day were willing to admit that evolution had indeed taken place as the scientists claimed, but that it had been directed by divine powers. They were quite willing to admit even that natural selection and the survival of the fittest, two key Darwinian concepts, had been responsible for evolution in the animal kingdom, and that chance just possibly had even played some part in bringing new species of animals into existence. But they could not bring themselves to believe that man, the crown of the created world, could have arisen from a chance mutation in some lower animal, millions of years ago; nor that he could have acquired his indisputably superior mental and spiritual characteristics by some chance mutations in higher animals in more recent times – thereafter proving so successful in the struggle for existence that his successors survived to dominate the planet, and all forms of life upon it.

So there has been a constant struggle between religion and science for well over a century, and it is scarcely settled, even now, in favour of science, especially not in many parts of the United States where efforts are still being made, sometimes successfully, to prevent the theory of evolution from being taught in state schools. As a result numerous denominational schools refuse to teach it as anything but a not very well founded hypothesis, with a scientific status no better than the biblical teaching. But if the Darwinist and neo-Darwinist schools of thought are still dominant (as they appear to be, especially in English-speaking countries), this is not because the scientific evidence continues to favour them. On the contrary there have been numerous devastating attacks on them from impeccably scientific quarters so that neo-Darwinism is quite clearly on the defensive. Indeed, it is difficult for the layman who studies the evidence provided by biologists (especially those who are engaged in the speciality of morphology), and the paleontologists, to come to any conclusion except that a large part of neo-Darwinian theory is now totally untenable. If the neo-Darwinists who have looked at the evidence have continued to cling to their theories, the main reason seems to be that they simply do not *wish* to believe it, or to draw the conclusions imperatively demanded by it. This is wholly understandable because the conclusions undermine the very foundations of the scientific materialism on which they have been nurtured. This materialism is the predominant dogma of our time, held by the vast majority of intellectuals, especially those who are professionally engaged in some scientific occupation.

Nevertheless it is highly significant that some of the most polemical anti-Darwinians, having examined the evidence with great care, and drawing what seem to be inescapable conclusions from it, are still unwilling to abandon their materialism or to adopt some other theory which would accommodate the operation of non-material factors in evolution, preferring not to venture into that kind of uncharted territory. An outstanding example of this hesitancy is provided by a recent book, the last to be written by the accomplished English writer and scientific thinker, Gordon Rattray Taylor, entitled *The Great Evolution Mystery,* a thoroughly documented work with an extensive bibliography (London: Secker and Warburg, 1983). Although Taylor concedes that natural selection was probably operative in some well known cases, the enormous weight of the evidence he cites makes it impossible to believe in the theory as a whole because it is incapable of explaining the evolutionary changes cited in such abundance in the book. As a result the whole concept of 'chance' mutation simply becomes untenable. Yet Taylor was quite unwilling to go further, to discuss the implications of his findings in the book – though he might have done so if he had lived to write another. He made it clear enough that he had no sympathy with the simplistic notions of the 'creationists', nor could he follow the neo-Lamarckians (believers in the inheritance of acquired characteristics who stress the evolutionary importance of behaviour), although he concedes a few points to them. Apparently remaining a materialist, and unaware of any other theories that could be thought of as scientifically respectable, he preferred, understandably enough, to avoid taking the subject further.

It is impossible here to deal in any detail with the kind of criticisms that have been levelled against the Darwinians. But even laymen raise such questions as why is it that all the planned and directed efforts of scientists using the most modern techniques have thus far been unable to create in their laboratories mutants with any survival value. Artificial mutations have certainly been achieved through radioactivity, but always retrograde ones, while favourable mutations, such as are made use of by stockbreeders and horticulturists, have always been natural ones. How is it that the expected 'missing links' have never been found, the intermediate organisms that *ought* to have existed if the theory had been true? Over 20 years ago Heitler pointed out that in a mutation-bound process it only needed one factor to "come out wrong" for the end result not to work at all. Furthermore, "the probability that all this does come out right by chance is so fantastically small that we would not expect to find a squirrel once in the whole course of evolution of life". Heitler* continued that if an upward mutation were to require a change in *only* 32 links (of the 10,000) in the DNA molecule then "we get odds of a particular arrangement (of) one to a hundred thousand billion". One

*W. Heitler published *Man and Science* in 1963 (Oliver and Boyd); he was then Professor of Theoretical Physics in the University of Zurich. The quotations are taken from pages 64–5 of this very interesting book.

doubts whether the earth itself has been in existence long enough for the necessary mutations to have occurred and survived.

As long ago as 1968 a book entitled *Biologie an der Grenze,* (Freiburg-im-Breisgau; Die Kommenden) appeared; the author, Werner Schupbach, was a biologist steeped in anthroposophy, and he criticised the neo-Darwinian theories from the point of view of anthroposophical biology, making use of much material provided by Rudolf Steiner. Schupbach's book is far from being as comprehensive or up-to-date as Rattray Taylor's, but naturally he made use of as much evidence as existed in 1968. In particular he stressed the evidence for what is called 'pre-adaptation', which was also one of the major concerns of Taylor, and which is quite beyond the possibility of fitting into Darwinian theory.

It would appear that in the course of evolution over millions of years *preparation has always been made in advance* for major mutations, as for example, the development of mammals (more exactly, the development of viviparous animals which give birth to their offspring in a live condition after having matured from embryos carried in the parents' bodies). Now it would appear that more than one solution for this problem was attempted by 'nature', and both solutions have proved effective. For example, kangaroos and all other marsupials have no placenta and carry their young in a pouch; whereas the usual system adopted by the mammifers has been to nourish the embryo through the placenta, while carrying it in the womb. A young kangaroo could not possibly survive if it did not have immediate access to its mother's milk while still in the pouch; because of this it would have been impossible for the marsupial species to have come about in the course of numerous tiny mutations (as postulated by Darwinian theory). The mutations could not in themselves have had any 'survival value'. There are numerous other instances of organs whose rudiments came into existence *before* there could be any possible use for them. Certain fish, for example, acquired lungs for breathing air and limbs for moving about on dry land while they were still aquatic – again they can have had no 'survival value' while their owners were still swimming about in the water. This kind of 'pre-adaptation' (only one of *twelve* serious inadequacies in the Darwinian system tabulated by Taylor pp. 137-138), makes it difficult to escape the conclusion that each evolutionary step was, in some unknown manner, *planned* a long time in advance, in preparation for the time when the actual step forward would be taken. For this reason some biologists – and not only anthroposophical ones – have felt obliged to adopt the hypothesis of some kind of an 'intelligence' at work. This seems easier for them than to accept the theory of the operation of pure chance, even when this chance is supposed to have been operative over at least a billion years. However, it is rather difficult to picture an 'intelligence' that does not belong to some entity possessing intelligence. Many materialistic biologists who are compelled to draw such conclusions as this would be happy indeed if this entity were eventually to be shown to be 'material'. However, it seems somewhat wilful to go on looking for this when all that is really necessary is to accept the notion of what has always been thought of as a 'spiritual' entity acting on the material world. Although such an entity is not perceptible through our mundane senses it is none the less there, it presents itself through its effects on the material; it is one of the many forces whose existence is inferred *because of* the visible effects.

In view of current trends in biology, the teachings of Rudolf Steiner (which form the major theme of this book) may no longer seem so fantastic as when first published in the heyday of materialistic monism, the early part of this century. Before taking these teachings for granted let us examine them. Steiner made revelations about a suprasensible world; these revelations he claimed were based on a direct perception (that could be developed by others if they followed his instructions for attaining it). As a result of his research he had much to say about the evolution of men and animals that can now be seen to be in accord with recent findings of science. His work provides the missing explanation for many of the facts that have been so conscientiously observed. Note that Steiner did not wish to challenge the *facts* as discovered by Darwin, Haeckel and other contemporary evolutionists, nor did he contest the fact of evolution itself. And he betrayed no sympathy for the fundamentalist 'creationists'. But he put forward the startling notion that man existed *before* any of the other forms of life – but in a spiritual form (and therefore not perceptible to the senses), thus necessarily leaving no traces in the fossil record. Although Steiner dealt with such questions on many occasions, there is, as it happens, a very cogent, and humorous, passage in a lecture given in 1909. He is speaking of embryologists:

"They would look, for instance, at a monkey, and doubtless experience the queer sensation that every normal human being would have – a certain sense of embarrassment. The judgement expressed through feeling means that the monkey is really a retarded being, having remained behind in the evolution of man. This feeling is nearer the truth than is the later judgement of the erring mind because it embodies the realization that the monkey is a being that dropped out of the human current, that had to be divided off from man if the latter were to achieve his goal. The moment our fallible mind approached this fact it inverted it: instead of realizing that the monkey was eliminated from the evolutionary human current it concluded that the monkey was the starting point of human descent."★

As will be recognized, Steiner was talking here about the fallible nature of human thinking, especially the thinking of the intellect based on sense perception. This kind of thinking, as we shall be discussing later in the book, is a

★Steiner, R: *The Wisdom of Man, of the Soul, and of the Spirit,* New York, Anthroposophic Press, 1971, pp 55–6.

relatively recent acquisition, which in fact became a possession of man right at the time when he was acquiring just that acuteness of sense perception characteristic of recent centuries that in turn made modern science possible. It is impossible for us to discover through ordinary sense perception, and the thinking that accompanies it, that animals, as Steiner insisted, are descended from man, and not vice versa. But the 'man' from whom they are descended was suprasensible – and 'perceptible' only to suprasensible, clairvoyant vision. According to Steiner not only has man's body evolved in accordance with a kind of predetermined plan (as some modern biologists are being compelled to recognize, whether or not they are willing also to attribute its authorship to divine beings), but his mind and his consciousness have also evolved – partly in order to keep pace with his biological evolution. Although it is not possible for us to discover any major physical difference between ourselves and the ancient Egyptians, Greeks and Romans, our consciousness – according to Steiner – is vastly different from theirs, close though we are to them in time. Even the consciousness of our medieval forebears is subtly different from ours, as the result of a major change that, according to Steiner, occurred in the human brain as recently as the fifteenth century. Though, unhappily, it does not seem likely that it will ever be possible to prove this assertion by means of anatomical evidence, it can scarcely be doubted that modern man has indeed looked at the external world in a manner totally different from his predecessors. But cultural and intellectual historians have seldom if ever found it necessary to *explain* this change which seems to them to be merely a natural consequence of the accumulation of knowledge, plus the need to devise new theories to take account of it. But why did knowledge begin to accumulate so suddenly, in such quantities? If they feel aware of the need for explanation most such historians fall back upon the pseudo-explanation that social life was changing, more people were beginning to live in cities, leisure became more easily available to the classes likely to interest themselves in science, and the like. Heaven forfend that any non-material explanation should be given houseroom in our all-pervading atmosphere of materialism!

According to Steiner the evolution of consciousness is a continuing process, both in the history of mankind, and in the life of all human beings. As consciousness evolved during historical ages of the past, so does the human being evolve ever new capacities in accordance with his own chronological age. Certain capacities he cannot develop until he has reached a certain age, though this fact is little recognized (even by psychologists who readily recognize how capacities develop during the years of childhood). It is one of the purposes of this book to discuss this evolution of consciousness and the capacities that accompany it, and in a later chapter we shall also describe the correlation between the historical periods of the past and the evolution of human consciousness within a single lifetime. Thus if social life changed, if more people began to live in cities, and if leisure became more abundant, the explanation, for Steiner, lay in the evolution of consciousness – as a consequence of which social life necessarily changed. Of course this evolution of consciousness did not take place at any one time, or in any particular place; it has continued over many centuries and indeed, consciousness is still changing today. Obviously if all this is true it has a most important bearing on the study and practice of psychology. The primary purpose of the book, as has been stated in the introduction, is indeed to provide information, derived from anthroposophy, for psychological consultants and counsellors who in all probability are not even aware that it has anything to say on their subject, even if they have vaguely heard of anthroposophy itself, and its founder Rudolf Steiner. But it must be admitted at once that many topics of interest to practising consultants will be omitted or given very slight attention, for the excellent reason that only those subjects on which the author feels that Steiner and anthroposophy have something pertinent to say have been included. For example, no attention will be given to conclusions drawn by some psychologists from the behaviour of rats. From the anthroposophical viewpoint such behaviour has little or no bearing on our understanding of human beings under pressure, analogous though it may appear when regarded from a purely external angle. As anthroposophists hold that man is a being of body, soul and spirit they see no worthwhile conclusions being drawn merely from the study of animal behaviour since the spiritual element in man is not present in animals. What may be called the 'soul' in animals is not influenced by its own individual 'I' since it possesses only a group ego belonging to its species, and, unlike the human 'I', this is not present as a separate entity within the individual animal.*

It will also be taken for granted that mental (or soul) capacities are, contrary to what is widely believed, *not* inherited through the genes. A tremendous amount of investigation has been carried out in the last decades, but it has never been established (and perhaps never can or will be established) that such capacities are transmitted from parents to their descendants, in spite of appearances to the contrary. Even in antiquity philosophers were greatly interested in the question, and asked why it was that great men such as Themistocles or Pericles produced such incapable progeny. There can, of course, be no question but that the colour of eyes and hair and other *physical* characteristics can be predicted within certain well defined limits in the same

*This apparently arbitrary statement will not be elaborated further in this book, which is devoted solely to human psychology. A short description of the contrast between animals and human beings will be found in my comprehensive book on anthroposophy, *Man and World in the Light of Anthroposophy* (Spring Valley, N.Y.: Anthroposophic Press, 1982 – pp 282-285). The bibliography at the end of chapter seven of that book gives further references to works on the subject by Steiner and other anthroposophical investigators.

way as similar characteristics are predictable with virtual certainty in the case of domesticated animals. The science of stockbreeding is indeed dependent on the accuracy of such predictions. But when it comes to predicting human mental and psychical characteristics on the basis of genetic heritage so little success has been obtained that the time may not be far off when researchers will come to the conclusion that they should look elsewhere for explanations of the apparent inheritance of non-physical characteristics by close descendants.

Bearing in mind the demonstrated and unquestioned fact that *physical* characteristics can be inherited, it is entirely reasonable for us to explain the appearance of musical talent in a family such as that of the Bachs by postulating the inheritance of an unusually sensitive ear. Similarly, mathematical talent may well be dependent on the structure of the inner ear, on which the sense of balance depends. It could even be that a particular kind of brain can be inherited. Though it does not necessarily follow that its possessor will think as well as his forebears, at least, in so far as his brain is concerned, he will not be deprived of the possibility of doing so.

But two other factors, one of them universally recognized, the other as yet not recognized at all by practising psychologists, may be far more important than the supposed transmission of talents through heredity. The influence of the environment, the provision of suitable opportunities for the development of one's native talents, is accepted and can scarcely be overestimated. But the particular environment into which a human being is born, and the talents that he possesses to cope with it, are *both,* according to the teachings of anthroposophy, matters of what is loosely called destiny (in anthroposophy, *karma* – a concept that will be developed in considerable detail in the last chapter). This 'destiny' is thought to result from deeds in previous lives. Reincarnation and karma are inextricably linked; once they have been understood and accepted they may in the not so distant future (within the limits currently possible) be taken into account by psychologists and psychological advisers, indeed they will need to be. This will mean that such consultants will never try to explain everything revealed to them by those who consult them in terms of a single life on earth.

However, it is not possible at the present time for any of us to know in detail anything whatever about the previous incarnations, still less the karma, of persons who may consult us. Such a knowledge, Steiner assures us, will be attainable by many in the not so distant future, even in the absence of consciously directed spiritual development. But as of now, to the best of my knowledge, only Steiner himself possessed the faculty of perceiving former incarnations, and the ability to investigate previous lives. Furthermore, he was by all accounts extremely reluctant to say anything at all about the former incarnations of living persons. This was for him a realm into which no one had the right to enter since it is concerned so profoundly with human freedom. Indeed, he regarded it as a wholly improper interference with a person's privacy to say a word about such matters, unless there was some vitally necessary reason for doing so.

Nevertheless it is surely valuable for the psychologist to be aware of the *fact* that the person consulting him has been incarnated before many times and will be reincarnated again in the future even though he knows nothing specific about any of these incarnations. It is surely also a helpful exercise for him to use his imagination, on the basis of what he has learned from anthroposophy, to try to picture the process by which the experiences of one life could have been metamorphosed into the present life pattern of his client – though he will never breathe a word of it to him.*

*But in the very doing of this he may succeed in earning some insights that he could never have obtained by any other means. I have said more on the subject of this kind of thinking, and from several different points of view, in the seventh chapter of my book *Man and World in the Light of Anthroposophy*.

Reincarnation and karma are key concepts in anthroposophy; an understanding of them leads one to see that a deeply significant relationship exists between one life, the next, and subsequent lives. Human beings have all been incarnated before, and they are the architects of their present earthly life, having willed it to be as it is when they were still in the spiritual worlds. Their determination to create this particular kind of framework for their present life resulted in large part from a desire to compensate for deeds performed in the last or earlier lives; but not only from this desire to make compensation. The particular *kind* of challenge presented to us by our environment may also be necessary for us if we are to make our present lives useful and meaningful, enabling us to make further spiritual progress which will bear fruit in subsequent lives.

As we have said, it is impossible for those without a very highly developed clairvoyance to read the past incarnations of anyone else, whether characters in history, or one's friends, enemies, and acquaintances. And least of all it is possible to perceive one's own. In recent years, particularly in the United States, there has been a growing readiness to accept the fact of reincarnation and repeated earth lives. Some psychologists have even been trying to develop techniques for discovering what it was in a previous earth life that created the troubles experienced by their clients in this. A far from negligible number of books have been written on the subject, to which a little attention will be given in chapter seven. Even though a few of them try to show how compensation is sought in the present life for evil done in a former one, none of the writers or investigators appears to have seriously considered Rudolf Steiner's teachings on karma, which are far more subtle and detailed than what they propose. In the last year of his life Steiner gave a large number of lectures on the subject of the karmic relationships of a number of persons whose former lives he had investigated. Although none of this information can, of course, be checked, it is possible for the serious student of anthroposophy to come to a *general* idea of how karma operates (also taking into account the many lectures Steiner gave on the general subject in earlier years). It is worth emphasising again that all that the psychological consultant can do at this stage is to be aware of and take into consideration the fact of earlier lives and the karma that was created during them. And it seems to me that such knowledge must be far more helpful in such work than any supposedly scientific knowledge about the hereditary factors that go to make up the personality of the individual human being who has come to him for help.

The word psychology, though it has been in occasional use for some centuries, has only fairly recently been used to denote a subject for scientific study. The word psychoanalysis was coined by Sigmund Freud as recently as 1896 to denote his own system of treatment for disturbed and neurotic patients. Both words contain as their root the Greek word *psyche,* which to the Greeks meant both life, in some of the senses of that word, and the soul of man as contrasted with his body. Yet curiously enough, many of those who call themselves psychologists, or students of the 'soul', do not even believe in the existence of an entity that may be called a soul, often preferring to speak of a 'mind' when they mean what others would call a soul.

For anthroposophists the word soul presents no difficulty, and they are quite capable of saying what they mean by it. However, they are unlikely ever to speak about the mind, which to them is not a definable entity but rather the activity of thinking, which with feeling and willing is one of the three fundamental attributes characteristic of all human beings, and one which indeed distinguishes them from all other living creatures. Very recently an excellent book on the human soul in all its many aspects, written by a practising Dutch anthroposophical psychologist, has been published for the first time in an English translation: *The*

Anthroposophical Understanding of the Soul, by F.W. Zeylmans van Emmichoven (Spring Valley, N.Y.: Anthroposophic Press, 1982). In this book will be found what anthroposophists mean when they speak about the soul. However, Dr Zeylmans does not discuss what constitutes the subject matter of the present book, namely how anthroposophy can not only contribute to our knowledge of the human being but may also be able to help those who may at some time in their lives be called upon to give advice to others. It is the contention of the present writer that suprasensible knowledge, as Rudolf Steiner once put it in the title of one of his own lectures, is a 'demand of the age', and its practical usefulness in human life needs to be known: this is why this book has been written.

We have no wish to belittle the achievements of the last century during which psychology has become a subject of surpassing interest to a large number of people and has been established as an academic discipline in universities and medical schools. In particular, considerable efforts have been made to understand the subconscious elements in man's make-up which do not readily reveal themselves to ordinary observation. This area was scarcely known at all before the work of the great pioneers, of whom the first and best known was certainly the Viennese doctor Sigmund Freud. Many of Freud's formulations have passed into the common language, and the technique of psychoanalysis that he invented is, with numerous modifications, still used by practitioners, sometimes with at least apparently beneficial results. Perhaps unfortunately, Freud's theories and those of his immediate successors were too often accepted as if they had been true and comprehensive insights, though in fact they could not be anything but woefully incomplete, because he and they did not have access to suprasensible knowledge. Moreover Freud, in spite of his undoubted genius, was seriously handicapped by being unable to escape from the materialistic and mechanistic preconceptions of his time.*

Today it would appear that the Freudian tendencies in psychology are on the wane, and more promising areas for investigation are being opened up, notably in developmental psychology. These newer trends take into account many of the aspects of human life that will be discussed in this book. Nevertheless, it is still worth while beginning our study with a relatively brief discussion of the work of the great pioneers, showing why it is now necessary to move beyond their theories, even though not necessarily abandoning all their practices as they have been developed by their successors over the years. We shall then give an outline of the life and work of Rudolf Steiner, showing why his findings are worthy of our interest and respect. These two subjects will therefore form the content of our second preliminary chapter.

*Of the three main pioneers of psychology – Freud, Adler and Jung – two are determinists. Freud, for example, through his notion of past traumas causing neurotic behaviour; and Adler through his will-to-power as manifested through the inferiority complex. By contrast, Jung sees behaviour as essentially goal-oriented, as endowed with a sense of purpose. Significantly, this is to include the notion of freedom of the individual psyche which, say the Jungians, strives for creative development, wholeness and completion. SC.

Chapter Two

From Freud to Steiner

BEFORE FREUD began his work in the later decades of the nineteenth century very little was known about the subconscious strata of the human soul; little attention was given to dreams, nor was it supposed that they could yield any reliable information about the subconscious. There had been little serious study even of insanity, and almost no treatment was available for the insane. Much fear and superstition lingered on from the days when hysterical women either had been regarded as saints inspired by God or had been burned as witches thought to be possessed by the devil. In later times sick men and women were shut away in asylums, in company with others who were similarly afflicted, thus sparing their sane fellow-men the pain of seeing them at large and having to look after or protect themselves from them. The psychotic, those who had committed crimes of violence for which they could not be held responsible because of their affliction, were confined in maximum security establishments – not so much for cure as for management.

Today a very wide range of drugs is available, and they are widely used, sometimes in conjunction with more or less intelligently applied electric or other forms of shocks; and in extreme cases surgery is used to remove those parts of the brain that are associated with behavioural aberrations. The work that has stemmed in the last hundred years from the pioneer efforts of Freud and his pupils, and the theories of these men (improbable and far-fetched as they sometimes sound) are still far from being totally superseded. One reason for this may be that they are not open to conventional methods of scientific proof or disproof. Furthermore, the whole area of mental and psychical disturbance is extremely difficult to investigate with the tools provided by modern materialistic science. While the physical sciences have progressed by leaps and bounds throughout the same century, the impact of these sciences on psychology has been almost negligible. The new drugs and the new tools and techniques for delicate brain operations have not succeeded in contributing significantly to our *understanding* of mental disturbances, as distinct from our ability to keep human behaviour within the limits found tolerable by society.

Freud himself cannot be thought of as a great scientist, and he was not particularly well versed in the science of his day, much though he admired it. But he was a man of very great intelligence and was genuinely interested in his fellow-men, and certainly he desired to bring his investigations within the framework of the science of his day, which at the time carried as much or even more prestige than it does today. Although he invented psychoanalysis as a technique for helping neurotics, he was never interested as much in his own practical successes and failures with his patients as he was in understanding how they had come to harbour their particular neuroses, and in creating wide and complex theories about how the physically unobservable subconscious operated. In the course of a long lifetime of devoted work he wrote a considerable number of books, revising and adding to his theories as the need arose, even trying to understand historical personalities and events of the past in the light of his theories. In the course of these efforts he often contributed remarkable new insights that were taken up and developed by men of lesser genius than he. And he forced people to think, even though they might disagree with every detail he adduced in support of his insights. Even today there is a curious branch of my own speciality, known as psycho-history, which owes almost everything to him. The insights of psycho-historians, like those of Freud can never be disproved because unlike other scientific theories they are in principle unverifiable through experimentation.

Even while paying tribute to Freud's great intelligence and insight I think we should always be careful to make a sharp distinction between his theories and his practice, while giving him full credit for the actual discoveries he made. The discoveries reached in an empirical manner may be interpreted without the aid of his theories, which often seem indeed to be rather loosely connected with the empirical data. Some of Freud's own pupils even went so far in developing the work of their master as to build different theories based on substantially the same data, and using some of Freud's analytical techniques. While we do not wish to occupy too much space in discussing these theories, it does seem necessary to devote at least a few pages to them, if only to enable the reader to see, and later judge for himself, in what respects the teachings of anthroposophy can correct and amplify them. The material on Freud is drawn mainly from his last published work *An Outline of Psychoanalysis;* this contained in an abbreviated form his main conclusions based on his lifetime of investigations. The book also contains his theories in their final form after many previous versions had been substantially modified or abandoned (including the so-called death wish).

According to Freud there are three elements that go to make up the human 'mind'. There is the '*id*', which 'contains' the instincts – some 'pre-conscious', or on the threshold of consciousness, and some totally unconscious. These latter, however, can be brought up into the pre-conscious, and eventually to the conscious. The second element is the *ego,* the real self that is the bearer of consciousness, whose primary function is self-preservation. Freud calls the ego the eternal striver. The third element is the *superego,* which acts as a kind of tyrant, continually forcing the ego to do unpleasant things for so-called moral reasons, which in themselves have no objective validity. They are, indeed, according to Freud, the sum total of the commands imposed at an early age upon all of us by those who exercise authority over us. The superego therefore reflects the social customs of a particular age, as filtered through the parents who wish to teach their children to live in conformity with them. The ego is therefore squeezed between two 'tyrants': the instincts on the one hand, and the superego on the other. It is thus in a state of constant warfare and finds it difficult to maintain equilibrium.

To use Freud's own words, the ego, as the bearer of consciousness was "developed out of the cortical layer of the id, and has brought under its influence ever larger regions and ever deeper layers of the id". The id itself, whether unconscious or pre-conscious, contains within itself as a primary instinct the *libido* or *eros* (desire) as well as the death wish. Many, perhaps most, psychologists would be ready to follow Freud in accepting the libido, which seeks for pleasure at almost any cost, as man's basic urge. The ego also is permeated, according to Freud, with the "pleasure principle" or the desire for pleasure, however it is forced by life experience to be more cautious and to put curbs on its desires when they are likely to endanger its safety. This accounts for the lifelong struggle between the ego and the id, from which at most only a precarious equilibrium can be attained. The death wish, on the other hand, makes a man unconsciously wish for death, and this contributes to his feeling of helplessness in the face of misfortune, especially when it occurs late in life. Men often unconsciously *wish* to fail in their enterprises, even while at the same time they are with their conscious mind engaging in apparent efforts to achieve their goals.

It seems evident that Freud saw man as a biological organism which has developed a power that it cannot really use and perhaps would be better without. Like other animals this developed human animal has as its main task to fulfil its natural urges and take its appointed place in evolution. But because of those elements in man that make him different from animals he does not seem quite 'fitted to survive' in a cruel world, though he must naturally try to do his best, having, after all, no other choice. There can therefore, in Freud's view, be no 'normal' human being because no one can avoid this struggle that goes on as long as life lasts. Using analogies characteristic of his age, Freud used to speak about 'mobile' and 'bound' energy (corresponding to the unconscious and pre-conscious conditions), and talked about erecting 'dams' to protect men against the overpowerful instincts of the id. Freud does not seem to have room in his scheme for the really controlled expenditure of 'energy' in free creative work, since the energy is at once consumed in the everlasting struggle between ego and id. 'Sublimation' of one instinct is certainly possible and the possibility was fully recognized by Freud. But sublimation cannot be more than a minor victory on a vast front.

After his explanation of how all life is a constant struggle between warring tendencies in the human psyche, Freud then charts the progress of the battle. It may seem more natural for us to think of a human life as influenced by various environmental factors – some constructive and helpful and others not – and the course of the life itself as largely determined by the choice of possibilities that are presented. But Freud does not seem to take very seriously the conscious, or even the unconscious responses to these circumstances – in this differing from most other psychologists. For him they are far less important than what he considered as the determining factor in human biography – the simple fact of being born as a boy or a girl. The girl, not possessing the male organs of generation, unconsciously feels herself inferior without them, while the male is afraid – also unconsciously – that he will lose them at the hands of his father. The enormous complications that occur in the very tenderest years of childhood thus determine the nature of the whole life-struggle, and, in Freud's view, shocks to the psyche at this time can never be fully healed or overcome. The Oedipus complex, desire for the mother and hatred of the father, and the reverse in the case of the girl (Electra complex) are also determining factors in life. Or, as Freud put it succinctly, 'anatomy is destiny'. From its very beginning the unconscious desires of the id are thwarted, parental disapproval constantly reinforcing the superego. The ego is cowed and may be defeated before it has even begun its task of developing consciousness. The major technique of the psychoanalyst is thus indicated. It is the analyst's task to uncover the repressions of the id, bring them first into the pre-conscious and then into the conscious state, so that the patient recognizes how he (or she) has misunderstood the nature of the struggle, and produced a whole lifetime of conscious explanations of his troubles that are simply 'rationalizations'. Therapy should help to dissolve these rationalizations and enable the patient to accept the bitter truth. He should then emerge from the analysis purged and ready to start again after having acquired a self-knowledge that had hitherto been withheld from him because of his false rationalizations.

It will be at once evident how well this theory of human life fits in with the Darwinian concepts of the nineteenth century. Man is an animal who has developed a special power not possessed by other animals, but he has not yet shown himself fit for survival in the struggle for existence. He spends his life trying not to be defeated by his animal characteristics which he has inherited from the not so distant past. In essence he is an animal with delusions of grandeur far beyond his real possibilities for achievement. But at least we are all in the same boat together and should not expect too much from ourselves or from others. This notion is consoling and it is in conformity with our human experience as most of us know it. If it is scarcely in accord with the idea of man as a child of God as held by most religions (and emphasised, incidentally, by Jung), it is certainly in conformity with at least one interpretation of original sin from which man cannot be redeemed except in the hereafter. Almost all religions have been pessimistic about the nature of man and the possibilities open to him of overcoming his heritage while on earth. If Freud was able to point to the fact of being born as boy or girl, with all its sexual implications in later life, as our 'original sin', at least the Bible attributed original sin to the same prehistoric period of time in human history when the first human beings were driven out of the Garden of Eden – after having for the first time, through eating the fruit of the tree of knowledge, discovered they were naked.

Alfred Adler, originally a follower of Freud, later diverged from his master's views in several important aspects.* However, to a large extent he accepted Freud's suggested chain of causation, and was scarcely less of a determinist than he. Adler held that at the moment of birth or soon afterward a child begins to experience a feeling of inferiority, called by him an 'organ inferiority'. This may be connected with the possession by the female of a rudimentary organ of which she may be subconsciously aware, or, more often, it is simply a vague feeling in a child of either sex of being too weak to survive in a hostile world. Such fears may have nothing whatever to do with sex but are based more often on the actual condition of a child that it *is* helpless and dependent on others. The feeling of inferiority thus engendered may persist for many years, or even throughout life. But according to Adler the more common reaction is for the child to register a 'masculine protest', which finds expression in the urge to 'compensate' for his

*Alfred Adler (1870–1937) and Jung both distanced themselves from Freud around 1912. Adler is the founder of Individual Psychology, particularly influential in America. See Adler A: *The Practice and Theory of Individual Psychology*, Kegan Paul, 1929. SC.

inferiority by effective action. Such action could be of two kinds. He may gain satisfaction by self assertion beyond his actual abilities, or he (or perhaps more often she) may obtain his way by exciting pity, lying down to be trodden on, or retreating into a dream world in which he is no longer inferior. The first path Adler calls overcompensation, the second undercompensation. Somewhere between the two is the theoretical 'normal' path of the average human being.

If a child is continually made to feel lonely and unsupported, and if there is a lack of love in his environment, then the initial and inevitable feeling of inferiority will be converted into what Adler was the first to call an 'inferiority complex', a term that, like Freud's Oedipus complex, has passed into the language. This complex, according to Adler, may become a powerful and irrational force working in the subconscious. The child, and later the adult, will struggle to master everyone and everything in the environment, using crude or subtle means according to the nature of the individual and the circumstances. Some of these insights are surely valuable for us all, whether afflicted or not, so common are the symptoms described.

The inferiority complex is a neurosis, and needs treatment; several of Adler's books are devoted to the various methods that can be adopted for the purpose. The important difference between his school (now called Individual Psychology) and the Freudian is that Adler's followers try to uncover the reason why the feeling of inferiority, which in itself is natural, developed into a deep seated complex, and they do not seek only for the sexual reasons for it. For the Adlerians the 'masculine protest', or desire for power, is fundamental, and sex drives are only one of its many manifestations. By contrast Freudians, as a rule, are inclined to view the drive for power as the expression of sexual frustrations.

Though Adler's explanations may cover a greater variety of human behaviour than those of the Freudians, the characteristic determinism of Freud is still visible. The feeling of inferiority is a necessary consequence of being born, but it is not so impossible in after life to overcome a feeling of inferiority as it is to deal with unsuspected sexual desires whose origin lies far back in childhood if not in the womb. Adler concedes that most of us do to some extent succeed in overcoming our feeling of inferiority long before it becomes a 'complex', though it is always possible that some serious frustrations will bring it to the surface again and convert it into a complex. Real frustrations with definite causes can certainly be removed, and Adlerian psychologists make serious efforts in this direction, for which they have often been criticised by Freudians on the ground that they are too rational. They themselves hold that neuroses are rooted in the deeper strata of the subconscious, and little or nothing can be achieved simply through discussion and rational arguments. Since most Freudians are convinced that neuroses have a sexual basis, and sexual repressions may well lie deeper than simply feelings of inferiority which can be freely admitted without undue damage to the psyche, it may be that Freudian therapy is more fitted to deal with sexual neuroses and Adlerian with other kinds. But it is not our purpose here to do more than indicate how these men thought, and it is no part of our intention to pronounce on their respective therapies.

Other psychologists have undoubtedly adopted less mechanical types of causation than the two men discussed here, and some of them have acknowledged the spiritual element in human life much more strongly than they. This was especially true of Carl Jung, who long outlived them and wrote even more voluminously than they. His work is less easy to follow because it is not mechanistic and includes some matters of a spiritual nature. Because of this he has, until relatively recently, been less understood and accepted, either by the public or by other psychologists, than were Freud and his followers. Though Jung came to some conclusions not unlike those of Steiner, his lack of a truly suprasensible perception led him to differ in several crucial respects from him; the two men did not have any great appreciation for one another. It seems to me that when Steiner's theories and perceptions are thoroughly understood and assimilated they can be of much more value in practical life than the many insights of Jung, and it is the main purpose of this book to show how they can in fact be used in practice.

There are many other schools of psychology, some of which get by on a minimum of theory. The Behaviourist school is a strong and important one. It stems originally from the nineteenth century work of Pavlov with rats. But it has now gone far beyond simply the study of the 'conditioned reflex', its initial field of interest. This school is necessarily empirical, thus contrasting strongly with Jung and also with Freud and the Freudians. But it is overtly materialistic in orientation, and attached to the Darwinian and neo-Darwinian theories of evolution. Aside from Developmental Psychology* mentioned earlier many other psychologists have concentrated on the inter-relationships between human beings and the society and groups in which they live. Such work has given rise to a social psychology which can be a source of many fruitful insights†, and help to explain many real problems that can lead to neuroses; and they do much more justice to the great variety of human life and to the frustrations that it is impossible for any of us altogether to avoid.

*Developmental Psychology is best known for its studies of age-related behaviour in children. Its methods are observation, psychometry (testing), and experiment. Developmental Psychology now includes work on the phases of adult development, 'life-span' psychology. SC.

†Wilber has shown that the various schools of psychology address different aspects or levels of personality, and therefore are not necessarily in conflict so much as more or less relevant at each particular level. The levels and therapies are shown in an interesting diagram which also includes religions in Wilber K: *No Boundary*, Routledge & Kegan Paul 1981, especially the first chapter. SC.

It must be obvious to everyone that the structures of western societies, with their emphasis on competitiveness and success in 'the struggle for existence', work great hardship on those human beings who are 'unfortunate' enough to possess personality traits that hinder success in this kind of struggle. As a result many men and women simply *withdraw* from society more or less involuntarily, and shut themselves up with their neuroses. Susceptibility to criticism from others varies greatly in individual cases because of our different personality structures – forced unemployment damages one person's self-respect almost beyond endurance, while others may be able to make a use of the leisure they had not sought and find themselves capable of enjoying it. It is not at all obvious that such cases, and countless others of the same kind, are in need of psychoanalysis. They can indeed sometimes be helped by advice given by trained and sympathetic psychological consultants. And as long as these consultants have a wide experience of life, it seems to me that they could also profit from the insights of Steiner that we shall examine later.

However, it may be conceded at once that something more drastic than simple consultations are necessary in the case of serious neuroses, irrespective of whether psychoanalysis is the best therapy for the purpose. For the most distinctive feature of a neurosis is the compulsive nature of the behaviour. The true neurotic may wish to lead a 'normal' fruitful life such as he sees his fellow men and women lead, but he simply *cannot* do so. Therefore he cannot even follow, except in a very limited degree, advice, even of people he respects, including the psychologist to whom he has turned for help. So it is no use trying to argue with him, and appeal to his reason, or, as it used to be called, his 'better self'. A second characteristic common to all neurotics, according to almost all schools of psychology, is that the neurotic, albeit usually unconsciously, has a consuming hatred of himself. This hatred may be concealed by all kinds of devices suggested by the subconscious. Even though the neurotic may have good and sufficient reasons for hating and despising, or at the very least disapproving of himself, it remains true that his self-hatred is by definition *irrational,* and not a consequence of reasoned objections to his own behaviour, which he could then make conscious efforts to improve. He cannot do this precisely because he *is* a neurotic, afflicted by a neurosis that makes him behave compulsively, and at the same time prevents him from overcoming it by his own unaided efforts.

There may be many reasons why a person may behave in what may seem to his fellow-men to be an abnormal manner. For example, in the society in which we live it is surely understandable that a person might wish to live alone in some desert spot, untroubled by the sick world around him. But such a man may be thought of as a neurotic, in the same way as some writers on psychology may suppose that early Christian hermits chose to escape from their earthly obligations and difficulties because they were neurotics. In fact we are in no position to judge the actions of our forebears, including the often (to us) curious behaviour of religious men and women whose beliefs we may no longer share. Even Christ himself was regarded as a pathological character by some nineteenth century writers. We may be in a slightly better position to judge our contemporaries – who may adhere to fringe political or religious movements – but once more the crucial question is whether or not their behaviour is truly compulsive. If it is not, then appeals may be made to their reason, and the consultant's role may be helpful.

The most terrifying forms of mental illness are the psychoses in some of which the patient cannot restrain himself from committing certain violent acts such as murders or rapes, and may engage in various kinds of sadistic torturing. Such cases are certainly beyond the range of people who can be helped by mere advice; and it is for these that the psychiatrist may seem most justified in prescribing drugs or even surgery to protect society from them. As a rule they also lie outside the range of the psychoanalyst, unless they are treated at an early stage of their illness. A seriously ill psychotic is scarcely able to exercise even a limited degree of freedom of choice in his behaviour; his every thought and action may be determined by his illness. Instead of positively *acting* he can only *react* to every situation. Consciously or unconsciously he finds his condition unbearable. He may fall a victim to fantasies which he sometimes attempts to bring to realization, almost invariably to his own detriment. Common to all such persons is a single-minded concentration on his own needs, and an inability to perceive anyone else except in relation to himself. This in turn makes all social relationships of a positive kind impossible, and those who have had such relationships with them may now have to protect themselves. On the other hand some less seriously ill neurotics often give the appearance of acting normally, and they may even go out of their way to help other people. However, their neurosis becomes visible when, as so often happens, they react violently if their proffered help is refused, and it can be seen how their real preoccupation is only with themselves, and that their pretended interest in other people was primarily, if not wholly, for the purpose of interfering with their lives. This enables them to experience a feeling of power – a very different thing from perceiving and responding to the needs of others for which they may wish quite normally to receive credit and approval.

It is perhaps not very often that such serious neurotics can be helped by the kind of advice that can be given them by consultants with an anthroposophical background. Their efforts will be directed toward helping their patients to act *uncompulsively;* holding out to them the prospect of pursuing freedom as a positive goal. This goal has been at least temporarily abandoned by the neurotic, who in the process of being 'cured' or rather curing himself must learn in the end not only to act uncompulsively but to think critically without being overwhelmed by his emotions. Instead of hating himself he must learn a positive appreciation of and understanding of himself – or, what used to be called in the best sense of the word, self-respect. Of course none of this can be achieved simply by talking with a psychological consultant. But at a certain point when the patient has begun on the upward path he may be given a different orientation by the consultant.

Freud himself was seriously underequipped for this part of the task because of his own determinist views. It is difficult to believe from a study of his writings that he truly believed in the possibility of freedom for man. Nor does he appear to have held any very clear picture of the meaning and purpose of human life. Without this he could hardly be expected to instil positive ideas on the subject into his patients. But when faced with feelings of guilt in his patients he might hope to relieve them of their burden by making it clear that no higher power is going to 'punish' them for their lapses; he could explain how the 'superego' has succeeded in internalizing taboos and laws imposed by society, making them feel guilty when they break them, while at the same time trying to persuade them that the taboos and laws possess no objective validity.

However, Freud would have wished to be judged not so much on the positive advice that he gave to the patients he believed he had cured, or helped, but rather on the technique of psychoanalysis which constituted his therapy. What he wished to do was to encourage his patients to remember those elements in their lives that he thought they were repressing and that were connected with the visible neurosis. In leading his patients back into early childhood, as he almost always found it necessary to do, he was immeasurably helped by analyzing their dreams which expressed in symbolic form various memories and desires that had been consciously forgotten but continued to live on in the subconscious, disturbing their conscious lives so much that they developed a fully fledged neurosis. If the analyst were successful the patient ought to become like a little child, clean and purged. But Freud quite early made the crucial discovery that in the process of regressing to childhood the patient developed a dependency on his analyst, somewhat as a child is dependent on his parents! It became an important and inescapable task of the analyst to release his patient from this dependence – a long process that took up much time, and it was by no means certain that this would lead to a condition in which the patient could truly take up an independent life of his own, without further need for the analyst. Indeed, rather few patients do achieve the necessary independence and it is a notorious fact that large numbers of them have to have recourse to analysis again. The analyst also has to instil into his patients good reasons for *wishing* to live independently – not only ceasing to repress their unhappy memories and their desires of which their 'superego' disapproves, but also trying to accept themselves, guilt and all, so as to march positively on into the future. The analyst can measure his progress by the different quality of his patient's dreams, and see whether he is free from his psychological burdens. But he cannot do more than this without having a more positive outlook on life (such as some of Freud's pupils, for example Erich Fromm, acquired) and without at least some of the spiritual knowledge that Steiner has provided.

Within the limits of their theories Adlerian psychologists have rather more to work upon with their patients, if only because they do not assume, as do the Freudians, that sexual repressions are the basis of almost all neuroses; nor do they in their analyses have to take their patients right back to childhood. Moreover, if they think of a neurosis as being the result of a feeling of inferiority (whether or not it has grown with the years into a real 'inferiority complex') it becomes possible to begin the positive aspect of the treatment at once, from the very first visit. An Adlerian psychologist tries to leave his patient after each session with a 'lift', a new sense of his own importance and value. The irrational 'compensation' posited by Adlerian theory can be shown to be something patients do not really need. They really *are* important in themselves, and do not need to be dependent on other peoples' appreciation. They should accept their own limitations for what they are and try to overcome them in a rational manner, in the process acquiring a new and genuine self-respect. As already mentioned Freudians tend to criticize Adlerians for being excessively rational and for giving too little weight to the subconscious irrational elements in man. They are also said to disregard in too cavalier a manner the evidence for the sexual origin of most neuroses. When the methods and theories of Adler appear to be confirmed by visible 'successes', Freudians may insist that the patients were either not really cured but merely given an ephemeral self-confidence that they will soon lose, or that the neurosis was an exceptionally benign one, or even not really a neurosis at all, and improperly diagnosed as such.

Quarrels and disagreements among the different schools of psychology are, for the most part, beside the point. It is our contention that none of the schools or their practitioners is in a position to effect a true and permanent 'cure' if they are unable to set their patients on a positive path, so that they can see their way clearly into the future and understand the course of their lives and how the problems that beset all of us can now and in the future be handled in a constructive manner. Even if we agree that seriously neurotic patients can be helped by traditional psychologists, psychiatrists and psychoanalysts, and that the worst symptoms of their neuroses can be overcome, this is really only the beginning. When these persons have begun to be able to behave in the kind of relatively rational manner considered as normal in our society, then their real *soul* therapy can begin.

Such a therapy based on anthroposophical insights will surely be brought into being in the future. As yet there have been only a few highly gifted individual practitioners (including especially the Dutch psychologist Zeylmans van Emmichoven, author of the book on the soul referred to in chapter one) who have worked in this area, and their findings have, as far as I know, never been brought together into a body of knowledge capable of being transmitted to others. But I believe no progress can be made in this direction without giving serious attention to the nature of the soul itself and of everything else that, according to anthroposophy, goes to make up man.

Conventionally trained psychologists who lack the insights that can be derived from suprasensible perception necessarily fall short because their knowledge of man has been acquired either by empirical means – observation and perhaps a certain amount of experimentation – or from theories about the nature of man that can never be verified. The notion, for example, of a subconscious realm of the mind that impinges on the consciousness and deeply affects it cannot be anything other than a postulate. Certain peculiarities of the conscious mind that cannot be otherwise explained are attributed to the subconscious, but it is extremely difficult for any of us to visualize, to picture to ourselves, such a subconscious except in spatial terms. Yet, when we think about the matter we know perfectly well that the subconscious cannot exist in space. Although it could be argued that anthroposophical insights rest on an equally unstable foundation, the essential difference is that even if very few of us now possess suprasensible perception, in the course of time the capacity will become widespread, and eventually universal, as it was in the remote past. The ordinary man does not now have to argue about whether anything perceptible to his senses is really there; he takes it for granted that it is. So, if we are to believe Steiner, suprasensible perception will be in the future, whereas such a nebulous concept as the 'subconscious' will, *even in principle,* be for ever unverifiable.

In other words it is certainly quite legitimate to describe, and even to base theories on human behaviour as it presents itself to us. But since we do not really *know* why people behave as they do, we have to struggle along in the dark as soon as we begin to postulate such invisible 'realms' of the 'mind' as the subconscious. Psychology as an empirical and theoretical science must necessarily be limited, and all that can accurately be stated has been derived from the material world. This is scarcely less true also of medicine, which has to make do with observations on how the body appears to function, and how it can be affected by drugs, surgery, physiotherapy and the like. Such theory as exists in medicine usually has to be based on the assumption that the human organism is in essence a kind of living machine, but machines are something we can really understand because it is *we* who manufacture and design them. Some schools of psychology also tend to regard the human being as a machine, as has already been noted; so just as medicine has made some remarkable advances without benefit of much theory, so has psychology. But it would be much more effective if it possessed some truly accurate knowledge of man as a *suprasensible* being. Unhappily, suprasensible knowledge cannot be acquired as easily as earthly knowledge, nor can we invent a machine to acquire it. The machine is necessarily limited by the knowledge we build into it, even the microscope is only a more penetrating and efficient human eye.

To the best of my knowledge no one except Steiner has in recent times explored the field of the human soul by means of suprasensible perception. His findings, in so far as he communicated them to his followers and associates, are so extraordinarily relevant to our understanding of human psychology, and even to the practice of psychotherapy that the rest of this book will be devoted to them. All that I shall say will represent only a very small percentage of what could be drawn from his works. I have not had access to all of these and so the selections I shall make, and the conclusions I shall draw from them are therefore my own responsibility.

Although Steiner's teachings are now fairly well known in much of Europe, especially in Germany, Switzerland and Holland, and though much practical work of all kinds is being done in accordance with indications he gave, there is still a very widespread ignorance of the man and his work in English speaking countries. And when something is known about them a marked prejudice is visible against a man who founded what he called a 'science of spirit' (*Geisteswissenschaft*), and claimed to work out of suprasensible perception. It may be noted here that in most anthroposophical publications the word supersensible is used for this kind of perception. However this kind of perception is 'above' the ordinary perception through the senses (supra = above), whereas the word *super-* sensible ought to mean perception through heightened senses. For this reason the word suprasensible has been used throughout this book. This kind of perception was possible for Steiner because he had developed faculties by means of which he could 'see' into a world that cannot be perceived by either our five ordinary senses (or even by the other seven senses recognized by Steiner – for example the sense of balance, of movement, and the sense for the 'I' of another). The power to perceive non-visible worlds has always been known as clairvoyance, but because everyone today does not possess it, those who do not, deny that it exists – as a blind man might deny the possibility of seeing through the eyes. Steiner tells us in his autobiography that he possessed clairvoyance as a natural gift, but that it needed to be developed so that he could make fully conscious use of it. It was also an exceedingly difficult task for him to find words precise enough to be understood by others. For this reason he did not speak of any of his suprasensible experiences until he was almost forty, having spent his earlier years working mainly in the field of philosophy, earning a doctorate in that subject, and winning a considerable reputation among those who knew him as an original, if unacademic thinker.

It is of course impossible for us to check what he said in so far as it was derived from his suprasensible perception. But it is always possible to use our faculty of rational judgement to decide whether what he said sounds 'reasonable' and in accordance with our actual knowledge and experience: to treat it, in short, as an hypothesis which we can try to substantiate or disprove through experience. It is also not irrelevant that Steiner was fully competent in earthly life, and became a master in several different disciplines and arts. The best advice I can give the reader is to take nothing on trust but to content himself with seeing if Steiner's teachings 'make sense'. He may find profit in seeing what suprasensible perception can contribute to the understanding of realms of human psychology that are closed to the ordinary investigator and therapist, however skilled they may be, and however familiar with the findings of workers in their own field.

Although we shall not be making much use in this book of the technical terms used in anthroposophy, it seems best nevertheless to begin with a description of how the human being appears to suprasensible perception. To this kind of perception man appears as a fourfold being, consisting of physical body, the only one perceptible to our ordinary senses, and three higher 'bodies'*, to which the usual names given in anthroposophy are etheric body, astral body, and ego. The last named is very different from the ego as postulated by Freud, from the word as used in common par-

*The use of the word body here is conventional in Anthroposophy. Those unfamiliar with this use are generally warned that not only is the word body a poor analogue but it is also misleading. There is no precise word for what is understood in anthroposophy by 'body' but some idea of it may be had by analogy with the iceberg, parts of which are not seen. These 'bodies' are our non-material, non-visible components or conformations. They are distinct and have quite different functions, qualities, and properties. SC.

lance. It cannot actually be 'perceived', even by suprasensible perception, in any meaningful sense of the word; but its presence can be recognized and its nature can be described with complete accuracy by the spiritual-scientific investigator. Since it is, in effect, the inviolable core of the individual self it is quite properly hidden from anyone else. It can be experienced only by its possessor who in all languages calls it by the simplest possible word: I, Je, Ich, Yo, Io, etc. Significantly enough no one can use the word to refer to anyone but himself, and a child comes to use the word of himself without ever being taught to do so. Suddenly, usually at about the age of three, he ceases to speak of himself by his given name ("Johnny wants", "Bobby likes") and says "I want" and "I like".

The ego or 'I' of man, according to Steiner, is spiritual in nature, and therefore is not subject to death. Death is marked, in fact, by the withdrawal of the ego, the astral body and the etheric body from the physical body, which thereupon becomes subject to the laws of decay which prevail in nature. Relatively soon after death both the etheric and astral bodies dissolve, leaving the ego alone to pass through the worlds of spirit before in due time reincarnating in a new body. This will be discussed in some detail in later chapters of this book.

It is only the ego that is immortal. The etheric and astral bodies together constitute what we call the human 'soul', which is neither body (the physical element), nor spirit (the I). Hence the human being can also be regarded as a threefold being made up of body, soul, and spirit, as indeed he used to be regarded in the early Christian centuries. The old division of the earthly world into four 'kingdoms' is also based on a correct perception. The mineral kingdom consists of nothing but the physical. Plants have a physical and an etheric body since they are alive; but they lack both the astral body and the 'I'. Animals possess physical, etheric and astral bodies, since they, unlike plants and minerals, are sentient beings. The human kingdom alone possesses an 'I', as well as the other three bodies, and it is precisely this 'I' which sets man apart from the animal.

The mineral kingdom is always lifeless. But plants die when their etheric body withdraws, as do animals and men. When the astral body withdraws from an animal the etheric body remains – the animal falls asleep, but remains alive. Similarly human beings fall asleep when their astral body and ego withdraw into the spiritual world, leaving the etheric body still attached to the physical, and therefore still alive. The astral body, which is the bearer of our feelings and emotions as well as of our waking consciousness acts as a destructive force on our physical body. Hence when it is absent during the night the etheric body which is the bearer of life can have a free hand in building up and restoring the body. The etheric body is also the bearer of our memory*, which, as is almost invariably the case, becomes weaker in old age, when the etheric body no longer possesses the life forces it had in our youth.

These insights of Rudolf Steiner can only be briefly touched upon here, but they hold much importance for the study of the successive phases in human life. A child does not truly develop the capacities of his etheric body until after the age of seven, nor does the astral body develop to the full before puberty. So, as the book progresses, a little more will be learned about these 'invisible' bodies whose existence we shall then take for granted. But it does not seem to be necessary to attempt to describe them or define them further until it has been seen how they act during life. In the next chapter we shall first consider the physical birth of the human individuality in the light of anthroposophy, and follow this with a discussion of the various phases of childhood until the coming of age at twenty-one.

*Interestingly, science is now revealing that it can find no specific part of the physical brain in which memory resides. It remains to be seen what will be made of this. See Pribram K H: *What the Fuss is all About,* in Wilber K: *The Holographic Paradigm, and other Paradoxes,* Routledge & Kegan Paul 1982. SC.

Chapter Three

The seven year life rhythms

From birth to twenty-one

IN THE FIRST chapter mention was made of Steiner's key concept that we are not living on earth for the first time, but have incarnated many times before, and will reincarnate many times in the future. We also spoke briefly of karma: the destiny we have all created in the course of previous lives on earth, and which determines the framework within which we shall live our present lives. Chapter seven will deal in some detail with karma and reincarnation, and how karma is created in the course of many lives and during our sojourn in the spiritual worlds between death and rebirth. We do not wish to anticipate here what will be said in that chapter, except to give a few essential facts drawn from anthroposophy and which have a special bearing on the subject of this present chapter.

It may seem somewhat strange to begin a discussion of life on earth by going back to a period long before conception, but since our individuality existed already in a previous life on earth it would also be arbitrary to neglect what Steiner tells us about how we come to choose our parents, who invariably also are connected with us through our karma and theirs. When we are born we arrive on earth with a heritage from the past, and when we die we shall carry this same heritage with us, modified by our stay on earth. In the spiritual worlds before birth we have (with the aid of higher beings whose knowledge and understanding are infinitely greater than ours) chosen as our parents precisely that couple who *can* give us just what we need – not at all the same thing as what we might have wanted if we had used only our feeble earthly understanding – in order for us to fulfil the particular series of tasks we have chosen for this particular earth life. Our parents in turn have also willed in the spiritual worlds before *their* birth to procreate just those children who are in fact born to them, though it is now possible in our present world to refuse to have them*.

It will be readily understood that bearing children and being born are two *karmic* events, that is to say, they will in almost all cases be in fulfillment of karma from former lives, and will certainly create karma for future lives on earth. A relationship built up in one life necessarily has consequences for later lives, but it is not at all necessary (and indeed is unlikely) that the same relationship will recur in two consecutive lives. So our relationship with our present parents was surely a different one last time, but once we made the choice of them in the spiritual worlds before birth, it is scarcely possible for our earth-bound imaginations to imagine how an almost infinitely large number of small finite events had to coalesce in order to make our birth possible. As far as our own individuality is concerned, during the life between death and rebirth we formed what Steiner calls a 'spirit-germ' ready to descend to birth at the right moment and enter our chosen mother's womb. If all has happened according to what was intended, our father and mother will have been brought together by their own karma (almost certainly from former lives) and will have ripened their relationship to the point where they decided to marry and found a family. The combination of their genes will then provide the incoming child with the physical organism he needs to fulfil his particular life-task. If a child needs to

*As will be discussed briefly later in the book, it may also be true that some children are now being born to parents who are not those originally chosen by the incarnating individualities as those most suitable for them since the opportunity for them to be born was for some reason denied them.

become a musician in order to fulfil his karma he will doubtless choose, as did members of the Bach family, to be born in a family in which the necessary genetic basis for musical talent was present. Therefore he does not *inherit* the talent, but incarnates in a family where the proper *physical* possibilities were provided.

It is at the moment of conception that the spirit-germ descends into the womb of the mother, and from that moment onward it is entirely true to say that a life will be extinguished if there is a miscarriage or an abortion. If an abortion is brought about intentionally, then the purpose of the incarnating individuality would be thwarted – if it is to incarnate at all it will not be to the parents it had chosen; at least unless they change their minds and decide after all to have the child on a subsequent occasion. As the physical body grows in the womb, so the etheric and astral body form themselves between conception and birth. The sex of the child will of course have been determined long before this; it is as well to recognize that the reincarnating individuality is without gender until conception, and it is customary, according to Steiner, for it to alternate between the sexes from incarnation to incarnation. He also tells us that a masculine physical body in a given incarnation will be endowed with a female etheric body, and a female physical body with a masculine etheric body, so that none of us are ever wholly of one sex – a fact that aggressively masculine personalities and feminists should perhaps bear in mind. It is also as well for both to be aware that next time they will incarnate in physical bodies to which they may have an aversion this time.

Clearly the information given in the last paragraph is of great importance, if true, not only for consulting psychologists but also to ministers of all religions who need it if they are to give informed advice. It is no part of my intention here to make pronouncements of a moral nature, but the fact that the intentions not only of several earthly individualities but also of higher beings who guide them are thwarted by an artificial abortion ought at least to be taken into consideration; it is also possible to imagine cases in which the earthly realities of life ought to be given even higher and more prolonged consideration. It is undoubtedly a part of human freedom that we may decide whether or not to have children, and not to regard ourselves as subject to inexorable necessity. It may also be that a clear distinction can be made between contraception and abortion on the basis of this knowledge. But in any event when a birth takes place that has been fully willed, even longed for, to a couple united in bonds of love, a child undoubtedly starts life on a quite different basis from one whose birth may both be unwilled and undesired. And even if the life of a much wanted child is sad or unhappy, even if, indeed, it is made so by the very parents it has chosen, we may conclude only that in the innermost being of the individuality this kind of life had been *desired*. Only through being born to this particular couple could the karma that this individuality chose for itself have been fulfilled.

With birth the child begins on its first life span of seven years. The whole of human life may be divided into these seven year periods; they will be discussed in some detail in the course of this and the next two chapters. Each such period comes to an end at a time when an important biological or spiritual change takes place, or a combination of the two, as at puberty. For example at the end of the first seven year period the change of teeth occurs. Ordinarily this change is not regarded as a particularly crucial turning point. But these teeth, designed to last for a lifetime (and often lasting as long as that among peoples unexposed to the delights of civilized man's food) are the hardest part of the human body, and they require a tremendous concentration of etheric forces to be produced. But as this task is being accomplished these etheric forces become available for use in thinking (which is not truly possible before the age of seven).

During the entire first twenty years of life the human being is engaged in the process of incarnation, of gradually learning to be at home in his earthly organism. For the first seven of these years it is his physical body that he is perfecting; and it is the primary task of the etheric body to make it possible for him in succession to walk, speak and begin to think. If one troubles to think about these three processes they cannot be thought of as anything but extraordinary feats. They are peculiar to man alone, as they are not a part of the make-up of animals. To walk means to rise from the horizontal position of babyhood when a child merely creeps along the floor to the vertical position in which he can and will walk upright to the end of his life. Some animals can briefly raise themselves to an upright position but it is not natural to them and they cannot in any circumstances learn truly to walk like men. To speak means to be able to convey one's feelings, and later one's thoughts, to one's environment, not in formless sounds like those of animals but in the form of articulated words conveying a meaning to others than himself, even if he is meeting the others for the first time in his life. The beginning of thinking occurs when a child feels, quite suddenly, that his real self lives within his body, as was mentioned earlier. It is at this moment that he first says 'I' to himself and ceases to look upon himself as an object in the world like other objects to which he gives names. These three tremendous achievements of early childhood ought always to be causes of wonder to us, so that we may repeat with the Greek poet Sophocles "there are many wonderful things but nothing more wonderful than man", to which he might have added "and nothing even in man is more wonderful than the way a child brings to birth his own specifically human characteristics in a wholly unconscious manner during the first seven years of his life."

It is well known that in the first seven years a child learns almost entirely through imitation; this is especially true of the early part of this period. He imitates gestures in particular, of course. But it is not so fully recognized that he also absorbs from the atmosphere around him all kinds of impressions, which in turn react upon his organism. Above all a child of this age lives in his will. He does not sit and contemplate anything; he does not admire a flower, he goes up to it to put his hands on it and if possible picks it. Pre-school and kindergarten years are therefore best spent in doing and making, and thus learning through doing rather than through instruction of any kind directed to his *understanding*. Likewise one cannot expect a child of this age to obey moral precepts. He will obey commands, but if he is to understand them it will be because he perceives the *practical* consequences of obedience and disobedience, not because of any ethical or moral content in them, however hard one may try to impress this aspect on him. The significance of the stages of child development is now more generally realised by child psychologists and others*, and it is also now more widely accepted that actual harm may be done if a child is encouraged to read too early. The soul forces needed for this do not really mature before about the age of six; especially if a child is taught by the prevailing methods etheric forces are called upon at a time when they are still needed for building the physical organism, and one sure result of teaching an abstraction such as the alphabet will be the stunting of imaginative and artistic capacities.

Such topics can be dealt with only very briefly here, and the interested reader must be referred to Steiner's books on education, almost all of which are fortunately available in English. He himself was instrumental in founding a new form of education, beginning with the first so-called Waldorf School in Stuttgart in 1919, in which he was helped by an extremely gifted group of pioneer teachers, not all of whom had ever previously considered teaching. The success of this form of education can be seen in its spread

*For example, the work of Piaget has prompted an interesting book by J C Pearce: *Magical Child,* Granada, 1979. SC.

to most countries of the western world – there are now nearly three hundred Steiner schools – so that it is now the largest complete private school system in the world. Its success is based on the fact that the education is in accord with Steiner's teachings on the nature of the human being, and pays full attention to the truth that the child is not a small man or small woman and that he matures gradually at a certain pace which in normal children does not greatly vary. Children in Steiner schools are taught according to their age, not according to some adult's idea of their supposed potentialities as measured by such criteria as the now almost discredited IQ test. This kind of education is not directed to the intellect alone, and when it is directed to the intellect in particular, as it is after puberty, this is because at puberty the intellect, with the astral body, is now ready to be nourished – the child is able to think independently – which was not true during the seven to fourteen period.

It may be noted here that as the physical body grows, so also do the soul forces. Therefore, perhaps it will be readily understood why it is impossible for students of the science of spirit to accept any of Freud's notions about sexuality in young children. These and similar ideas held by others are simply the intellectual constructions of adults. No pre-school child ever told Freud or anyone else about what he was experiencing while he made gestures that could be construed (by adults) as sexual because they *seem* similar to those made after the awakening of sexual forces at puberty. Nor did a child explain to Freud what he experienced while innocently exploring and becoming familiar with his own body. Such adult fantasies about penis envy, castration complexes, anal eroticism and the like among young children may be safely dismissed as rubbish, even if the dreams of older children as reported to psychologists may seem to bear out their ideas. Furthermore, it was also simply assumed by Adler that small children suffer from an 'organ inferiority' because such an assumption was needed to bolster his theory about the will to power, the masculine protest and the like. It is not possible to psychoanalyze children of this age, nor could an attempted psychoanalysis be of the slightest use in revealing what the analyst hopes to discover. It is only much older children and adults who supply the material for the analysts' theories. When a young child shows symptoms of what would in an older person be considered a neurosis, it is much safer to work on the assumption that his symptoms are the result of the fact that at one time he was *genuinely* frightened by something that he perceived as a threat to him. Or perhaps he was thrown into confusion by conflicting demands from parents or teachers, or by being punished for something he did not know was forbidden, or by any of the myriad other events that take place in a child's environment.

In short, it is far more profitable to take account of what actually happens to a child through the impact of his environment and the people and places that surround him in childhood and especially how his parents have treated him, than it is to fantasize about his apparent sexual desires and how they were frustrated during childhood. A psychologist who is also a student of anthroposophy will take into account the whole destiny of the child in so far as he can picture it in his imagination and give even some thought as to why the child chose the parents he did for the sake of fulfilling that particular destiny – not excluding even the possibility that he was not born into the family destined originally for him. Of course he will not speak of these things, even to the parents, and least of all to the child in question. But as he ponders the advice he is to give he will use all the imagination of which he is capable to perceive the child in his totality as an individuality striving to develop his talents, learn from life and fulfil his destiny. He will bear in mind, in so far as he can, all those possibilities of which he is aware from his study of anthroposophy, as well as all the details of the particular environment of the child that he can learn from its parents, and from his own direct observation of both child and parents. But he will not waste time and effort in trying to uncover the child's unconscious sexual fantasies and traumas as thought up by Freud and other adults for the purpose of fitting them in to their general theories on the nature and universality of the human libido.

After accomplishing the herculean task of bringing forth his second teeth a child enters a new seven year period that comes to an end with puberty (though the actual physical and visible changes at puberty are not so important as the accompanying soul changes that mark the age of thirteen to fourteen). It cannot be emphasized too strongly that biological growth is necessarily accompanied by the development of soul forces that are not so easily recognized as are the physical changes in his bodily organism. If efforts are made to force a child forward by giving him the kind of work he should not do until later when his soul forces have ripened, various consequences will ensue that are almost always damaging to him, though the effects may not be visible until much later in life. Hence in a Steiner school the age at which various topics are introduced is carefully planned. For example, not until at about the age of eleven to twelve can a child recognize that the mineral is truly different from the plant or animal, because it has no life in it. From this age therefore it becomes possible to teach geology, whereas geology at an earlier age would have no meaning for him, although of course he may collect and admire rocks and stones for their beauty and variety. All through this seven year period the effort is made to teach imaginatively and artistically because such teaching appeals in particular to the etheric body, which is at its strongest during this period – as may be seen by the rarity of serious diseases, and the very low mortality rate for children of this age everywhere (excepting of course accidents). The curriculum of Steiner schools is based upon the soul forces developed by children at particular ages, and these need to be nourished at least as much as the body. Prematurely intellectual education may, and almost always does, weaken other capacities in a child's life of feeling that could have found expression in some form of art. At twelve he is different in essential respects from what he was at nine, not only because he has lived through another three years but because his consciousness has changed in subtle but unmistakable ways. And this applies whether he is (or appears to be) specially gifted or talented or not. Between seven and fourteen the forces contained within his etheric body are being developed, with relatively little interference from the astral body that will take over at puberty – though, especially in our modern age, puberty already casts its shadow over the last years of this period.

Even more important than what is taught in these early years is *how* it is taught, and a special effort is always made to appeal to the life of feeling before that of thought. Indeed, the same subject may often be taught later during adolescence, but it will then be taught so as to appeal to the child's developing power of judgment and understanding. In the years from seven to fourteen ideally it will be the same class teacher who is responsible for the same group of children, thus giving him (or her) the real possibility of developing a feeling relationship with the children. Such class teachers, though they should of course possess whatever knowledge of the subject matter may be necessary for their work, need imagination and artistic talent much more than knowledge as such. Contrary, of course, to what is generally supposed both by parents and teachers, it is never the task of a teacher of children of this age merely to impart knowledge. It is his true task to nurture the soul forces of the children which then find realization in talents and capacities which can be used to the full both in the later years of their education and throughout their subsequent life. After all when a young person applies for entry to a university at the age of eighteen or nineteen it doesn't matter *at what age* he has learned a particular branch of a particular subject. What matters now is what he has acquired and truly learned during the last years of adolescence, building upon the talents he had developed earlier. It is entirely beyond dispute that children who have been educated from the age of seven to fourteen at a Waldorf School are fresher in mind and body, as well as more artistically inclined and ordinarily more developed socially than others of their contemporaries who have been educated elsewhere. They are able to support tremendous programmes of work when in the upper school without tiring; and this more than makes up for the fact that they were not called upon to absorb vast quantities of pure information when they were younger.

Toward the end of the second seven year period of childhood sexual awareness really awakens. The actual age differs in individuals, and particularly in individuals of different ethnic stock. However, aspects of puberty other than the purely sexual do not necessarily, or indeed usually, appear at the same time, more often waiting until the full fourteen years have passed. It is the heightened activity of the astral body which is responsible both for purely sexual development and the new possibilities for intellectual work and the exercise of judgement that arise at this time; this activity is so powerful as to force the etheric body, with its upbuilding forces, into a relatively minor role by comparison with the previous seven year period when it could exercise its activity virtually unhindered.

The experience of these later years of childhood is one of the most crucial in the entire life, as well as being in so many ways the most difficult to live through. The adolescent needs to feel independent and he (or she) resents all kinds of authority and discipline whether exercised by parents or teachers. While it is true that he is for the first time truly able to exercise his (or her) individual judgement it is also true that he may, and probably will, acquire an excessive confidence in it even while he is at the same time struggling with his emotions. These are more powerful than they have ever been and are likely to cause him (or her) much suffering, and will be accompanied by difficult physical changes that are equally disturbing, though in different ways, to adolescents of both sexes. Particularly in the early part of this period there is a great need to love and be loved, but it can well be disastrous if it is thought that only sexual love is of any consequence. It is also possible to develop a love for all nature, for animals and plants and for great heroes in literature as well as in life – even for great ideals. School life should of course be so ordered that the expression of other kinds of love is encouraged, and the understanding of both parents and teachers becomes especially vital during these years. The difficulties of adolescence have been so much observed and studied by psychologists and educators that there is no need to go into them in more detail here, especially since anthroposophy does not have so many new insights to offer that have not already been noted by specialists in this field. However during the last two or three years of adolescence, from, say the age of eighteen to twenty-one, anthroposophy has much to say that is important, since the full significance of 'coming of age' at twenty-one is rarely appreciated by non-anthroposophists, who do not know that the ego of man does not truly incarnate before that age; nor do they understand just what this ego is. So an effort will be made here to explain the nature of this ego and how its approach influences all the last years of adolescence.

Reference has already been made to the crucial moment in a child's life when he suddenly starts to speak of himself as 'I'. He is not taught by his parents to say 'I'. Surely no one has ever heard a parent say to a child, "Now, Johnny, you aren't a baby any more and you shouldn't call yourself Johnny, but say 'I'. Now say 'I' after me. That's right, now you have it". No, the child spontaneously says 'I' and the moment marks an actual change in his *consciousness,* a moment comparable with the moment in the far remote past when man was first endowed with the ego by higher beings, and could also for the first time say 'I' to himself, and, as the Bible puts it so magnificently, he "knew that he was naked". For the first time he could distinguish himself from all other beings in the world, and he surely at once became aware that only he could use the word 'I' of himself.

Although from this moment about the age of three Johnny and Mary will call themselves 'I' and feel themselves to be separate individualities, this does not mean that their 'I' is able so early in life to function as a wholly independent and autonomous entity within the other 'bodies', the etheric, physical and astral bodies, and act, so to speak as their helmsman. This 'I' will live in these bodies and allow their needs to predominate for about eighteen years more before it can truly operate as helmsman, determine the kind of life it will live, plan and take thought for the morrow, and put these plans into execution. Indeed, the human being is not truly 'on his own' until just about his twenty-first birthday, plus or minus a few months. Then he will have 'come of age' as most earlier societies before ours recognized, when at that age they permitted a young man to speak as an autonomous individuality in councils and sometimes, in democratic ones, permitted them also to vote. The Latin word *infans,* the word from which the English infant and the French *enfant* derive, pointed up this absence of the right to speak before twenty-one, and until very recently English law spoke of a young person before that age as an 'infant', and perhaps still does so.

If today most western societies allow eighteen year olds to vote and make their own decisions on such questions as marrying, and if they are proclaimed as 'of age' when they reach their eighteenth birthday, this is primarily because of quite extraneous considerations such as the desire on the part of governments to conscript them as soldiers, which may seem unfair if they do not have any say in the matter through their votes. It is also widely thought that young people today are much more mature than they were in earlier ages. But this is true, if at all, only in subsidiary matters. They may or may not be physically more mature, but it is doubtful indeed if they are more mature in their judgements. When children were put to work at the age of twelve they matured in certain respects very rapidly. But none of these considerations is the important one. It remains true that the ego incarnates at the age of about twenty-one as it has always done. External signs of maturity ought to be disregarded if the young person is to be fully understood as he approaches this age – whether or not one thinks that he should be given the vote or be allowed to marry at eighteen without the consent of his or her parents. Early marriages without consent do not appear to have been an outstanding success in any western society, and relatively few young people even trouble to exercise their right to vote at eighteen when they have been granted it.

Speaking now personally, I may say that I have known many hundreds of university students aged from eighteen to twenty-one, some of them quite closely, and I am convinced that, all appearances to the contrary, no young person I have known has ever truly reached his egohood at an earlier age than just about twenty-one. More careful observation has invariably revealed that the apparent ego of an earlier age was not the true and veritable ego, but a deceptive facsimile functioning in some respects as a true ego, but in other, and much more crucial respects merely masquerading. Of course the nineteen year old would not agree that he does not yet have his ego. Quite the contrary, he is almost sure to affirm with great vehemence and unquestionable sincerity that, whatever the *usual* circumstances, he undoubtedly possesses his ego. But if one then is privileged still to know the same young person a few years later and after the age of twenty-one, scarcely any of them will deny that they have changed; and it is not unusual for them to say that they wonder how they could have accepted the old simulacrum for the genuine article!

In order to develop this theme as it deserves, it now becomes necessary to go a little more deeply into some esoteric material from Steiner which is of the utmost relevance to this subject. According to Steiner, the highest being who takes part in earthly evolution, the Christ, incarnated in a human body almost two thousand years ago at a crucial turning point in earth evolution when it was necessary to give an upward impulse to humanity. It had always been the intention of higher beings that man should eventually take charge of his own future evolution; that he should develop *freedom,* the one quality that divine beings do not know, and in the fullness of time also develop love, which is in essence possible only for a free being.

Nevertheless, according to Steiner's teachings, the first impulse toward human freedom was given in remote antiquity, not by Christ but by a fallen angel who, unlike Christ, does not love man or particularly value him. This was the being known in the western world as Lucifer, the light-bearer. Lucifer is indeed, in a limited sense, the light-bearer, and he bears also other magnificent gifts that he is quite willing to bestow on man. He fills man's astral body with delight in beauty and art, with a rich and wonderful life of feeling, with emotions of all kinds that can be used for good or evil, desires and longings to reach out beyond himself to the world of the stars. Lucifer wants man to be more than human, to experience the heady delight of freedom – as he, Lucifer, understands it – not bound by any moral imperative but anarchically free to follow his desires, those desires that Lucifer himself has bestowed on him. But Lucifer has no access to the true human ego, *which man was not given in the beginning.* We have seen that a child speaks of himself as 'I' from the age of three onward, and as he approaches the age of twenty-one he increasingly feels himself to be an 'I'. But what he actually feels is Lucifer within him, or what we may call his 'Luciferic I'. The true 'I' is divine and not human, and in so far as it was bestowed on man it was bestowed by Christ, who gave man, so to speak, a spark of his own divine ego. Man never possesses his 'I' fully because it retains its link with the divine ego of Christ. But as he develops his free moral life – the only aspect of man that is of interest to divine beings – his own human ego that throughout repeated earth lives is the bearer of his individuality becomes ever more developed – and thus ever a little closer to its source in Christ.

Before the Christ through his life, death, and resurrection, and through the event of Pentecost when the Holy Spirit, sent by him, became active in man, had made possible man's true freedom, men created numerous civilizations. But all were under the leadership and inspiration of Lucifer, for the spirit and impulse of Christ were not yet within man and could not work in him until Christ himself had become man, and in so doing penetrated into the whole of humanity for all ages to come (or, as he himself said "I will be with you until the end of the world ages"). Of all pre-Christian civilizations surely the most comprehensive of all was the Greek, and it was the one most permeated by Lucifer – Lucifer at his best and most inspiring. The Greeks were a people obsessed with beauty in all its forms, and they also taught mankind for the first time to think. How the Greeks could think, how they could even play with thoughts in a way scarcely ever equalled by later humanity – as if thinking were a kind of game! As indeed it was at that time when thinking was in its infancy. No idea was taboo to them, though some ideas might be dangerous to hold in cities run by conservatives, especially if they ran contrary to established ideas of religion. Plato allowed every thought that anyone had ever had to occur either to Socrates or one of his companions. Socrates took them all very seriously, though he might dismiss some of them with a light touch. Read Plato's *Euthydemus,* in particular, in which two Sophists try to convince Socrates of their totally outrageous ideas, while Socrates himself, with a straight face no doubt, pretends they have indeed convinced him. Such a caricature of sophistic thinking surely contained elements of truth in it.

On the other hand consider how utterly ruthless the Greeks could be in dealing with their fellow-men, how mercurial their likes and dislikes were, how lacking in common sense and logic so many of their actions were; although as often as not they might try to defend them by using false and inapplicable logic. The Greeks, in short, with the possible exception of Socrates and one or two others who were precursors of the future, born, as it were, out of due time, had one terrible and ineradicable weakness throughout their history – they could not *discriminate.* Discrimination is a capacity that belongs to the ego, and only to the ego. To the astral body one thing is as good as the other; it does not and cannot discriminate. The Greeks had, indeed, no internalized moral sense, any more than the other leading people of that epoch had. The Hebrews also did not possess an internalized moral sense; their task was to *obey;* and their laws were received from Jehovah through inspired prophets and priests. They obeyed *just as if* they had had a moral sense, but their morality was *imposed upon* them. It had not come to them from within, as it could not. It could not because the true ego had not yet been given to mankind. From the Garden of Eden to the coming of Christ mankind possessed what we may call a Luciferic ego, a false ego that was from beginning to end incapable of overcoming *self*ishness, the cankerworm in the heart of everything that comes from Lucifer – including the greatest of Luciferic civilizations.

By this time we hope that the relevance of this historical interlude has become clear to the patient reader. For we have been describing nothing other than the last years of adolescence before the coming of the true 'I', a time when the young person possesses only a Luciferic 'I', which indeed reaches the highest point of its influence just before it has to yield place to the true 'I'. When such a young person begins to suffer from what is today called an identity crisis, when he ceases to feel himself in charge of his own life and in a very real sense cannot find his 'I', it is often the approach of the true 'I' and the partial expulsion of his Luciferic 'I' that he experiences. He longs for independence but does not know what to do with it and too often yields to the dictates of his astral body, filled as it is with false Luciferic notions and Luciferically inspired desires. It is heartrending to see so often the efforts made by young people to understand things which they do not yet have any possibility of really understanding, for lack of what they will without doubt receive a year or two later. The melancholy and moodiness that used to be known in America as the 'sophomoric blues' (about nineteen to twenty) are part of the same problem. The young person simply doubts the value of life; he will no longer – and rightly – accept authority, nor anything that comes to him on the basis of any authority, however exalted. But probably he will be able to produce hundreds of rationalizations of his attitude and behaviour, often contradicting each other. This is an age that presents the greatest and most insoluble problems for the ordinary consulting psychologist because it is impossible truly to 'cure' any of the symptoms, and very little can be done to alleviate them. In fact the only thing to be done is to offer support and wait for the phase to pass, meanwhile trying to prevent anything truly disastrous and irremediable from happening. Perhaps the watchword for the consultant at this moment is to indulge in 'masterly inactivity'. For there is hope, indeed a virtual certainty, that the phase really *will* pass.

At the age of twenty-one a young person truly 'comes of age'. In earlier times young men, with few exceptions, were then expected to launch themselves on their career, and large numbers of young women were already married, and had perhaps started to bear children. Biological maturity had been reached; the organism had ceased to grow, and all biological capacities were active and functioning. In our western civilization, and particularly in the United States, young persons of this age are far from ready to launch out into the world, even though forced to do so by economic necessity. Most college seniors, and a large proportion of juniors will already have passed their 'coming of age' before they graduate, and their work will in most cases be clearly marked by the fact that they have passed this milestone. Nevertheless their continued financial dependence may present problems, as do all other forms of dependence after twenty-one. In particular the young person should be encouraged to spend at least part of his life at this time in independent work since, among other things, he should also be making every effort to think as independently as possible and not rely on others, or be motivated exclusively through feeling.

It may be noted here, to conclude this chapter, that Steiner drew attention to a very important historical fact – in earlier civilizations the age of maturity occurred much later in life than it now does. But, as he also explained, this does not mean that young people remained dependent for a longer period than they do now. The contrary was true. What he meant by maturity was that men reached biological maturity later, and *with it* a kind of psychological maturity. *Through no effort of his own* man's soul capacities continued to develop and evolve until relatively late in life, whereas now, at a relatively early age, man has to develop his soul capacities by his own efforts. From that time onward he will not grow any wiser simply by becoming older, as he used to do in earlier civilizations – hence the respect paid in them to elders who acquired a certain wisdom without having to work for it. A person's life experiences in our present age are not necessarily absorbed and digested, *used* fruitfully for spiritual growth. They may simply *occur,* and no great effort may be made to understand and profit from them. But today it is necessary for us to make serious efforts to understand our lives. We are unlikely to receive any help from spiritual beings if we do not open ourselves to such a possibility through inner work. By contrast, in earlier civilizations spiritual beings poured wisdom into men, and all they had to do was be receptive to it.

In our time men have to take their own self-development in hand or they will simply not develop at all. The age beyond which men cannot progress if they do not make the effort has now fallen to between twenty-six and twenty-seven, whereas even for the Greeks it still fell as late as the early thirties. Thus if man is to continue to mature and bring fully to birth those soul capacities to which we give the name of the intellectual soul and the consciousness soul, to be dealt with in the next chapter, he cannot rely on divine beings, consciously or unconsciously, to do the work for him. But it will still, for a long time to come, be the divine beings who breathe the ego into him at the age of twenty-one, and for this, as already indicated, he has only to wait. He does not need to exercise a conscious and controlled effort to bring this process about, any more than he has to induce puberty by his own efforts. And unless he suffers from some abnormality, perhaps as a result of his personal karma (this will be discussed in a later chapter) he will at more or less the proper time receive his ego. Far off in the future perhaps it will be necessary for man to make an effort to reach his personal ego, and it will not come of itself. But by that time our consciousness also will have changed, so that it is idle for us to indulge in any speculation as to the means which man will use in those times to bring his ego to birth. For now it is enough that it will come, and when it comes it should be welcomed.

Chapter Four

The seven-year life rhythms

Twenty-one to thirty-five, the development of the human soul

IN AN EARLIER chapter we spoke of the human being as threefold: made up of body, soul, and spirit. In the first twenty-one years of life the body completes its growth, the next twenty-one years from ages twenty-one to forty-two are occupied with the development of the soul, while after the age of forty-two the spirit ought to shine into the now developed soul from higher worlds, making a true spiritual unfolding possible. Only in this way can a human being work for the benefit of mankind, leaving his selfish and egotistic impulses behind and no longer working for himself – not even for his own development, which will come as an incidental result of what he achieves for humanity. From twenty-one onward the ego is at work and should unceasingly win mastery over those impulses that could not be effectively controlled during the period before the ego had fully incarnated and that may still be active in the astral body. But the later epochs of life will be fruitful only if during this middle period from twenty-one to forty-two the soul has been truly developed, in the same way that the body should have been brought to full strength in the years up to twenty-one.

In his early book *Theosophy* (1904) Steiner explained at considerable length a most important concept which is entirely original with him. Human soul development, he tells us, passes in the early years of manhood through three distinct phases, as the ego assumes an ever firmer control over the individuality. The ego works first within the life of feeling, and Steiner calls this the period of the 'sentient soul', then within the life of thinking the 'intellectual soul' (a soul to which he also gave other names, as we shall see), and lastly through the life of willing 'the consciousness soul'. Thus three soul capacities are developed successively, first feeling, then thinking, and, in the consciousness soul, the willing. This chapter will be devoted to the first two of these phases of soul development, and an attempt will be made to show how they are to be differentiated one from the other, and the kind of experiences that should be expected if the development proceeds in a relatively normal manner, as well as the kind of trials and tests that are usually encountered on the way. Obviously this kind of knowledge, if true, is vital for the consulting psychologist to have; and though many psychologists have discovered some aspects of these phases, their writings, which are necessarily empirical, do not as yet form a coherent body of knowledge for lack of this particular kind of theoretical framework provided by Steiner.

The years twenty-one to forty-two are of crucial importance in forming the *character,* and how the second half of life can be lived depends on how the experiences of these years have been assimilated, learned from, and metamorphosed into new and usable faculties of soul and spirit. The body, by contrast, has ceased its growth and no aid can be sought from it. The physical body must necessarily degenerate through the remainder of life, though it too will grow more mature and formed during these middle years. Better use can be made of it by the soul and spirit as long as its necessary degeneration is recognized and accepted, and it is not forced to do what is no longer within its power. The etheric forces are constantly engaged in an ever more difficult process of rebuilding in sleep what is destroyed by the astral forces in the waking life, and nothing is left over for other purposes. Least of all is it safe to waste these forces wantonly by acting in later life as if one were in the early years of the sentient soul.

These first years after twenty-one are a period during which the newly born ego delights in its heritage, its new capacity to guide and direct the feeling life, to enjoy a kind of springtime without the melancholy and uncertainty of the years of late adolescence. This is the time when for most people the senses are at their liveliest, and everything can be directly experienced with the greatest intensity – an intensity to be distinguished sharply from the kind of intensity made possible by mental maturity, which will come at a later stage of life. The period from twenty-one to about twenty-seven is a period when there may be much falling in and out of love, more serious love affairs than in adolescence; marriages contracted in these years may well last longer than those contracted during adolescence. There is perhaps nothing more conducive to the life long happiness of a married couple than to have experienced the love of the sentient soul together, then passing together into the different kind of love of the intellectual and consciousness souls, both growing together and neither leaving the other behind in soul development. In this period also mistakes can be made in the choice of a partner which can still be rectified without life long damage. If 'wild oats' are to be sown this is the period for them. This is surely also the best time of all for the first children to be born – always provided the right choice has been made and there was truly a karmic connection between the two young persons that *required* that they should be married, and that was unconsciously recognized by both (as will be discussed in more detail in the later chapter on karma).

But above all there should never be any assumption that there will be an eternal springtime, nor that it is possible to recreate a springtime when the time has passed. There is a special danger in our civilization which so much admires and caters to youth that older persons, even those not at all old but well beyond the twenty-one to twenty-seven period, should try to appear and behave as if they were still in the epoch of the sentient soul when they in fact are older and now have other tasks to perform. If perhaps they have never truly enjoyed their youth and lived out the twenty-one to twenty-seven period to the full, they try to pretend, both to themselves and to others, that they are young because they are 'as young as they feel'. Those who have loved deeply during this period but for some reason, often a karmic one, were unable to form a potentially lifelong attachment, may well feel that the kind of experience they had during this period of their life is the only kind of experience that is possible for them. They may try with all their might to *renew* that experience of the past with another person, and expect it to be the same or even better. But they are deceived. Other new experiences are entirely possible, even 'better' ones, but they will be of a different nature because they are older. Yet they may well at the same time *not* be more mature – just because they are older. Their soul may not have matured while their body was growing older because, as was explained at the end of the last chapter, in our epoch of time it is necessary for the ego after the age of twenty-seven to make the effort to *achieve* maturity, not to expect that it will come of its own accord. Higher powers, especially that being (who until recent centuries was always known to exist) called by tradition our personal guardian angel, is ready to help, but he will do nothing if he is not asked. It is we who must take the first step. *We* must do the work necessary before he can contribute his aid.

By the time we reach the age of twenty-seven the guardian angel and other higher beings who are concerned with us will have completed such work as they had to do for us without being called upon by us. From this age onward *we are in charge*, and this fact we must recognize in the depths of our being. It is for us to transform what we have hitherto simply received, so that after forty-two we can use our developed soul forces for the good of humanity. It was for this task that human beings were first created by higher beings, so that we could form the tenth hierarchy, the hierarchy of freedom and love.

The above considerations may explain why the sentient soul period is likely to end in a crisis, which may not be recognized as such, even in retrospect, because we have simply slept through it. But, whether or not it is recognized, some crucial change is seldom if ever altogether missing from a normal life just about the age of twenty-seven to twenty-eight. It is brought on by what is, usually but not always, a subconscious feeling that one truly is on one's own, and that one probably has many decades of life still to be lived without the forces of youth which have hitherto been so much enjoyed. It is likely to be accompanied by a desire to know more about life than one has yet learned. Life may suddenly have ceased to be meaningful and one may now begin, perhaps for the first time, to wonder seriously whether there is any purpose in it, whether one's career really contains enough in it for one to be willing to continue with it for the rest of one's life. The intellectual soul period is especially characterized by the search for truth – as the sentient soul was preoccupied with beauty and the consciousness soul will be with goodness – and it is this search that causes the young person of twenty-seven to twenty-eight to feel faintly uncomfortable, or even disgusted by the kind of life he has lived hitherto that begins now to seem a little empty. He is therefore especially open to new ideas that purport to tell him about the true meaning and purpose of life, not only his own life, but all life and even the world itself. It is therefore no accident that so many people who find their way to anthroposophy do so at this age because it answers the deepest needs of the soul at this particular age.

Steiner once said, while speaking of the transition to the age of the intellectual soul, that those men and women are especially fortunate who are permitted, if their karma has prepared them for it, to meet someone who will speak directly to their mind and soul and tell them just what they need to know at this time, even though they may never have formulated their need, even to themselves*. As a result the transition is greatly eased, and they can take up the tasks of the intellectual soul without even soul-searching, and certainly without any serious crisis. At the other end of the scale there are other young people who are, so to speak, *forced* into an awareness they might otherwise never have experienced, through having to undergo a serious illness, which may even have endangered their lives. This too may have been a blessing in a very unpleasant disguise – if they profit from it to begin their search for truth.

Many of us go through some lesser experience, or begin – apparently spontaneously – to ask questions. If these questions meet with answers that satisfy us, then we may enter upon a new path of which we do not know the end. This process can be quite painless, if we are truly ready – or very painful if we find ourselves compelled to give up ideas we have long cherished or to perform deeds that we formerly regarded as repugnant. Perhaps many more young people who are in truth ready to embark on such a new journey fail to hear the quiet voice of their angel at this time, or sleep through whatever experience comes to meet them. They will of course have many more opportunities offered to them later in life, but it may be more difficult to catch up then to the point they ought to have reached before. Some who have slept or not listened wilfully continue to live within the sentient soul, and perhaps remain within it, their development arrested, for the remainder of their lives.

It is not at all unusual to meet quite elderly persons who think and feel in a manner scarcely any different from a person in his twenties. They will repeat the latest theory

*An anthroposophically trained consultant can sometimes give some crucially important advice at this time.

heard on radio or television as if it were their own opinion because they never truly learned to think for themselves, or have never exercised their independent judgement – because, in fact, they never did consciously pass through their intellectual soul period. They may still be able to enjoy, in a passive kind of way, entertainment directed to the sentient soul and amuse themselves (or comfort themselves) with the pretence that they have remained 'young in heart'. Unhappily they are not only failing to move forward and failing to develop further, they are obeying the inexorable law that in life there can be no standing still – they are slowly regressing, but do not even feel the need for a psychoanalyst or psychologist to help them. Being fast asleep in their souls, not even the best members of the profession could awaken them; but they will not be called upon to do so. They are more than content with their slumber – though they may be an almost unbearable burden to their hard-pressed and long suffering family who scarcely know what to do with, and for, them.

Thus far we have spoken of this new period as that of the intellectual soul, but this adjective stresses only one aspect of the soul, and perhaps not its most important one. Steiner used several different German words to describe and characterize it, and all of them add something to our appreciation of it. A second word is the 'understanding' soul, more commonly used in French, where this soul is ordinarily known as *l'âme d'entendement.* Another word in use is the 'responsive' soul which stresses yet another aspect. The most beautifully exact German word used for it is the *gemütseele,* the *gemüt* itself being totally untranslatable into English, which can give only approximate characterizations that are scarcely exact equivalents. The activity of the *gemüt* is a kind of combination of thinking and feeling, a kind of warm thinking, far different from what we usually mean by intellectual thinking, which to us is primarily a mental activity not necessarily warmed by the thinking of the heart, as the *gemüt* is. So though we shall follow the usual English practice here and call it the intellectual soul, all the meanings just given should be used in any concept we try to create for ourselves. For the same reason we cannot say that this soul simply searches for the truth, as the sentient soul was preoccupied with beauty, and the consciousness soul with goodness. The truth for which this soul searches is not scientific truth, the search for which properly belongs within the epoch of the consciousness soul. It seeks rather for truth that it can apprehend by both heart and mind at the same time – the kind of truth that may be perceived in a flash of intuition, not discovered through trial and error or by experiment.

It was mentioned in an earlier chapter how the development of the individual mirrors the development of civilizations. But since humanity as a whole is still only in the first third of the consciousness soul epoch, we cannot find a parallel between civilizations and the individual beyond the age of thirty-eight. Yet it remains instructive to consider the historical ages when the sentient and intellectual souls were developed by the leading peoples of humanity and see how the characteristics of these civilizations are indeed mirrored in the individual. It was during the epoch called by anthroposophy the third post-Atlantean (circa 3100–747 BC) that the sentient soul came to birth and found expression in the Egyptian and Mesopotamian civilizations. In those epochs there was as yet no true thinking, certainly no speculative thought of the kind developed later by the Greeks*. Instead there were great and beautiful symbols and rituals that appealed only to the feeling, but could in a certain sense be understood by the heart, which conveyed its meaning to the participant at a profound level of the subconscious. When in a great ceremony a Sumerian king moulded the first brick for a temple, all the people, who had been ritually purified

*For more on this see Easton, SC: *Man and World in the Light of Anthroposophy*, 1975 p 39ff.

for weeks prior to the ceremony, rejoiced at the perfection of the moulding, then some understanding of man's relationship to the gods was surely conveyed, just as surely as by the symbolism of the Egyptian pyramid and temple, and by the ceremony of the coronation (which could only take place at the time of the rising of the Nile).

In the historical epoch that followed the great civilizations of Greece, Rome and the mediaeval west (this age began with the founding of Rome in 747 BC and ended with the mission of Joan of Arc, born 1413) for the first time the intellectual soul developed. The most important cultural leaders of Greece – not the ordinary mortals of whom we spoke earlier – were deeply interested in the mysteries of life and sought to discover its meaning. Men such as the great writers of tragedy were preoccupied with questions of destiny in relation to the individual. Other Greeks of towering intellect, like Thucydides, tried to find a meaning in history and to discover why mortals behaved as they did in peace and war, under stress or in prosperity. For the very first time works of philosophy – which by definition seeks wisdom and understanding – were created by Plato and Aristotle, working on foundations provided by Socrates. Also for the first time a system of universal law was created by the Romans, a law whose principles should be applicable equally to all mankind. Mediaeval churchmen, following in the same tradition, engaged in metaphysical speculation and tried to prove through metaphysical arguments the existence of God, while Dante wrote his *Divine Comedy* in which he tried to sum up all the truth of philosophy and religion in one magnificent poem. Yet at the same time the Greeks, to a lesser extent the Romans, and the men of the Middle Ages *also* sought for beauty. But the beauty, unlike in our day, was always in the service of religion, including festivals that warmed the heart, thus providing the intellectual soul thinking of the age with a counterpoise, and helping to save this thinking from degenerating into arid and sterile speculation; a temptation to which thinkers of the later Middle Ages sometimes succumbed.

All these achievements of the intellectual soul civilizations are to be reflected also in the human intellectual soul period which lasts from twenty-eight to thirty-five. It has often been pointed out that mediaeval religious and philosophical thinking reached a height of pure thinking that has never been equalled in the centuries since. Thinkers such as Thomas Aquinas wrote enormous *summae* of what was at the time considered to be knowledge, but it rested very little on any material basis, and was the result of nothing but logical thinking about metaphysical questions. Something not dissimilar can be found in the intellectual soul age, during which the young thinker is often inclined to believe that he (or she) has already reached the heights of all that the human mind can attain. Indeed, the early years of this phase may be marked by a cocksureness that will almost certainly soon be lost as the age of thirty-five is reached, and at this time it is safe to predict that very little attention will be paid to the views of older persons, not excepting the consulting psychologist! It often happens also that in these early years of the intellectual soul the personal selfishness that goes with the cocksureness will reach its height. These years are, indeed, the last that may legitimately be lived for 'selfish' ends before a new seriousness is forced upon the young person as he enters the second half of life.

It should be emphasized that the word 'selfish' is not necessarily used in a pejorative sense. Nevertheless, it certainly is unusual for a person of this age to wish to devote himself to altruistic aims; too often when such aims are professed it will be found that they are not genuine, and may well mark a hidden selfishness – the wish to appear interesting or to be admired. Or the opposite may appear – a self-depreciation that may mask a hidden neurosis, or at the very least show that the self is insufficiently developed. The self *ought* to be developed as fully as possible during these years, and there may well never be another period in later life when it seems so easy to study and understand. It must be admitted, as a part of the phenomenon we are discussing, that more 'know-it-alls' are probably to be found at this age than at any other; a reliance on thinking and tendency to argument are noticeable. To the intellectual soul of this period *all* problems seem soluble, and are often expected to yield to simplistic solutions, because such young people still lack the life experience that would bring them to a more mature outlook. It is still very difficult for them to perceive the other person truly and clearly. They are more likely to see others through their own still undeveloped selves rather than as they really are. In short, the intellectual soul is still from every point of view 'subjective', because the consciousness soul, whose task it is to attain to 'objectivity' has not yet become part of one's being, and to attain to it one must first surmount all the difficulties that present themselves so forcibly at the end of the intellectual soul period. The consciousness soul has to be brought to birth through the exercise of the human will. It has to be created, as it were; it does not come of itself. It is possible, and not at all uncommon, never to pass beyond the sentient soul stage, and therefore to fail to develop even the intellectual soul. However, at least the opportunity to develop it presents itself, and the development does not therefore require a special effort of will. But to attain to the consciousness soul a very great effort is needed, requiring an outlook on life that will in many ways be fundamentally changed if one is to move onward into the second half of life with those forces needed to enable one to continue to develop. And this effort is by no means always made, not even by the British and Americans who have it as their task to develop the consciousness soul, and for whom it does not represent such an enormous effort as it does for some others.

About the age of thirty-two, or maybe a little later, a subtle change begins to take place in the young man or woman which is not likely to be noticed at once unless they have been told to expect it. When the writer of Psalm 90 (traditionally supposed to have been Moses) said that "the days of our years are three score and ten" he was certainly repeating an old and true tradition, since the ordinary life, at least in earlier times, usually did extend to seventy years, if not cut short by illness or accident. The psalmist indeed added "and if by reason of strength they be fourscore years, yet is their strength labour and sorrow, for it is soon cut off and we fly away", but we do not need to suppose in the present time that our remaining years will be only "labour and sorrow" as we shall hope to show in later chapters.

The life span of man does consist of seven decades, or, less abstractly, ten periods of seven years each, the first nine under the influence of sun, moon and planets and the last period under the influence of the fixed stars. At the age of seventy, actually soon afterward, the particular star under which we were born is again in the same place in the heavens as when we were born. Before the seventy-first birthday this complete cosmic year has passed – as Steiner puts it, our personal star has come out from behind the sun. This is an apt symbol for the fact that we are now no longer bound by karma from our previous lives. Although we have all through our present lives been preparing also for our next life on earth, after the age of seventy-one to seventy-two we concentrate on it. We can now look back on our life and recognize it as in all essentials completed. Exactly half way through our usual span therefore we reach our thirty-fifth birthday, and this does represent a true watershed between the before and the after. We have constructed our building, we must now live in it and use it. It is no accident that various distinguished personalities in history experienced this year as a crucial one in their whole lives. In the opening lines of Dante's *Divine Comedy* the poet tells us that "in the middle of *our* life's journey" he "found himself in a dark wood". We may also think of Descartes who in his thirty-fifth year experienced the onset of doubt, which he lived through with great intensity, systematically proceeding to doubt everything he thought he knew and everything he had believed – until finally he realized that he actually knew nothing at all for certain except that he was doubting. Or rather *someone* was doubting and he knew intuitively that it must be he! As a result of this experience he coined his lapidary pronouncement "I think, therefore I am" (according to Steiner, he would not have made such a statement had he realized that we ourselves are not actually present in our thinking and so cannot prove our existence by supposing it is we who think!)

Perhaps the most common unwilled and spontaneous experience in our inner life as we approach our thity-fifth year is indeed the experience of doubting, the disappearance of the cocksure attitude we had so recently. At twenty-seven to twenty-eight we should wonder about the meaning of life and try to find answers. But at thirty-two plus we begin to wonder (or ought to begin to wonder) if we have really made any progress at all in our understanding. One of our most overwhelming experiences may well be that *all* our knowledge, such as it is, has been acquired from others. Nothing is authentically ours. This piece of information, we realize came from that book, the other from another book, or we heard a lecturer and believed what he said. But is it true?

During this seven year period we have searched for the truth – we may have searched with the utmost conscientiousness, as was our proper task. But did we find it? Didn't we pick up only some scraps of information that we may have been proud and happy to parrot and show off to others, but never truly made our own? We doubt the value of the work we are doing, we wonder why we ever involved ourselves with it. But too often we dare not leave it because it, at least, is a safe anchor. If we do leave it, events seem to gang up on us, and nothing better ever seems to present itself. We may look at husband or wife with new eyes, and ask ourselves how we could ever have linked ourselves to that *stranger*. All our previous certainties seem gradually to become uncertainties.

It may also be that something happens to our memory, especially if we used to have a good one and were rather proud of it and showed it off. If we go far enough with our introspection we may even suddenly appear to ourselves as rather disgusting and wonder why anyone pays attention to us, especially to our opinions. Why don't they see through us? However little of all this may be consciously noticed or fully experienced, at the very least there is almost always a lack of ease, a time when little or nothing seems to go right for us, and with this there is very often indeed a temporary paralysis of the will.

If the young person nearing the age of thirty-five knows what is likely to happen it would be possible for him to help the process on, and thus gain far more from it. If it were more widely known that the experience simply *must* take place, whether or not it is passed through consciously, then it could be pointed out to friends and families that they could help greatly by not expecting too much at this time, by treating apparent aberrations with compassion and understanding. The need for this extra measure of understanding is especially evident in the case of married couples. If one partner is at least seven years older than the other and thus has already passed through mid-life experience, he or she can be very helpful to the other partner through the understanding he or she will have of the other's experience. If they are both within the same seven year period, and thus pass through this mid-life experience together, it will prove enormously helpful if a consultant can explain to them both what is happening and what can be expected.

It was said just now that the young person passing through this experience has the possibility of helping the process and co-operating in it. The kind of thing he might do is to admit himself at once that the knowledge he has acquired thus far is secondhand, and as a consequence he should make no attempt to hold on to it. All he has read and not made his own may well return to him afterwards (then he could indeed *make* it his own by understanding at the level of the consciousness soul or at even higher levels what has been taken in from the time of puberty up to the age of thirty-five). If he so wills, he can learn to *accept fully* what is happening, and not try to prevent it, for example, by racking his brains to remember something he is on the point of forgetting or has already forgotten — and not trying to understand again something he had once understood but can understand no longer. Instead of following his impulses, which may become quite wild, even frantic because of a growing feeling of powerlessness, he could quietly tell himself to wait patiently, recognizing that in time, if he waits and does not *fret,* it will pass. He should be very hesitant to take major decisions at this time, especially those that may involve his whole future, because the chances are very good that they will turn sour. It would, in my opinion, be a specially serious mistake to undergo phychoanalysis at this time because the process of living through his 'repressed' memories back to childhood will actually take him further away from this thirty-five point, which he must pass and in fact cannot escape except by real regression into childishness. Nothing whatever is likely to be uncovered in analysis that will help him over this hurdle, which must be met head on. Even a shoulder to lean (or cry) on is of doubtful value unless it is that of a loved one who sympathizes, best of all wordlessly, and makes no attempt to interfere.

I believe that all that a psychological consultant can do to help at this stage is to tell his client that this is a necessary trial for him to pass through, and that it is always passed through in loneliness and anguish if the full fruits of the experience are to be garnered in the second half of life. He might add that the more awake and aware a man is while it is happening the easier it will be to 'come through on the other side'; that those who sleep through it or have no worthwhile experience at all at this time will be poorer for the lack of it all the rest of their lives. Not everyone has *deserved* special attention from the spiritual beings who are concerned with us and our lives, and those who have not deserved it may indeed be those who are incapable of profiting from it.

Perhaps enough has been said to indicate the *kind* of crisis this is, and further details are unnecessary. But there is another point of great importance that must be stressed. In almost all cases recovery (the descent from the thirty-five peak) is gradual and neither regular nor immediate. Recovery may indeed last for the entire seven year period during which the consciousness soul should have been brought to birth. If the person is aware of what he is going through and has been through, it will probably take much less time. But I have known many people who even at forty-two are still thrashing around without having acquired their consciousness soul, for lack of the necessary understanding and effort. This especially applies to those men and women who never passed through their sentient soul period (from twenty-one to twenty-eight) in a positive manner, but remain at forty-two still looking for a renewal of what they experienced then. Or perhaps they failed to experience then what ought to have been possible for them, and now deeply feel the lack of it. It is exceedingly difficult for such people ever truly to grow up at all unless they come to perceive very clearly *how* they failed during those earlier years, and allow themselves now after forty-two to say goodbye for ever to that phase of their life – and by very great efforts of their true (and higher) self to come to a new maturity on a different level. This may well be accomplished *only* if they now turn, with all the will and all the attention they can muster, to the proper task of the second half of life: to work for others and for humanity and not for themselves. It cannot be denied that this course will require a self-knowledge and self-discipline that were conspicuously missing before. Without such self-knowledge a person can easily be deceived that he has attained a goal when actually he has taken only the first step. It could be pointed out to him that without self-discipline it will not be found possible to put a resolution into effect, even though it has been taken with the best will in the world.

For others who have followed until thirty-five a more normal development (including those who have passed the thirty-five 'hump' with full consciousness of what was being asked of them and what they have done) there are still likely to be many unsure paths and many false starts on the way down the mountain. In the days before there was automatic transmission with noiseless gear changes, I used to describe this path from the summit, in the picture of a driver who has been cruising silently in neutral but without real control of his car; on trying to put the car into gear while its speed was still excessive he found he could not do so – the effort resulted in nothing but an awful grinding noise. But when the road flattened out and a lower speed was reached, then at a given moment the driver could slip the car into gear, and at once he resumed control of his vehicle. I still think it a good image and though we no longer have such primitive gearboxes I offer it again, since it describes so clearly what happens to most of us in the years immediately following thirty-five. For a time we simply let ourselves be carried along, letting events more or less take their course. But at a given moment we may try to resume control of our lives, especially if a decision is required that may prove fruitful for the future. But this may be quite the wrong moment; it may be better to wait until circumstances arise which show more clearly that the road we are choosing is the right one.

Such a false start is perhaps most likely to occur at about thirty-seven when we feel a new excess of energy and want to make use of it. But often enough we find we were wrong and life simply teaches us the necessary lesson. Later we try again, and this time we know, and for certain, that something has changed and we are on the right road again and in control. We seem to have successfully slipped our car into gear. But, if we are wise, we go slowly, having learned in the last few years to take no chances, and then, as a rule quite imperceptibly, we come to recognize that our own 'I', our self that we had mislaid for a season, is with us again, unmistakably, and we are again in charge. The faculties, especially memory, that were conspicuously enfeebled as we passed through the thirty-five period, are likely now to return to us, strengthened, and we shall probably find they are now more conscious than before. Our former abilities are restored to us, and we find we have lost nothing permanently, though it is likely that we shall acquire no new abilities in the second half of life that we did not develop in some degree in the first. Best of all, we find that our restored ego has a greater control of the astral body: our life of feeling and our emotions are more under its guidance. They are no weaker, surely, but they should be very different in their nature from before, less diffuse, less easily dissipated, as well as being more consciously directed.*

It has seemed to me that the best way I could describe this thirty-five period was to devise a kind of general scenario (which will of course always differ in details for different individuals). I am convinced, from having studied many examples, that especially in the case of persons of a serious nature who have an important life-task to perform and who

*If any reader should come across a novel I wrote many years ago but recently revised for publication called *Vigil,* he will recognize in the young heroine the description I have given here of the passage from late adolescence to the coming of the ego at twenty-one, and equally that of the hero who had passed the age of forty-two. This particular case, as is made evident throughout the novel was a karmic relationship of a very special kind which both hero and heroine lived through to the end in what appeared to be a tragedy, but in spiritual reality was not — both having learned the karmic lessons, which it was the purpose of their lives on earth to learn.

do not sleep through the crucial transitional period in their lives, the life-path during these years will follow somewhat the pattern just given. If they carefully read this scenario they will indeed find that parts of it match what they did indeed experience during these years. Also, if they have not yet reached the thirty-five period but are in the preparatory years leading up to it, the scenario may prove helpful – above all if they can bring themselves to avoid making major decisions until at least the 'hump' has been well passed, and if they can learn to *wait* with as much patience as they can muster for the spiritual powers to indicate to them the path that is going to be best for them for the second half of their lives.

Chapter Five

Soul development in the second half of life

ATTENTION was drawn earlier to the fact that the various epochs of civilization since the sinking of Atlantis correspond to the development of the successive soul configurations in individual human beings. The sentient soul, for example, was developed during the Egypto-Chaldean civilization, and the intellectual soul was developed in the Greco-Roman civilization and during the Middle Ages in the west. We explained how the capacity for thinking that developed during the epoch of the intellectual soul is mirrored exactly in the individual from the ages of twenty-eight to thirty-five. But the epoch of the consciousness soul began only in AD 1413 and it will last, like the other epochs, for about 2100 years (the period during which the sun passes from one constellation to the next in accordance with the phenomenon known, since the time of the Greek astronomer Hipparchus, as the precession of the equinoxes). We are therefore only a little more than a quarter way through this epoch and have by no means fully developed those qualities that belong to the consciousness soul. So we cannot study the civilization of our epoch as we might study the civilizations of the Greeks and Romans and earlier people in order to discover more about the human soul in *its* twenty-one to twenty-eight and twenty-eight to thirty-five periods. However, it is not only possible but also very rewarding and enlightening to study just what *has* been achieved by mankind since 1413, and in the process we shall learn something about the nature of the consciousness soul itself as it comes to birth in individual men and women from thirty-five to forty-two. The successes and failures of this the fifth post-Atlantean epoch do indeed reveal much to the discerning eye about what we do and what we ought to do – or make a beginning toward doing – in our individual lives at this period, and it is precisely those successes recorded for our civilization that are likely to be those spheres in which we do best also in our private lives.

The first and most conspicuous aspect of the consciousness soul as it appears in our western civilization is the progress it has made in knowledge of the external world, in so far as the world may be regarded as material. Until very recently, virtually the whole scientific establishment was materialistic in outlook. Though ordinary man may apparently *believe* in some non-materialistic religion, he is almost sure to be a *practical* materialist. That is to say he does not take the non-material into consideration in his daily life, but keeps it for Sundays, so to speak. He may believe that God created the world – even that he created the world and man in six days – but it never occurs to him that his own belief itself implies that behind the external world that he sees – and interpenetrating it – is an invisible and intangible world of spirit. But the ancestors of both the scientist and of the ordinary man did take the spiritual into account at all times and even perceived some elements of it, as does the overwhelming majority of the so-called primitive people, especially the sub-Saharan Africans, even today. As we mentioned briefly in an earlier chapter, it was not until the early fifteenth century AD that higher beings created *an organ* in man which enabled him to perceive the external world as separate from himself – *objectively*, as we say.

It now becomes necessary here to allude to something that may appear absurd to materialists (or at best an interesting myth that may be considered even enlightening as long as it is not taken for a reality). But it explains so much about the modern world that mention of it can scarcely be avoided. We have already said something about that spiritual being whom, following tradition, we called Lucifer. He it was who in pre-Christian times helped man along the path of freedom by providing him with a self that was like Lucifer but not like the true ego, of which man was later given a spark by the being we call the Christ. From Lucifer came all the enticements that made man experience this self, in beauty and art, and in knowledge, incomplete and one-sided though it was. These gifts of Lucifer made it possible for man to become *self*-ish, as Lucifer was, and proud of himself because what Lucifer gave him made him, as the Bible puts it, "like the gods, knowing good and evil". When Eve, and then Adam, ate the fruit of the tree of knowledge, they set foot on a path that could indeed lead to freedom, of a kind. But they could not, in spite of all that Lucifer was willing to give them, learn to love, because Lucifer does not love; it is not a part of his nature. He does not love man, but would nevertheless like man to become his permanent possession, living not on earth but in a spiritual world which would be ruled by himself. He does not therefore want man to become attached to the earth, and so everything that takes him away from the earth into a nebulous world of spirit Lucifer gives to man in the greatest abundance.

But Lucifer is not man's only tempter. There is another who is in all essential respects the polar opposite of Lucifer, whom anthroposophy, following ancient Persian tradition identifies as Ahriman, the lord of darkness, Lucifer being the lord of light. Steiner speaks of Ahriman as the greatest, most all-encompassing intelligence in the universe: his intelligence is limited to the material and thus to the earth, in so far as it is material; and he insists to everyone who will listen that the earth is *only* material, and that he is its lord – as indeed he truly is in so far as the earth is material. In pre-Christian times he was not able to tempt man as effectively as Lucifer could because until fairly late in history men were actually able to perceive the spiritual world. Long after they had lost their direct perception men continued to believe that heavenly cosmic wisdom had been built into, been incorporated into, the earthly world. When they thought, it seemed to men of an older epoch that they had access to this cosmic wisdom, and did not in fact think themselves. They borrowed it, so to speak, while on earth, for the duration of their lifetime, but did not *own* it. A reflection of this notion is explicit in the great Muslim philosophers such as Avicenna and Averroes, and implicit in Plato and Aristotle, this being the true meaning of Plato's so-called 'theory of ideas'. But when, through the deed of Christ, it became possible for man to reach his true freedom, then it became necessary to darken his former vision and make it impossible to perceive directly the world of spirit other than after a long and severe training. If man had possessed direct vision as he had in earlier ages then he could not have denied its very existence. He would always have felt himself to be linked to the spiritual world, himself a part of it, and so would not have been strictly *on his own*. This was what divine beings wished him to feel, as an essential part of his own freedom. Freed from the link with the worlds of spirit he would no longer feel *coerced* into doing as spiritual beings directed and wished – as for example, the Hebrew people had been in the time of the Old Testament.

This ignorance of the world of spirit was reflected in the obscure decision of the Church Fathers in the ninth century AD to condemn all teaching of the human being as threefold (made up of body, soul, and spirit) therefore denying the working of Christ in man as this had previously been understood, as for instance, by St Paul. The Holy Spirit was henceforth regarded as a being external to man, and not at all as a part of his being. Thereafter, rather rapidly, the world of spirit became totally dark and all clairvoyance virtually ceased, with the result that even a highly developed personality and thinker like Thomas Aquinas could deny any personal knowledge of the spiritual hierarchies and the spiritual world itself, being forced to rely, as he admitted, on tradition for all his knowledge of them. Dante, who lived at the end of the same century as Aquinas might well find himself in a "dark wood", for that is what the spiritual world had indeed become for him until a guide came to help him.

This darkening of the spiritual world was, as may be supposed, a great triumph for Ahriman, and presented him with unlimited opportunities for his work. Even in the later Middle Ages men were becoming ever more oriented to the earth, and some of them, like Roger Bacon in the thirteenth century, became deeply interested in it and wanted to learn more about it. Meanwhile another great culture which penetrated strongly into the western world at this time was found very attractive by many highly developed westerners who did not and would not dream of accepting its religion. Contrary to appearance this Islamic culture was fundamentally non-spiritual even while it acknowledged the rulership of a single all-powerful God, whom it called by the name of Allah, essentially a law-giver similar to Jehovah, the God of the Jews (whose culture mingled with that of the Muslims). In these cultures Ahriman found a terrain very much to his liking and he bent every effort to making it his own, endowing them with a science far ahead of anything available to the west, but of a wholly materialistic nature and totally earthbound.

When therefore, as we have seen, spiritual powers in the early fifteenth century endowed men with a different soul capacity through an actual modification of the brain, the wisdom that men (in the west) had once thought resided in the spiritual world now became discoverable by men who could think as Ahriman thought; they no longer had to be inspired directly by Ahriman as had been hitherto true of the Muslims. By virtue of this new kind of brain man could now look at the world as if it were a body totally external to him, totally foreign, and at once western philosophy began to show signs of the influence of this new kind of thinking. This culminated in Kant, who could not come to any other conclusion than that it was impossible for man to know the world except indirectly. He knew only pictures in his own mind of what the world seemed to be to him. Only by inference could he suppose that an unknowable external world created the mental pictures in his consciousness. Though philosophers might hold that the mind was indeed what they thought of as spiritual, and even that thinking was a divine kind of capacity, it was not connected by them with any actual spiritual world. As a result, by the nineteenth century there were scarcely any people in the west capable of challenging materialism. They could only *believe* in a God or in the truths of religion, but could not know them, and not a few of those who professed an other-worldly Christianity came to live and act as if they were materialists. They ceased trying to justify their beliefs at the bar of reason when faced with the apparently certain verities of the scientists.

The scientists, starting relatively slowly with the work of Copernicus (who was able to show that the hypothesis that the earth moved round the sun was mathematically simpler than the reverse theory that had been held for millennia*) and continuing on with the work of Brahe, Kepler, Galileo, and finally Newton, were able through these centuries to carry along with them almost all the serious thinkers of the period. Other branches of science and engineering began to flourish, especially from Galileo onwards. At the beginning of the seventeenth century Francis Bacon made himself the publicist for the potential *usefulness* of science, and urged ever more and more experimentation, so that there would

*Steiner discusses the Copernican and Ptolemaic systems in some detail in Lecture 6 of the cycle *Spiritual Hierarchies* given at Dusseldorf in 1909, showing how the former system is true at the present time from a physical point of view, and the latter from the spiritual viewpoint.

be ever more inventions to change the quality of human life. He and others were listened to, and in every field scientists began to acquire more knowledge of the material world and how it functioned, while technicians and engineers did their best to make use of it in practical life.

None of this would have been possible if men of science and other thinkers had not regarded the external world as a legitimate field of action (making knowledge useful, as Francis Bacon had insisted) and if all new theories had not been verified as far as was possible, by planned experiments. If a scientist works on the basis of his own preferences, and can find no evidence in the external world to support them, then he soon ceases to be a respectable man of science. His work must be *selfless* in the sense that his personal self must not intrude into his work and mar its objectivity. To hold any prestige in his field a scientist is compelled to publish his theories and the experiments on which they are based, whether made by himself or by others; and he must then allow everyone to pick holes in his theory or even prove it wrong by imagining and carrying out other counter-experiments. This is the only acceptable scientific method in today's world, and its success is wholly dependent upon *allowing the facts to speak for themselves,* not intruding anything from his own inner being into his work. His devotion to truth is of course essential, and a certain warmth of enthusiasm that probably animates him in his pursuit of it, is certainly worthy of admiration; and it may well fortify him in his long hard work of research. But in essence, the character of the scientist, his virtues as a man, have nothing to do with the objective value of his work. A cold-hearted man who cares nothing for beauty, or art, or religion, and who is a tyrant in his domestic life, is in no way precluded from contributing as much or more to his science as a man with profound cultural interests who may also be a paragon of felicitous domesticity. Personal human qualities are simply *irrelevant* to the kind of science that alone is acceptable as true science today. The reason for this is that science of this kind has been taken over by the lord of the earth, by Ahriman, the "greatest and most encompassing intelligence in earth evolution" who, it may be supposed, proposes to scientists, in the silence of the night, the solutions to problems their brains as yet have been unable to solve unaided.

This picture has been presented in such detail here because this coldness of thinking and the separation of himself from the world around him is not only an occupational danger for scientists, but it is also the besetting danger for the man or woman entering the period of the consciousness soul. While scientific selflessness and its objectivity is a necessity for the advancement of science, as we have seen, *other* kinds of selflessness are required for human beings, not only in the period of the consciousness soul from thirty-five to forty-two, but for the remainder of the second half of life. If the consciousness soul is to come to full expression it must also be able to breathe love into all one's work, and this should become intensified throughout the rest of one's life. By this time a man or woman should have achieved selfhood, he should know who he is truly, and he should now both respect and have confidence in himself. Precisely because of this achievement, he should now be able truly to *perceive* the other person, recognize his or her 'I'. It becomes possible now, and for the first time, to love another person, recognizing him or her as an equal, not making the self-ish demands that alone were possible in the first half of life (however much we may have deceived ourselves at the time into believing we truly had the welfare of the other as our very first consideration).

All this is not to say that anyone will at once be able to achieve this selflessness in love. What may indeed happen, and only too often does, is that one looks at the other person, perceives him or her objectively enough, to be sure, but not with the warmth that alone makes such perception bearable to the other person. Some of the most devastating quarrels between husband and wife may occur at this time and on into the forties, just because of this clear-eyed vision which is unaccompanied by the warmth of true love. It is an act that can only be termed an act of aggression and cruelty to perceive, and then probably criticize, another if it is done without warmth; and the other has a total right to do his or her best to conceal their inner being from the other – whereas it can be one of the greatest of all human joys to allow oneself to be known by another because we know we are loved.

In discussing the development of science since the beginning of the consciousness soul epoch Rudolf Steiner pointed out that the cold objectivity of the first centuries of this epoch, dominated as they have been by Ahriman, must in time be transformed into an understanding of the external world which will be no less objective, but no longer cold and Ahrimanized. A pioneer in the new way of looking at the world was Goethe, who was a scientist as well as a poet; and perhaps because he was the greatest poet of his time his scientific work was understood and appreciated only by a few, because it was so out of tune with the scientific work and methods of his contemporaries. Rudolf Steiner, while he was still a student at the Vienna Institute of Technology, came in contact with Goethe's scientific work, and during the rest of his life he made constant efforts to develop Goethe's methods himself and laid a philosophical basis for Goethe's concepts which the poet had not rigorously worked out for himself. Such an interest in Goethe's scientific work, unique as it was in the 1880's brought Steiner to the attention of a publisher who was preparing a collected edition of all Goethe's works. Steiner therefore was selected as the editor of Goethe's scientific works and later spent several years in Weimar in the newly opened Goethe archives. Goethe, according to Steiner, had believed that only through a kind of imaginative perception could the natural world be truly understood in its entirety, and that the understanding of it by the intellect alone, the path of accepted science, was one-sided and could reveal only a part (the Ahrimanized part) of the truth. What was necessary then was for man to develop his faculty of imaginative perception (perception 'warmed' by the imagination, as Steiner put it), and then selflessly to allow the phenomena to *reveal* themselves in the wholeness that they possess in nature.

A major part of Goethe's work was a study of the metamorphoses in the plant world*. Some of his contemporaries did indeed recognize the value of this work, even for ordinary science. After all, it required only heightened observation, and for this it was not necessary also to analyze the mineral constituents of a plant after having first reduced them to ash, as was the accepted scientific procedure. To recognize how each part of a plant is a metamorphosed leaf nothing whatever has to be *done* to the plant, no experimentation is necessary. But the observer has to *perceive* the process, and in a sense live through the metamorphosis in himself, through his imagination. In this procedure the observer is just as objective as the analytical scientist, but he has to participate personally, through indeed making himself *selfless* in relation to what he observes, although his own self, his ego, is fully at work. After immersing himself for many years in his work of observation Goethe was able to picture to himself something that Steiner was later to define as a suprasensible/sense-perceptible reality that did not exist in the form Goethe perceived it in the *external* world, but was nevertheless a reality. Goethe insisted to his friend Friedrich Schiller that he really *did* see it, and it was not a mere idea in his mind, as Schiller insisted it must be. This was the famous *Urpflanze,* the archetypal plant, ridiculed by so many scientists as the fantasy of a poet. When Goethe later 'imagined' through his method the intermaxillary

*His short study *Metamorphosis of Plants* was edited with an introduction by Steiner. An English version of this introduction appears in *Goethe the Scientist,* NY, Anthroposophic Press 1950.

jawbone in the human head which had not yet been discovered by anatomists, claiming that it *must* be present because the form of the head as it existed in his 'imagination' required it, the scientific world likewise refused to believe in its existence until the anatomists – no doubt shamefacedly – then discovered it. To traditional scientists, however, it was no more than the lucky guess of an amateur, and proved nothing about the method – thus lapsing as scientists at all times have been known to lapse, into something less than complete objectivity! So Goethe had to wait for Rudolf Steiner's work more than fifty years after his death to receive recognition from a reputable scientist, and very few other scientists outside the field of anthroposophical research have followed Steiner with similar appreciation for his great predecessor.

The truth is that Goethe and Steiner have shown the way – and a difficult way it is – by which the consciousness soul can overcome its initial coldness; or, as Steiner put it, the light element that dominated in its early centuries can be filled in the centuries to come by the warmth element which is an integral part also of the consciousness soul. In this way the study of the natural world can be freed from the Ahrimanic prison in which it has hitherto been enclosed so that the light *and* love of Christ can shine into it. It might appear that the Goethean method has an obvious application only in the organic world, the world of the living, which mankind cannot truly understand at all unless the principle of living metamorphosis is recognized. The intellect with its analytical method is qualified in a limited way to understand the world of the lifeless mineral world; and it can certainly work all kinds of transformations in this world, of greater or lesser benefit to mankind. But even its limited knowledge of the world of the living is often attained only by first killing it, so to speak, putting parts of it under the microscope and engaging in calculations – making full use of the gifts of Ahriman, indeed almost exclusive use of them, to see the world as Ahriman sees it. But as time has passed a strong reaction has grown to this method of working, even though it has given us chemical fertilizers, insecticides and herbicides; a host of drugs synthesised in the laboratory; laser beams in space and vehicles to explore the planetary system; and of course the 'atomic' bomb and nuclear weaponry. As some counterpoise to these Ahrimanic successes, the modern world has seen the birth of the science of ecology which tries to emphasise the interdependence of the world of nature, and assumes that nature, on the whole, knows better than man. It has also given birth to the environmental movement which tries, among other things, to preserve natural resources for the use of a hoped-for posterity that we personally will never know, and to other movements such as that for various alternative medicines. These efforts may seem quite insufficient by contrast with the all-pervading onslaughts of Ahriman and his hosts, but who would be willing to bet that they may not in the end prove too much for him – even if the end is still a long way ahead?

Now if we apply these insights to the life of man in the early consciousness soul period from thirty-five to forty-two, it is at once apparent how he too is faced with the same problem. How to escape the pitfalls of his new capacity for objectivity, while using what he is acquiring because of what it can bring him in the remainder of his life. He is now, for the first time, fully in possession of his ego, and is therefore now capable of directing his own life. Now it is quite possible for him to begin a whole new career if he wishes, after exercising the kind of reasoned choice that was so difficult for him before. He can use his will in a new way to bring to fruition what in his mind he has decided. But at the same time it has *also* become necessary to look at his fellow men and women, and the world in a new way. Not to regard them, as he may have done before, consciously or unconsciously, as fields for his own exploitation, for his own benefit. This is a major temptation offered him by Ahriman, who comes most fully into his own after the human being has passed the age of thirty-five.

For while Lucifer with his gifts previously tempted man into the paths of selfishness (often disguised as self—realization) there was then something legitimate about it. As long as man is on the upward path of his personal evolution, and has indeed the task of providing himself with a fully developed self capable of work in the world, it is permissible to be *self*-ish in the best sense of the word. But after the age of thirty-five this is no longer true, since one's own talents, everything one has acquired up to this point, have now to be used for work in the world. They now have to be placed at the disposal of the world, and it is no longer proper for a man to use them exclusively for himself. Lucifer was always a less dangerous tempter than Ahriman because *his* gifts could in fact be metamorphosed into usable talents and capacities as long as they had been accepted and developed in the pre-thirty-five years, and not *simply* enjoyed for their own sake and for personal self-gratification. But now Ahriman offers *the world* to the man over thirty-five to use for his own benefit, but without telling him that these gifts ought not to be used for himself, nor without care for the wellbeing of his associates, or the preservation of the earth. In so far as the earth is material Ahriman is its lord, and if man misuses it that does not concern him. Money and earthly power are the gifts offered to men who will serve him, and if these are not enough then Lucifer will be more than willing to suggest other means of self-gratification. In particular Lucifer tries to lead men to deceive themselves over their motives in using money and exercising power. There is no possibility of prevailing over such adversaries and tempters if a man does not use his higher faculties and his newly developed ego to create for himself a true moral sense based on the very best understanding of which he is capable. He is now able for the first time truly to think, and above all he must exercise this thinking in the moral realm – something that was never possible in earlier ages before man was given this capacity that had formerly belonged only to higher beings. This is what Christ meant when he told his disciples that they would in future, through the Holy Spirit, come to know the truth, and the truth would make them free.

The man or woman over thirty-five can and should, as already indicated, be able to perceive all other beings in the world as separate beings in all respects equal, each having the right to exist without being exploited – and this applies not only to other men but to the world of animals and even plants. They can be perceived truly, however, only if all subjective preoccupations are left aside – for example, any calculation as to their commercial value, usefulness, rarity, or the like. It is now necessary for man in the age of the consciousness soul to learn, like Goethe, to make himself selfless and receptive, and in so far as this is possible for him, to use a developed imagination in his perceiving. Thus will he allow the external world – of man, animals, plants and even minerals – to speak to him, and in this way he will become capable of truly knowing them as they are, *in the process of becoming,* and not as something fixed and permanent, like insects preserved in amber. The ability to develop this kind of perception over the rest of one's life is the best, and perhaps the only way, to 'keep young', to keep one's etheric forces alive and active – for what has been described here is perceiving with the etheric body – the first stage in the development of suprasensible perception. But it is not possible to develop it, nor even to perceive truly, unless a man develops warmth in his heart, so that he can kindle *love* for the being he is perceiving, and so awaken the *light* of his understanding. This then is also the task of the consciousness soul in the world of our time and in the centuries to come. Or, to quote Steiner's words shortly before his death: "In its essential nature the consciousness soul is not cold. It seems to be so only at the beginning of its unfolding, because at that stage it can reveal only the light element in its nature, and not as yet the cosmic warmth in which it has indeed its origin".* Historically, the consciousness soul epoch began with cold, objective science, which ruthlessly exploited the earth. If it is to reach its goal it must change direction – as we ourselves are also called upon to do in the second half of our life.

The seven-year rhythms continue during the second half of life, each bringing its own series of possibilities, but such details lie beyond the scope of the present book. In a very real sense the entire second half of life can be regarded as a whole, with an orientation always toward the use of one's talents for the benefit of others, not for oneself. This orientation should begin about the age of thirty-five and continue for the rest of one's life. But it scarcely needs to be said that virtually no one has a fully developed consciousness soul at the beginning of the thirty-five to forty-two period and very few have acquired it by the end. Indeed, for most people the first seven year period up to the age of forty-two is one of the most difficult in the whole of their lives. Although there may be quite a strong subconscious wish to place oneself firmly on the right path for the future, as it has just been described, there will almost certainly be much bungling and many tentative efforts, often meeting with failure, and a great deal of indecision. I am convinced that Shakespeare's Hamlet, that familiar literary figure, was of the age thirty-five to forty-two, and indeed behaved in a manner typical of it. The lower self, egged on by both Lucifer and Ahriman, will constantly intrude in our efforts, but one of the very best fields for our endeavours is surely within those human relationships which are familiar to us and to which we have become accustomed. *All* human relationships must necessarily be different after thirty-five from what they were before, and a conscious effort can always be made to change

***Anthroposophical Leading Thoughts*, Rudolf Steiner Press, London 1973, page 139.

the nature of a given relationship to bring it more into accord with the new insights that should have been acquired with the full development of the ego.

The recognition of one's own newly acquired freedom ought to be accompanied by an equal recognition of the freedom of the other. In a human relationship after thirty-five neither party should be *dependent* on the other; nor does either have the right to make *demands* on the other, or even expect gratitude (least of all demand it overtly) from the other. Each is entitled to be allowed to *give* love, and even give gratitude – which is after all only the recognition of a gift – *freely,* or even to withhold it. This recognition of the other's right to withhold what one offers freely oneself is extraordinarily difficult to achieve when one loves, and the other does not, or has ceased to love. Yet this right must be recognized by both *as a right* of the other, and the necessary consequences drawn in the most open possible discussion between the two. Indeed, one of the most difficult of all failings to overcome is jealousy, one of Lucifer's most effective weapons. Actually, the only way of overcoming it is by recognition of the other's ego, even if the possible consequence is unspeakably painful. This is because it means that in the depths of our soul we must recognize the right of the other person to prefer someone else, however mistaken we may believe his (or her) judgement to be. We must be willing to face courageously every consequence of this choice by the other, and leave it to the future (and to the karma of each) to decide whether the choice *against* oneself is permanent. Such considerations apply equally to decisions concerning our work: for example, we may be passed over for promotion when we believe we have merited it, so that an all-too-natural jealousy intrudes. Nevertheless it may happen that the effort to overcome jealousy in the only way possible may occasionally bear wonderful and unexpected fruits. It is never in our power to influence this *directly,* but it may just, in a most extraordinary way, 'appear to happen'.

Most of us have experienced something like this at some time in our lives.

In circumstances like these the role of the consultant as adviser may be vital because at this stage of life it is possible for us to handle a difficult human relationship, perhaps a marriage that seems to be in the process of breaking-up, as mature and adult human beings, not merely giving way to jealousy or wounded pride, not just standing firm on our supposed rights or stubbornly and blindly insisting on our own viewpoint without even being able to see the struggle the other person may be having too. It is especially important for the consultant to keep in mind any age difference between the two parties, and what may be expected of each at this time, giving advice accordingly – never adopting the viewpoint of either but speaking out of his own objective understanding of the situation as it presents itself to him. While having the utmost sympathy for both as human beings he should try at all times to speak directly to the higher ego of the person consulting him, knowing that this ego is there waiting to be brought to life – even if at the moment it may seem to have retreated out of sight. At this point he may find it helpful to make use of some of the techniques developed by psychoanalysis in order to persuade his patient to unburden himself of what may have been troubling him for years and preventing him from taking an effective hold on his life. More will be said on the latter point in the next chapter.

In the series of lectures on karma given in the last year of his life, Rudolf Steiner drew attention to something of great importance that could have been discovered only through suprasensible perception. The higher beings above man, among whom – apart from the Christ – we have thus far mentioned only the guardian angel, are constantly pouring spiritual forces down upon us beings of earth in order to enable us to become truly human by acquiring those capacities of soul and spirit that we need to this end, and to make the spiritual progress that is possible for us during our earthly incarnations. Whatever we may think, we are never alone in the universe, man being, in Steiner's extraordinary phrase, the 'religion of the gods'. But these higher beings who in earlier times were known to be ranked in various hierarchies and even given names by the clairvoyant initiates of the past, are not equally active at all times in our lives. As might be expected, we are most in need of their aid when we are very young, as when we are learning to walk, speak, and think – activities that would not be possible for us if spiritual forces did not pour into us from higher worlds. All through the first half of our lives different powers are awakened in us through the activity of these higher beings, but at a certain stage in our life we are, so to speak, left alone with what has been given and required thereafter to make use of these gifts and develop them further for ourselves. If we are to receive any more help then we have to earn it. The spiritual worlds are not cut off from us, but now we must find our own way to them.

To explain how our higher faculties can be developed (especially in these later decades of our life) would take us far beyond the limits of this book. The subject has been touched upon here only because Steiner mentioned the age of forty-nine as being the time when higher beings altogether cease working directly upon us. From thirty-five to forty-nine the highest of all the hierarchies are active, but they are able, even in these years, to help us only if we have made serious efforts to work with them (orienting our lives in the way we have been indicating in this chapter) even if we are totally ignorant of their very existence and may have no belief in any being higher than man. It is within the most deeply hidden part of man, his will, that these highest beings work, and thus their interest is not only in our changed attitudes after the age of thirty-five but in the *deeds* through which we express them.

It is therefore not haphazard that during our first years of being 'left alone' many men and women experience crises in their lives, though of course they cannot know what lies behind them. As a rule these crises are concerned in one form or another with the tremendous task of deciding how to spend the rest of their lives in a truly fruitful manner. Our karma from the past (described in the last chapter of this book) has by this time been very largely fulfilled, and though we are already preparing for our next life on earth we should still have at least two decades during which we can bring forth our ideas and ideals from within ourselves and try to bring them to fruition in the world. All the faculties we have brought to activity within us during the first half of life should now gradually be metamorphosed (recognizably the same faculties but at a different stage of development) and again they should now be placed in the service of others, and be for their good. We should also recognize that our physical powers are now on the decline, and our senses are no longer as acute as they were, and also need to be transformed*. Though we should be developing inwardly as consciously and conscientiously as we can, we should not permit ourselves to concentrate on inner work to such an extent that we cease to interest ourselves in the outside world and other people. The two should go hand in hand. It is just *because of* our inner development that we should be able to be more helpful to others; our interest in others and in the external world should be constantly growing – including a lively interest in those persons we meet who seem at first sight to be unconnected with us, who do not belong to our family, and are not friends from earlier periods in our life. These may well be our new companions in this life and the next, and we must be careful not to pass them by.

It cannot be overstressed that it is unwise to concentrate

*On this subject the uniquely valuable book of Norbert Glas entitled *The Fulfilment of Old Age* (New York: Anthroposophic Press, 1970) should be consulted, especially Chapters 3 to 5.

on our spiritual development when we seem to ourselves to be making progress in it. Lucifer is always at hand to tell us how wonderful we are and how very 'spiritual' and unusual. He may even suggest to us that we are now ready to use what we have gained in order to enlighten, or even 'heal' others. We should be extremely wary of such 'advice' and be very sure that we are not deceiving ourselves and 'enjoying' our new found 'spirituality', and that our sudden desire to 'enlighten' the world is not a disguised form of our old enemy, excessive interest in our own self, another word for which is egotism. The willingness to place ourselves in the service of others of which we have spoken may also tempt us into this path, but in almost all cases it should be resisted, especially when we are in our early fifties. There are other ways in which we can be of aid to others just in our ordinary life, through our regular work and our constant consideration for others among whom our destiny has placed us.

Also from Lucifer is the desire to shine, to be looked up to and admired, to appear young and beautiful as of old, in spite of our years, and from Lucifer and Ahriman together is the willingness to take advantage of such admiration as is offered to us. However, in general these later years subject us more to temptations of Ahriman than of Lucifer, especially the quest for money and power. If through our work money and power accrue to us we are always in very great danger. But there is no reason to fall a victim to them and pursue either of them for their own sake, or for our own sake. We must never forget that both are to be used for ends that are dictated to us by our own moral imagination*, as we try to develop this quality ever more fully. It is then possible to abuse neither, but to use them for purposes that we know (or at least know within the limits of our mental

*Moral imagination is a key concept in Steiner's philosophical works written before he began to teach anthroposophy. It is impossible to describe it adequately in a few words; the reader is referred in particular to chapter twelve of Steiner's *Philosophy of Freedom*.

and moral capacities) are good. In these years it is at last possible to be truly altruistic, as was never fully possible in the first half of life; it is from such altruistic deeds that we can alone win true satisfaction, and ultimately serenity.

None of us lives a completely fulfilled life. Talents that we had in earlier times may lie dormant, and not be metamorphosed as they should be in the second half of life. Outward success eludes all of us in some measure. But obstacles can also be sources of strength – and not necessarily because we overcome them. They may prove too much for us, even for the will we have now developed. We can learn to accept what appears to be ill fortune or ill success, and perhaps even grow stronger through the acceptance. Also, what appears to be our ill fortune may provide an opportunity for others that might not have presented itself to them had we insisted on having our own way and fought beyond the real necessity for fighting. At a certain point we must be ready to call it a day; and if we know deeply within ourselves some of what will be said about karma in the last chapter of this book, we shall know that the struggle was worth while, and that the fruits will be harvested in another life on earth.

This, it seems to me, is all that needs to be said at this point on the later years of life. In the last two chapters we shall discuss the problem of guilt and the development of conscience, and how to learn to accept ourselves as we are. Above all how to transmute those feelings of guilt and insufficiency that we all possess into a more positive outlook for the future. This problem, so widespread even in our apparently permissive and not especially moral epoch, is one that faces all consultants almost every day of their lives, and anthroposophy can tell us many helpful things about it. We shall then conclude with an extensive discussion of that special contribution Steiner made to the understanding of human life: his formulation of karma and repeated earth lives; we shall see how this knowledge, above anything else, is essential in our time.

Chapter Six

Conscience – guilt and sin – shame and acceptance

ALTHOUGH not all parts of this somewhat comprehensive chapter owe much directly to the work of Steiner, what he had to say on the subject of conscience and its origin, and the evolution of human moral consciousness, seems to me to have important implications for psychology, including the advice and help that may be given by consultants to those who are troubled, even obsessed, by feelings of guilt. It is in my view especially important to go beyond Freud's understanding of conscience as a tyrannical 'superego', more or less internalized but deriving in essence from religious teaching and moral preachments characteristic of our western culture. There is certainly much truth in Freud's descriptions of how most men and women usually arrive at their moral judgements, with the devastating conscious and unconscious effects of the feelings of guilt that result from having contravened them. But it is very far from being the whole truth.

Conscience is, according to anthroposophy, a spiritual reality. It came into existence at a particular moment in man's history, and it will be an integral part of man's being for a long time to come. Though some men and women can live their entire lives apparently without suffering any 'pangs' of conscience, this does not mean that they are without it. It may only be that it has not been awakened in their day consciousness, or it may simply have been lulled to sleep in the daytime. But as soon as we are asleep it becomes no less active in those who are unaware of it when they are awake, than it is in the rest of us. Therefore it is important to know just what it is, and how it acts and evolves when our consciousness is extinguished in sleep. One of the reasons that Freud gave conscience as much attention as he did was because he recognized how much our dream life reveals. Indeed, he used his understanding of dreams, limited though it was, to uncover its workings in a way scarcely attempted by his predecessors. But his conclusions had to be partly erroneous because he did not truly understand the nature of dreams*, and he lacked the suprasensible knowledge necessary to complete his understanding both of dreams and of conscience.

As a preparation for our discussion it is worthwhile spending some time on the two separate and unconnected strands of thought that eventually led to the recognition, and even the description of human conscience. The Greeks were the first to create a word for it during the course of the fifth century BC. But it is mainly through the Hebrews that the common meaning of conscience as an inner awareness of having sinned became incorporated into western culture. According to Steiner the reason the Greeks invented the word is because some of the most advanced personalities among them actually did for the first time experience conscience as an inner voice just at that particular time. As evidence of this Steiner contrasted Aeschylus and Euripides in their treatment of the crime of Orestes. Aeschylus, who lived in the early part of the fifth century, and Euripides who was born a few decades later, used the same theme for one of their tragic dramas – the murder of his mother by Orestes as retribution for her own murder of his father – but they treated the aspects of guilt and punishment quite differently. In Aeschylus' play Orestes, after avenging his

*What Steiner has to say about dreams may best be studied in Lecture 4 of *The Evolution of Consciousness*, a cycle given in Penmaenmawr in 1923, and Lectures 7 and 8 of *Anthroposophy: an Introduction*, given in Dornach in 1924.

father at the behest of the god Apollo, is immediately set upon by the Furies whose task it is to punish a matricide. These are evidently suprasensible beings experienced by Orestes as his actual pursuers. He is unable to escape from them until he takes sanctuary in Athens, where eventually he is freed from the curse through the intervention of Athena, the tutelary goddess of the city. She is also able to pacify the Furies by converting them into beneficent beings (Eumenides) in the service of the city.

In Euripides' play there are no external beings, suprasensible or perceptible. But Orestes, after committing his crime, is ill at ease as he wanders from city to city unable to find peace of mind, though no one is seeking to punish him for his (presumably justifiable) act of retribution. When at last he reaches Sparta, King Menelaus, his uncle, the brother of Orestes' murdered father, asks him, simply enough, what ails him. Orestes replies "It is my conscience (*synesis*), because I know I have done terrible things". The word synesis (used in this sense for the first time in any extant Greek work) means a kind of inward knowing; it is later translated quite literally into Latin as *con-scientia,* from which comes our word. St. Paul in his letters uses a slightly different word with substantially the same meaning (*syneidesis*) and this is the word invariably used in the New Testament. Five centuries after Euripides conscience had become widespread among human beings, and the word had therefore come into common use, both in Greek and Latin.

Crimes like matricide and patricide had always been taboo among the Greeks, and it was expected that the gods themselves would punish them. Thus certain families were afflicted with terrible destinies from which later generations could find no way of escaping. In his drama Aeschylus is interested in this problem, as also in the moral problem of conflicting duties. He settles this in his own way by allowing Orestes to be freed by divine intervention. But Euripides, who was somewhat sceptical about the gods (and surely had no belief in suprasensible beings) nevertheless knew that a man like Orestes would suffer pangs of conscience. The old divine laws are therefore shown by this example to be in the process of becoming 'internalized' – Orestes knew inwardly that he had 'done terrible things'.

Yet it is also true that the Greeks did not have a concept of 'sin' as disobedience to the law, at least not to man-made law. There were certain divine laws to break which was to bring on divine punishment. When Christians later needed to translate the word 'sin' into Greek no word was available that expressed the same concept, because the concept itself was alien to Greek thought. In the New Testament therefore the word used is *hamartia,* which means a mistake or failing, a word used by Aristotle to describe what it was in the character of Oedipus and other tragic heroes that led them on to their destruction. Of course the Greek city states passed laws that their citizens were required to obey, but in no sense could they be thought to be 'binding in conscience', a concept of law favoured by the later Catholic Church. Law-breakers would be punished by the state, but the Greeks did not expect these laws to be 'internalized', so that a man would feel he had committed a 'sin' when he broke them.

It is therefore from the Hebrews that we have inherited our concept of sin and guilt, and it is not surprising therefore that Freud (brought up in the Jewish tradition) should have stressed so strongly the role of the superego, a role indeed not unlike that of Jehovah as he is represented in the Hebrew religion. Historically this religion was established in the era of the sentient soul, many centuries before human beings began, with the coming of the intellectual soul, to think clearly for themselves. Nevertheless, according to Steiner it was necessary for the idea of morality to be implanted in men. Although they could not as yet develop a morality from within themselves, Moses was given the task of transmitting to the Hebrew people a knowledge of what God expected of them, and the Ten Commandments, originally all negative, telling them what *not* to do, consisted of instructions in morality, capable later of being internalized. In short, the Hebrew people were told to behave *as if they already had an ego* to guide them but before the ego was as yet incorporated within them. The Hebrew leaders were expected to punish men for breaking the laws thus given to them, and on occasion, according to the Bible, Jehovah himself punished the people as a whole because they had *disobeyed* his law. Thus grew up the new concept of 'sin', defined as disobedience to God's law.

It is possible to detect from the Bible the actual moment when it began to be predicted that this law would become internalized. There is a passage in the book of Jeremiah, a prophet who lived in the late seventh century BC, a century or so after the coming of the intellectual soul, in which Jeremiah tells the people that "after these days, saith the Lord, I will put my law in their inward parts and write it in their hearts, and I will be their God and they shall be my people" (Jer 31:33). This relationship between God and the people will constitute a 'new covenant'. Many centuries later St. Paul was to take up this same theme. In his Epistle to the Romans (2: 14–15) he explains that the Gentiles, who did not have the privilege of receiving the law directly from God, nevertheless unconsciously obeyed the precepts of the law 'written in their hearts', adding immediately afterward that they also 'bore witness' to the working of the law in their 'conscience'. Although Paul in his other writings and speeches referred often to his conscience (always in the sense of the Freudian superego) telling him what not to do, in another well known passage he also insisted that the time for 'obedience' to the law was over. Men should indeed continue to follow the precepts of the law but now as free beings. "The Law was a schoolmaster to lead us to Christ", he tells us, "that we might be justified by faith. But after the coming of faith we are no longer under a schoolmaster" (Galatians 3:24–25). This passage is followed by a long discussion about freedom as contrasted with bondage, in which he makes it clear that there is no contradiction between the law and freedom, because the free man would behave morally out of his freedom, and this behaviour would turn out to be in accordance with the law given by God.

Steiner tells us that it was only with the incarnation of the Christ, and his death and resurrection (all of which is usually referred to by him as the *Mystery of Golgotha*) that the possibility arose for man to become truly free, with his own personal ego within him, but linked with the Christ being, who is the higher ego of all mankind. This fact was sensed by Paul who in the same epistle to the Galatians speaks for the first time of the Christ within himself, a phrase that Steiner was to refer to on innumerable occasions throughout his work, stressing always that it is now possible for man himself to allow this Christ impulse to live within him, and thus to act out of his higher ego, free from the influence of Lucifer and Ahriman. He does this when he exercises his 'moral imagination', and performs acts in response neither to internal nor external compulsion but solely for the love of the deed itself – after having taken into account in the fullest possible way all the knowledge, earthly and spiritual, sensible and suprasensible, that may be available to him*.

This does not mean that conscience is no longer necessary for us, still less that it may be disregarded. It is impossible for us to bring all our acts into conformity with our moral imagination. Perhaps only a very few acts in all our lives are in accordance with it, and thus are totally free. Conscience therefore remains our guide, but it is more like what Erich

*This statement can be appreciated only after the attempt has been made to work through Steiner's book *The Philosophy of Freedom* (in some editions: *The Philosophy of Spiritual Activity*) which is concerned with the nature of freedom. The whole of the second half of the book deals with how man can attain the ability to act freely and exercise his 'moral imagination'. The subject is too far-reaching to be more than just touched upon here.

Fromm, one of the more enlightened among Freud's pupils, called the 'humanistic' conscience than it is like the stern tyrant described by Freud. It is just as aware of our failures to do good as it is of those deeds regarded as evil by the older form of conscience. The Catholic church (whose leaders have at all times been only too well aware of the undeveloped moral nature of the vast majority of human beings) when it inherited from the Jews the Old Testament and the concepts of sin to be found in it, assumed for itself the prerogative of adding to and interpreting the laws that supposedly came from God. And its own laws, and their interpretations, were held by it to be binding on human consciences, thus allowing man only a very limited freedom in the moral realm. It has continued to this day to make pronouncements on the subject. Catholics everywhere are too often obsessed by unnecessary feelings of guilt, believing that when they break God's laws they are endangering their salvation in an after-life. Catholic priests usually welcome these feelings, from which indeed they may themselves have suffered since childhood, seldom giving much weight to the psychological disturbances that so often result. Protestant churches, almost without exception, in turn assumed similar authority, especially the various Puritan sects, which are inclined to feel it to be their main task to supervise the morals of their congregations. It need scarcely be said that, however justified such attitudes may have been in the era of the intellectual soul (before man had fully come into his egohood) they can no longer be justified in the epoch of the consciousness soul, when it is man's task to develop his highest faculties in such a way that he can eventually determine his own morality for himself.

Nevertheless man does not determine all by himself and without aid whether his deeds are good or evil: higher beings are deeply interested in all that he does. Steiner has explained how every night when we are asleep these higher beings pass judgement – or, to use his vivid expression, they 'rain' down their approval or disapproval on our deeds of the previous day. We are unaware of their verdict because we are only conscious when the astral body is united with the etheric and physical bodies. But the knowledge is nevertheless contained within our astral body, and after we awake a kind of residue or extract of the night's experience percolates into our daytime consciousness. We may experience it consciously as joy or sadness, or simply lack of ease that does not seem attributable to any known cause.

Our first experience immediately after death is a memory picture of our whole life in reverse order, this memory tableau being in effect the content of our etheric body, which has all through our life remained attached to the physical body. After about three days the etheric body dissolves, returning to the etheric world from which its substance was originally drawn before birth. The astral body and ego then remain together for a period that ordinarily lasts for about a third of the lifetime we have just spent on earth. This period is not an arbitrary one. We spend about a third of our lifetime in sleeping, and after death the experience of our sleep is recapitulated, including the judgement of our conduct by higher beings. But after death, when the etheric and physical bodies have been cast off, the experience is more vivid than during our nights on earth because of the living memory picture we have just experienced. Such an experience is never possible with such intensity during our earthly life because during life the astral is still attached to the physical and etheric bodies. For this reason we are never either fully conscious of what we have experienced during the night, nor are we totally unconscious of it.

Our conscience is therefore essentially nothing but our unconscious experience in waking life of what we have experienced during sleep. With every sleep we actually add to the content of our conscience, and at all times when we are awake we can, if we listen, hear our conscience speak. So it is a very true intuition when conscience is described as a voice, the 'voice of conscience'. But the voice must be listened to and heard if we are to take any profit from it.

When we seem to know 'instinctively', as we say, that something we are proposing to do is wrong, it may be that we are remembering what higher beings have disapproved of at some earlier time in similar circumstances. When our conscience tells us that we are not doing something that we ought to have done, that we are not realizing our potential, not doing as well as we could, such a realization may well come not from our experiences of the night but from the whispering of our guardian angel whose task is indeed to guide us along the path we have chosen for ourselves before birth, a path determined in accordance with the possibilities offered us by our *karma,* as will be discussed more fully in the next chapter.

The full understanding of what we have done in life and how this has been experienced by others enables us to build our karma for the next earthly life, and indeed other subsequent lives, during which we shall compensate in some measure for what we have done in this life. Without the help of spiritual beings we could never know how to make this compensation, but we can freely make the resolution (on the basis of our experience after death) that we *wish* to make compensation. Within certain limits we can also compensate for some of our actions in this life, when these actions have been disapproved of by our conscience. Even so, it is quite improper for us to look upon our conscience as a tyrant, a 'superego' in the sense given to it by Freud. It is in no way imposed upon us, as we have seen, by parents, teachers, conventions and the like, 'internalized' in such a way that we feel badly if we do not obey what it 'dictates'. It is certainly possible for us to feel guilty when we do something forbidden by such as the Ten Commandments, but this is not the same as when we feel 'ill-at-ease' or even guilty because we have done something that is disapproved of by higher beings during the night that follows our action. These higher beings know more than we do, and among other things they know the consequences of our actions and the effect they have had on others. Thus the human conscience is far more subtle than the simple 'superego' of Freud, and if it is to be 'heard' it must truly be 'listened to'. It is a quiet voice and can easily be drowned, whereas commandments imposed on us, and perhaps dinned into us since childhood often push their way into our consciousness where they can indeed behave like tyrants. Our conscience, however, and this cannot be too strongly emphasized, is necessarily *personal to ourselves,* and is not to be equated with the accumulated moral heritage of mankind. Even though such a serious thinker as Aristotle held that slaves were an inferior breed of mankind we do not have to accept his viewpoint; and it is even possible that some of the commandments given by Moses could be modified by circumstances in a much later age. For example, it is not inconceivable that some very well established practices in modern life could be regarded as theft, thus breaking the eighth commandment. In certain circumstances I could also conceive that the seventh commandment, and more certainly the sixth could be broken without misgiving because of the special circumstances. It is just these special circumstances that make the human conscience truly personal; perhaps only higher beings can say whether or not one is justified in breaking them. In our age it is our task to use our moral imagination; if we are mistaken then we shall be judged by higher beings. But no other man can determine what these higher beings will say later in the quiet of our night; it is only my own lamp that lights the way.

The above considerations are not intended in any respect to deny the reality of *guilt,* as it is experienced by the human being, but rather to suggest that the concept of guilt should be totally distinguished from the concept of *sin,* as it has been generally interpreted by ecclesiastical authorities. Our discussion of the Greek attitude toward morality was intended to point up this contrast, and to remind us that the Judeo-Christian idea of sin is peculiar to our culture, and other cultures closely connected with it. The Greeks, who are popularly supposed to have had a word for everything, had no word for sin for the excellent reason that they did not have a concept of it, and thus no need for a word. Guilt, however, is an entirely different matter and it is based on a reality: the recognition by our consciousness that we have committed some act regarded by our conscience as evil, or of having failed to perform other acts that we feel we could or ought to have done. If, for example, we have allowed our comfort to stand in the way of something we ought to have done, even if it entailed some discomfort, then our conscience, if it is active, will make us feel ill at ease. But in our age the judge of such deeds and omissions ought only to be our own selves, not anyone else, whoever he may be and whatever authority he (or she) may pretend to hold. We have, in fact, offended against our own conscience and those higher beings who have created it. When the old Hebrew psalmist said to his God "thee only have I offended", he was speaking what was indeed the truth at that time. As yet his higher ego was not within him, and he could not offend against this ego, or against his conscience which he also did not yet possess. All he could know was that he had offended against what he believed to be the commandments given to him and all men by the being he thought of as his 'God'. In those days a man felt guilty because he had broken such commandments and it was therefore natural enough to ask God to show him mercy, even to pardon him; and it often happened that he came to believe that God had indeed done so. Today men can also ask God to forgive them, but they cannot, or at least should not, expect 'God' to answer. The only being who now in our age can forgive sins is not God but the sinner himself. Those persons he has wronged can perhaps recognize his contrition, his sorrow at the harm he has caused. Conceivably in certain circumstances they can even agree to be compensated for the wrong, and such acceptance may help the 'sinner' to forgive himself.

We have argued that the notion of 'sin', and the form that it takes in our minds, are an integral part of our culture. We are conditioned from childhood to believe that certain actions constitute sin, whereas in other cultures the very idea of sin does not exist. But, whether or not the feeling is associated with sin, the feeling of guilt is an essential part of our make-up, and this is not confined to western Judeo-Christian culture. It is difficult to deny that almost all of us feel within ourselves that there ought to be a higher 'justice' that will some day pronounce judgement on our deeds, however little confidence we may have in earthly justice as meted out by ordinary men and women. One major reason for doubting human justice is the necessary ignorance of judges. They simply cannot *know* enough about any case they judge; they can never know *all* the circumstances of the case well enough to pronounce justice on any fellow human being. Least of all can they know enough to decide whether a man thought to be guilty of a crime should live or die. It is no doubt for this reason that men have looked up to God as the final judge, and have pictured some 'Last Judgement' presided over by God the Father, Christ Jesus, or some other superhuman being possessing superhuman knowledge and wisdom (as would certainly be necessary if a man were to receive his 'just' deserts).

It is more than probable that rather few modern men and women, even among professing Christians, believe that such a procedure will literally take place after death, and if it were true it would surely be unsatisfactory, according to human notions. What kind of rewards and punishments could such a superhuman judge hand out? If they die in the odour of sanctity their salvation (whatever that may be) would of course be assured; while if they have committed a preponderance of unrepented sins they would be condemned to... what? Perhaps their 'sentence' would be lightened because their good deeds can be subtracted by the judge from their much more numerous evil ones. If, as is believed by Christians, Christ has taken over the burden of their sins, do they then not have to compensate for them at all? Or if God has mercy on them and they do not receive the due punishment for their evil deeds, where is the justice for which each human being longs in his heart? How can any of these beliefs assuage the feeling of guilt that is experienced, and which it is so difficult to conjure away? But whether our feeling of guilt is justified or wholly irrational, it is a reality for us. Even the psychologist who undertakes the task of trying to help his client overcome the burden of guilt that is oppressing him, must himself have his own residual feelings of guilt unless he has forgiven himself completely and irrevocably. How is he to comfort a new patient who has reached the stage where he can no longer live with himself unless he pours out the story of his guilt, as he experiences it? And after he has poured it out, how can he comfort him? Can anthroposophy help in this task?

The consultant who is also an anthroposophist will naturally know all that has been said here about life after death, especially the backward review of life that takes place immediately after death, and the period that follows it usually known by the Sanskrit word *kamaloka**, during which the experience of the nights on earth is relived, likewise in backward order. He will be aware of the fact that all acts, good and evil, that have been done by us in our lifetime will now be judged not only by higher beings but also by ourselves because we live through them again, but *as if they had been done to us*. Thus not only do we feel within our own souls the wrong we did to someone else, but we experience also in our own souls the good we have done to

*The *lokas* of the Hindu system are a range of regions (some material – the *rupa-lokas;* the others spiritual – the *arupa-lokas*) set aside for specific purposes. SC.

others. If we have hated we now experience the same hate but now directed against ourselves; if we have loved we are now loved in return, and this is experienced as bliss. These experiences will come to all of us after death, and as a consequence we make the resolve to compensate for them in our next life on earth. Furthermore, the consultant will know something that is only very rarely understood by Christians, that the Christ did not absolve men from their guilt nor save them from undergoing the consequences of their earthly deeds. All such deeds have made the *universe* less perfect, and the damage they did to it would have had the effect of handing over a part of it to Ahriman, the lord of evil. But the Christ took upon himself the consequence of these deeds as far as the universe is concerned, and through this act became its redeemer. But man's own sins remained with him and in the fullness of time over many earthly lives they are to be compensated, redeemed by him. This was made possible also by the deed of Christ who is now the Lord of Karma and sees to it that men indeed have other chances and other possibilities in their lives to come*.

It is always possible that the man or woman who comes to the anthroposophical consultant may be in need of this knowledge, as will be shown by their questions. But as a rule he must carry it only within himself as part of his own understanding. It is his primary task, as we shall see, not to try to help his patient to seek the forgiveness by others of his sin and guilt, not even by the Christ. The patient must eventually learn over the process of time to *forgive himself*. Once that has been accomplished he is then healed, as much as he may be healed in this one life. If he wishes he can then try to repair the evil he has done in so far as this may be possible, and he can compensate for his evil deeds of the past by doing good deeds in the future in accordance with his moral imagination.

*For Christ as Redeemer in this sense see especially Lecture 3 given in Norrköping in July, 1914 entitled *Christ and the Human Soul* (London: Rudolf Steiner Press, 1972).

It seems to me that the first step of this process will be for the consultant to help to arouse *shame* in his patient – not an overwhelming feeling of guilt that may be too much for him to bear in his present condition, but a recognition at the deepest level of his being, in his ego, that he has done something of which he should indeed be ashamed. It is one of the most difficult tasks of a consultant to arouse shame in this way without inflicting any damage. He must be perceptive in the highest degree, while never ceasing to be firm, and above all open and candid. It goes without saying that he must have, in the best sense of the word, sympathy and indeed love for the struggling self of his patient, always aware that the human ego is in its essence spiritual, linked to the Christ, however enmeshed it may now be within the astral body, with all its imperfections. In trying to arouse shame what the consultant is trying to do is to awaken into consciousness the true knowledge of our failings that is present at all times in our conscience. The higher self is actually aware of these failings, but up to this time it has not been consciously aware of its knowledge. If it can now be brought to consciousness, the patient may suddenly experience the most intense feeling of shame at what he has done or not done, and the consultant must be prepared to deal with such a crisis, knowing that it is in reality the recovery of what higher beings have taught him during sleep when they approved or disapproved of what he had done. It is no part of the task of the consultant to condone any evil of which the patient becomes aware and confesses; still less should he be a judge of it. From his knowledge of life as well as of anthroposophy he will be ready to offer advice if it seems to be needed. But the next stage of his task should be entered upon as soon as possible, and this is a realm in which almost all the work falls upon the patient. There is nothing more to be gleaned from the conscience. It has performed its task, as has the consultant by his successful efforts to bring it into waking consciousness.

What is now needed is an effort of will by the patient.

This is not as yet the will to repair the evil he has done. That should follow as the result of a successful next step. The patient must now be encouraged – and *encouragement* in the literal sense of the word is all that at this stage is needed – to *accept* what he has done, and leave it to the future, to karma and later earth lives to take care of the past. The past is over, but it must now be *experienced* as over.

Let it not be supposed that self-acceptance is easy. It needs courage not only to acknowledge what has been done in the past, but to say to oneself "I did that, and I am willing to pay whatever price is necessary. I will accept without making any excuses all that I have done, and I will change my life accordingly". It is not so very difficult to recognize through our thinking, our intellect, how badly we have failed, how far short of our ideals our actions have been, our moral weaknesses. Excuses can so readily be made including all those about how external circumstances have hindered us, excuses that have surely been used often in the past. It is for this reason that it is necessary to pass through the stage of experiencing in the feeling a real sense of shame before we can reach acceptance, and why courage, strength of will, is in this last stage so much needed. It sometimes helps if we do over and over again one of the exercises given by Rudolf Steiner in *Knowledge of the Higher Worlds,* the exercise of trying to see our own actions as objectively as possible, *as if they had* been done by someone else – in this way not only experiencing in advance what will later be our experience in kamaloka (seeing the consequences of our deeds through the eyes of others) but perceiving our life as a whole from the beginning of consciousness to this present moment. Then the present can indeed become a turning point, a watershed between our life up to now and the future.

Having reached this point, with the perspective of our whole life before us, we can learn ultimately to forgive ourselves, and then we are indeed ready for the future.

Chapter Seven

Reincarnation and karma in the light of anthroposophy

IT IS not too much to say that the central theme of anthroposophy is reincarnation and karma; not simply the notion of repeated lives on earth – a notion that is taken for granted in most of the world east of Europe and is becoming increasingly accepted in the west – but the link between these earth lives that alone gives them some meaning. Therefore before we enter on the subject of what the science of spirit has to say about reincarnation, it will perhaps be as well to explain as clearly as possible what reincarnation is and what it is not, and to show in what respects the anthroposophical concept differs from all others.

Man, as we have seen, consists of four separate 'bodies', all working together and inseparable during waking life on earth. These are the physical, etheric, and astral bodies, and the 'I' or ego, the central core of the human being. Of these, only the ego is immortal and persists throughout all our incarnations. After death the physical body, like all formerly living creatures, becomes subject to the same processes of decay that prevail in the physical world. When a new incarnation begins, a new physical body will have to be built up from elements existing in the physical world at that time. The etheric body (which gave life to the physical and contained our memories during earthly life) whose 'substance' was drawn, from the time of conception onward, from the non-physical world of formative forces, returns after death to that world. Its formative forces are then reunited with the entire pool of such forces in the universe. The etheric body ordinarily dissolves after about three days, during which the entire life tableau just completed is lived through in reverse order by the surviving astral body and ego. These two 'bodies' then remain together for the experience of kamaloka, an echo of which has survived in the Catholic church, which has given it the name of purgatory.

As described earlier, during kamaloka the experience of our sleep on earth is lived through again by the astral body and the 'I'. This is a period of inestimable importance for us all since during it we learn to know the effects of our earthly deeds by experiencing what we have done as if it had been done to us. We also know how higher beings have regarded these deeds. Because we no longer have a physical body, but continue to have our body of desires (our astral body), we experience everything with much greater intensity than on earth. Now, in proportion to the strength of these desires at the time of our earthly death we suffer an equivalent deprivation, lacking as we do the physical body through which alone desires may be satisfied. However, as we progress through kamaloka (for about the same period of time that we spent in sleeping when we were alive) the desires grow weaker and have dissolved altogether by the time we leave it for our journey through the spiritual worlds – after having eventually reached the stage of babyhood on earth when our desires were of the most simple and primitive kind. In this way the astral body also is cast off from us, but not in quite the same way as the etheric body was dissolved earlier into the etheric world. In fact, a residue of the astral body remains in the astral world as a kind of astral corpse. However, it is detached from the ego, which cannot subsist in the highest worlds with its burden of desires, sin and guilt. The ego therefore goes on alone, retaining only a kind of extract of both the etheric and astral bodies which help to preserve a memory of the recent earth life in the earlier stages of the journey through the worlds of spirit.

It can easily be understood why the church fathers, although no such experience is mentioned in the Bible, elaborated the idea of purgatory as a period during which the human being destined for salvation is required to 'purge' himself of his sins* before being permitted to enter heaven. It is indeed true that the burden of sin is left behind before the higher worlds can be entered, but this is essential because of the very nature of these worlds, which cannot tolerate the presence of evil in them. The experience of kamaloka should therefore in no respect be regarded as a *punishment* for earthly deeds. Its purpose is to impress the lesson of our lives on our ego, so that we may resolve to make compensation in other lives for our deeds that have harmed others and the world, thus laying the basis for our karma in future lives on earth. In the depths of our being our 'I' takes the resolve, not because a divine justice requires it of us, but because we truly *wish* to make this compensation as the result of what we have experienced in kamaloka. We are, of course with our weak human faculties unable to decide, *how* to make the compensation. That is a task for higher beings who work at creating our karma for us as we pass through all the realms of the spiritual worlds (realms which are in the science of spirit given the various names of the planetary spheres).

For purposes of this book it is not necessary to describe the different experiences in the different planetary spheres of the spiritual world, as revealed by Rudolf Steiner in

*Here and everywhere in this chapter the apparently masculine possessive adjective and the masculine form of the pronoun will be used. Of course the form is common to both sexes, as is the word 'man' itself, but under the influence of feminism the somewhat absurd custom has been growing up of substituting a more obviously common word like 'person' for the more convenient 'man'. It should be clear that unless there is a specific distinction to be made between man and woman in this chapter the words he, his and him are intended to refer without distinction also to her, whether pronoun or possessive, and to 'she'.

many lecture cycles*. It is sufficient to say that there is a certain point of time between death and rebirth, known as the 'cosmic midnight' after which we begin to retrace our journey, through the spheres we traversed earlier. In the last stages of this journey back we cooperate with higher beings in choosing the two human beings whom we will have as parents, their destiny being likewise moulded by our choice before they were brought together, through the work of our guardian angel and theirs. To bring two people together, perhaps from distant parts of the world, so that they could unite to bring into existence the physical body and the earthly environment needed by their children, and at the same time to enable these parents to fulfil their karma, is a task the magnitude and scope of which we can only with difficulty imagine. And to understand how all these webs could be woven lies far beyond the possibilities of our feeble earthly intellect, clever though we have recently grown in handling quantities of disparate data in our computers.

At all stages of our life in the spiritual worlds we have been working on our future karma, with the aid not only of spiritual beings but also excarnate human beings with whom we are united by karma. In a general way, according to Steiner, we pass through our lives with substantially the same group of persons as before. But on each occasion we encounter some individualities who are new to us, and our karma with some others is finished and we do not meet them again. Thus we are together with our 'karmic companions' also in the spiritual world and we all cooperate in making possible our reunion next time we are on earth. However, very seldom indeed do we have the same

*Of these my own choice for further study on this subject would be a short lecture cycle given at the Hague in 1923, which bears the title *Supersensible Man*, London: Anthroposophical Publishing Co., 1961. Here Steiner goes into many deeply esoteric matters which it would be inappropriate to enter into in this book though serious students will not find them difficult to understand. Similar material is presented from a different point of view in the *Inner Nature of Man* (forthcoming from Rudolf Steiner Press, London) especially the introduction given to the public.

relationship as before, and we do not necessarily know the same persons at the same time in our lives. According to Steiner our parents in one incarnation were probably encountered last time only in middle life so that at most only half our lifetime was spent with them then. But the vast majority of the individualities with whom we are karmically connected were in a broad sense our contemporaries, and we are most unlikely to be connected with historical personages of the recent past whom we may admire in this life and wish we had known. As an example Steiner spoke of how he had always admired Goethe, and he never lost the opportunity of quoting from one or another of his works, which he seemed almost to know by heart. Yet this did not mean that he had ever been Goethe's contemporary, and in speaking of this possibility he once said humourously that it would have been 'unbearable' for him to have known Goethe personally when he had a double chin, and was a stout privy councillor of the Duke of Weimar. Though he knew Goethe's poetic and scientific works so thoroughly, it would have been quite a different matter to have had to pass him in the street and take off his hat to him.

Since we are linked by our karma only to those who live in the same epoch, it is understandable that we are in the spiritual worlds at the same time and are aware of each other as spiritual beings, and also that we should even play a part in helping to elaborate their karmas as well as our own. The historical personalities whose incarnations Steiner investigated, especially those of whom he spoke in his series of eight lecture cycles of 1924 (entitled *Karmic Relationships,* 8 vols., London 1972-5) were almost always the same individualities but in different relationships on each occasion. It is very difficult, Steiner explained, to investigate the former lives of persons in history, and only those who have attained the degree of spiritual development required for reading the spiritual record known as the

Akasha Chronicle*, are able to make such investigations. Even so the difficulties are such that it is essential for the spiritual researcher never to speak about any of his findings until he has rigorously checked them by various means which Steiner discusses in different contexts in these lectures. It is, he said, difficult to perceive one's own former incarnations because there are so many pitfalls, so many possible delusions stemming from both Lucifer and Ahriman, which can deceive even the most conscientious investigator. He once remarked that he had known at least two dozen persons, almost all of them women, who believed they had been Mary Magdalene, and as many others who claimed to have been Cleopatra or other well known personages. But the astronishing thing about Steiner's investigations was how very rarely any of the karmic links could have been predicted.

It is therefore with extreme scepticism that we should regard the recent spate of books dealing with reincarnation, in which professional psychologists, psychiatrists, mediums and others claim to have uncovered – often by very simple means such as hypnotism – the previous incarnations of their patients who have come to them for help. In some instances the psychologists claim indeed to have helped cure these patients by revealing to them their former incarnations, a subconscious knowledge of which was plaguing them in this incarnation. There may of course be a few cases of fraud, but there seems no reason to doubt that the vast majority of the investigators were respectable practitioners and trained observers, and they did not invent the case histories they describe. The patients, whether in trance or not, quite clearly had access to an historical knowledge

**Akasha:* a Sanskrit term referring, in Hinduism, to a universal medium similar to 'ether', the fifth element. It is widely referred to in western occultism as a subtle medium in which every thought, feeling and action is imprinted to form a record which those with higher consciousness can 'read'. It is very similar to the 'cosmic reservoir' suggested by the pioneer philosopher-psychologist William James. See Easton, SC: *Man and World in the Light of Anthroposophy,* page 22. SC.

that neither they nor their psychiatrists had ever possessed in their conscious lives, and this knowledge can be objectively checked for accuracy. What the British psychologist and physician Dr Guirdham calls 'far memory' is indeed, at least sometimes, a real memory that is apparently fixed in the subconscious of his patients and does not arise merely from the suggestions of the psychologist. But it remains a very big step further to assert that it is the memory of the patients themselves, something they personally experienced in a former life, and that this hypothesis is the only one worthy of being taken into consideration. In Dr Guirdham's case he believes that he and a group of his patients (and other persons who came to him for advice or got in touch with him on account of his writings) were incarnated with him in the thirteenth century, and that most of them were Cathars who were burned at the stake at Montsegur in 1244. Then, it is said, they reincarnated in the twentieth century with a common memory of the fate they had suffered, including remembering numerous details they had not learned of in their life in the twentieth century. Not very many of them were even acquainted with each other in their present incarnation before Dr Guirdham investigated their cases. Nor, aside from Guirdham himself who has at least investigated all their cases and written several books on the subject, do they appear to have had any important tasks to do together in their present life. It would be most presumptuous of me to dismiss all these cases as delusions, but I must also comment that if what Steiner says about reincarnation and karma is true, then these cases, with no exceptions that I have been able to find in the literature, do not fit into the framework he has given. And of course none of the investigators even claims to possess the kind of clear and trained suprasensible perception to which Steiner had attained by 1924. Moreover the techniques they have devised for investigating the supposed former incarnations of their patients are for the most part quite primitive.

All the details of the life between death and rebirth as Steiner revealed them, the work with spiritual beings in the elaboration of karma for the next life, are of course absent from the works of these modern writers on reincarnation. Indeed, almost all of them appear to be aware only of reincarnation and know nothing of karma, even if some of them do speak of compensating in this life for what was done in the last one. But the very essence of Steiner's teachings on karma is that seldom, if ever, is anything the same in another incarnation – the same situation, with the same actors playing the same or very similar roles, the same parents engendering the same children, and the like. A talent in one life is metamorphosed into another different talent in the next, and Steiner states it as a general principle, if with many exceptions in the cases he investigated, that the sex alternates between two incarnations, as was described earlier. The experiences of men and women are essentially different, precisely because of their sex, and both experiences are equally necessary for the human individuality.

Yet almost none of the cases cited shows any sign of a major metamorphosis. In the case of Dr Guirdham's Cathars, one would think that the severe test of faith and fortitude involved in going willingly to the stake to be burned for one's beliefs would have shown itself in some outstanding way in the next incarnation. Yet most of his ex-Cathars led peaceful and ordinary lives, mostly in rural England, during the twentieth century, whereas one would have supposed that the fact that they had all endured martyrdom together would have been a preparation for an important destiny together in a later life. In most of the American cases reported, the reincarnations seem to have taken place with extraordinary rapidity, leaving no time for metamorphosis and for working out a new destiny in the spiritual worlds; yet according to Steiner even two incarnations in rapid succession are rare. Far too often the same relationship is reported in a subsequent incarnation, or sometimes a very obvious inversion of roles, for example as husband and wife. It is often difficult to escape the conclusion that any writer with a quite mediocre talent could have invented these destinies, almost none of which seem to have any wider significance or to lead the reader toward any deeper understanding of human destiny as a whole – in this differing most noticeably from the cases reported by Steiner from his own investigations.

However banal the stories may be, this is of course no conclusive argument for their untruth. But they may suggest to us that some beings whose interest lies in preventing men from giving serious thought to the subject have been at work trivializing what, if Steiner is to be believed, is one of the most profound of all mysteries concerning man; in which higher beings play a constant role in helping mankind to fulfil its mission through repeated earth lives; in which new lessons are learned and the possibility of higher development is always present. The deceivers Lucifer and Ahriman do not sleep, and it is easy for their invisible helpers to insert themselves into the unconscious lives of men and women, especially when they are in trance, under hypnosis, or ill; including when they are sick with anxiety and their consciousness is dimmed – or when they suffer from the various psychoses for which they have sought help from their psychiatrists. In certain circumstances the astral corpses of the dead may be used by these beings and within these corpses is the knowledge acquired when the human beings who have left them aside were alive. Indeed, the lives recounted by the patients when they awake may have been drawn from these corpses in which case they would not represent the actual former incarnations of those who now tell the tale. None of these possibilities can be dismissed out of hand, so little is known in our materialistic age of such entities other than man, or indeed of the nature of our consciousness and how it can be transferred from one person to another. But it is certain that if what Steiner said on the subject of reincarnation and karma is true – as we are assuming it is for the purposes of this chapter – and if it is as difficult to investigate former lives on earth as he insisted it was, then the stories reported do not represent the truth. Truth cannot be attained by the methods now being used so widely, and the unwary reader should not be persuaded into accepting the trivialization of the subject. In the consciousness soul age it is too important and vital for mankind to know the truth as it really is, to allow oneself to be diverted from the search, and from the path of understanding indicated by Steiner.

A last word should be said on the difference between karma as it was explained by Steiner and the older oriental teachings on the subject. The Hindu and Buddhist religions and philosophies have always been well aware of the fact of karma, but their attitude to life is such that they are inclined to regard it as an inescapable destiny, the result, indeed, of former lives on earth, but, like caste, to be accepted at best with equanimity and at worst with resignation. Particularly in Hinduism earthly life is regarded as something to be endured, not made use of for improvement in a positive sense, because it is in the last analysis only an illusion, a *maya*. In the Buddhist view the aim of life is to escape the wheel of rebirth by reaching such a condition of enlightenment that it is no longer necessary to incarnate again; this was the condition attained by Gautama, the great Buddha who could remain for ever in Nirvana. Unhappily, according to these eastern teachings, our karma from previous lives binds us to a cycle of rebirths from which we may only be liberated by coming to see the illusory nature of existence (and therefore of attachment) following enlightenment. Thereafter we may remain in the spiritual worlds, our true home.

This is, of course, an oversimplified picture of oriental beliefs which are and were by no means uniform. But it will be recognized how incompatible it is with Steiner's positive picture of reincarnation and karma which is essentially in accord with the present-day consciousness soul. By contrast the oriental tradition dates from pre-Christian times when there was more truth in it than there is now because the higher ego of mankind had not yet lived in an earthly body. That deed changed the nature of earthly existence and of the earth itself, thus making all future progress on it possible.

Earlier in this book we mentioned that the psychological consultant who is an anthroposophist should be fully aware of all that Steiner taught on the subject of reincarnation and karma – though not necessarily aspiring himself to become a personal investigator in this realm. That is a role that very few can fill, but it is possible to develop on the basis of knowledge and personal effort a living faculty of imagination, so that the karma of patients is always in the forefront of thought and feelings. The consultant will know that the problems on which he is being consulted are seldom if ever to be understood on the basis of a single earthly life, and that the patient's karma will have played a part in his difficulties. It may be only quite rarely that he will be able, to be or feel that he should be explicit on the subject. But he should nevertheless allow his imagination to encompass, for example, a difficult marital relationship, to see whether or not it would be wise to try to effect a reconciliation. Or, to take an entirely different situation, what he should say to parents with a defective child for which they, or one of them, may be blaming themselves. Indeed, the possibilities are endless, and an anthroposophical consultant will always give advice on a different level because he is aware of so much more than his materialistic colleagues, however apparently enlightened they may be. Since almost all the persons who come to consult him have problems that involve human relationships, it is these interpersonal relationships on which he should be most fully informed – and these may well involve karma in one context or another. He will also take into account the age of his client (as already discussed in chapters four and five) and the main characteristics of our present age of the consciousness soul, during which all relationships are more fluid and mobile than they were in earlier more settled ages. More and more people, whether they are fully conscious of it or not, are seeking for more meaningful ways of leading their lives, and have a greater need to bring their many potentialities to realization.

It has already been mentioned that there is ordinarily an alternation of sexes between two incarnations. Thus all of us are men in one life and women in another, even if there is no strict alternation of sexes in successive earth lives. As numerous psychologists have noted, children are inclined to inherit different faculties from father and mother, a boy being especially connected with his mother and the girl with her father. According to Steiner this observation is quite correct as far as it goes, but the faculties inherited from parents are metamorphosed and do not appear in the same form in the offspring. The inner qualities of the mother become outer faculties in her son, and the outer faculties of the father become inner qualities in the daughter. The soul qualities of the mother become physical qualities in the son, his abilities and talents, whereas the personality of the father and his achievements become soul qualities in the daughter. This observation of Steiner's provides food for much thought. It is given here largely as a striking example of what he calls metamorphosis, and the particular qualities needed by the incarnating individuality will surely affect his choice of parents, as will be discussed a little later.

Before leaving the subject of the different sexes, which was dealt with briefly in an earlier chapter, a few observations on the changing role of each sex in the light of anthroposophy should be made. Until almost this present century a woman's role in the world and society was strictly circumscribed. But as society changes, as it must in the age of the consciousness soul, the particular qualities she possesses as a woman may now be increasingly needed in a world that has been so largely made by men, who are more often endowed with talents suitable for dealing with the external world (however perniciously they may have been using them in recent times), talents that are not shared equally by women. Women today feel that their special qualities are not being fully used, while as a result of numerous inventions, almost all devised by men, they have more time and energy to devote to life outside the home. Many women therefore become 'feminists', leading numerous men to over-emphasize their masculinity. Without attempting to comment on how necessary women's special qualities are in our machine-dominated materialistic world (in which so many masculine bodies are, through the influence of Ahriman, becoming rapidly hardened) we think it worth while emphasizing again the probability that the sex of almost all of us is likely to be different next time. As a consequence the sexual experience of the next life will complement the experience of this one.

Similar considerations apply to racial and national choices that we make in the spiritual world before descending into incarnation. For example, an individuality born this time as a Jew, an Oriental, or an African, and living in the western world, is unlikely to choose the same ethnic stock for his next life. If, for instance, he should be an aggressive Zionist, even taking the side of his racial and religious heritage against his nationality, it may be as well to remember that he will probably not be a Jew next time and might even be inclined as karmic compensation to become an anti-Semite, while a black American from the ghetto might well become one of that white upper class, that he may now despise, and perceive the world from that standpoint. Only through the complementarity of experiences can we make real progress through our earthly lives, and it is one of the purposes of karma to give us this possibility.

It may be difficult to understand how it is that a child can actually choose his parents long before they even know one another on earth. Yet Steiner assures us that this is indeed the case. In a sense the child loves his parents before he is born, and it is this that draws him to them. This love is also experienced by the parents and it is this that often helps to bring them together and makes them welcome him as a loved child before he is born. However, it should be recognized that the choice is made by the incoming individuality, not by the parents who provide only the *means* by which he may be born, and, as we have seen, the talents that he will need that can be inherited from them. It is very important to realise that in no sense does a child *belong* to his parents. He is not their property, as some suppose. They have only been given the opportunity to welcome and care for him. He belongs to *himself* alone. While he is still young and dependent naturally he should not be entrusted with the knowledge that he has chosen them. He lives his life with them, and he loves, appreciates and is grateful to them, or he may resent and sometimes have little love or appreciation for them. But the parents, who probably spent the second half of their lives with him last time, can certainly be told of the choice he made when he decided on them as his parents; that can make a real difference to their attitude toward him, and their treatment of the difficulties they may be experiencing with him. In the deepest part of their being they may come to realize the responsibility they incurred when the child made his choice, not by himself alone, but with the aid of higher beings who knew his karma. The incoming individuality may indeed choose as parents a couple that will give him no material advantages, and he may even have a need in his karma for a childhood that will be difficult. But this in no way affects their responsibility to do their best for him, and the karma they now create with their child will have its own karmic effects for themselves in a later life on earth. It could even be that the child who has just been born was father or mother to one or both of them in a former life in the not so distant past.

It can, however, be – as was discussed briefly earlier in this book – that the parents an individuality chose for himself before incarnation fail to make it possible for him to be born. If they practise contraception, as almost all married couples do in our present age, at least for a time, it is always possible for him to wait until they change their minds and allow him to be born. This will mean only that he will have to spend longer in the spiritual worlds than was necessary for him. But after a child has been conceived in the womb of the mother he has chosen, she may have an accidental miscarriage or may have the child aborted for any of a number of reasons – some of them perhaps good ones, others based solely on various earthly considerations. Steiner once explained in a lecture to a group of doctors, that the surgeon who performed abortions would have to bear the karmic consequences of his interventions. But in 1924 abortion was not so easy or so common as it is today, and it seems hardly believable that he would say today what he said then, when he observed that a child in these circumstances would usually be born later to the same parents – or, as he delicately put it, would "return to its appropriate channels"! It can scarcely be doubted that today, when millions of abortions are performed every year, the incoming individuality will sometimes be born to parents who were not those destined for him, in preference to renouncing incarnation altogether for what may well be a very long time.

For our present purposes the important point is that it is possible that a consultant will be faced with what may seem to him to be a case of this kind, in which the karma of *many* lives may have been thrown into disorder. A child may not only be born to parents not originally destined for him, but may even have the sex not destined for and needed by him when he made his original choice. If a consultant suspects that such may be the case he can scarcely speak of it. But his advice could nevertheless be couched in such a way that it might help to solve the problem for parents and child, enabling them to accept and even love the individuality who is undergoing this painful destiny while he appears to them, as he may well may, as a kind of changeling in their home. In this way some order may be restored to the karma of them all and good eventually come from their adjustment. The angel of the child may also help in this task since he may have guided him to these parents when those to whom he would have guided him made that first task impossible. As Steiner added to the doctors in his lecture: "Such questions are not to be answered in general, depending as they do on the individual case. But deep, tragic life-conflicts can occur as they often do in life, when karmic ties are broken".

If we regard human life wholly from the earthly point of view, it is often very difficult indeed to understand either our own or anyone else's. It is also understandable that, even if we have been studying anthroposophy for decades and have tried to make it part of us, we too are sometimes at a loss to offer any explanation for certain aspects of our own lives – to say nothing of those of our friends and other persons with whose biographies we may be fairly familiar. I believe the right course is for us always to try to imagine how higher beings (including our own angel who has the most direct knowledge of our karma) may look upon our life, always bearing in mind their deep interest in man as a whole, and how he fulfills his task and what progress he is making toward his ultimate goal. The consultant who is an anthroposophist will always have in mind when he gives advice that the person who has sought his counsel has not only chosen the particular path of life he is pursuing, with all the obstacles to earthly success he may meet, but that he also has a longer term goal that makes every struggle, however difficult, worthwhile. Whether conscious of it or not, he is trying to make spiritual progress in the course of his earthly lives, and it is in pursuance of this spiritual progress that, with the aid of higher beings, he has chosen the karma he is now fulfilling. But he does not know what is in store for him, and at the present stage of earth evolution he is subjectively entirely free, that is to say, he can choose what to do in the next and at every later moment of his life. What he cannot do is determine for himself the result of his actions, which may be quite different from what he has envisaged. Thus karma is not *fate;* he is not blindly following a path laid out for him before he was born, and simply making the motions of deciding what he will do when in fact the decisions he thinks he is making are all predetermined. What he chooses to do within the framework of his life he can do – and he will also experience the consequences.

The same considerations apply to his human relationships in life. Higher beings and his karma will bring him together with those persons with whom he has a karmic connection. But what he decides to do after he has met them lies within his freedom. He may be brought together with a person with whom it will be best for him to share his life. But this does not mean that he and the other person will necessarily make that decision. They may reject one another and thus lose the opportunity presented to them, which if followed up would have borne good fruit for both. Nevertheless, it is also true that in such a relationship there will almost invariably be a moment when each recognizes the other, if not always consciously. Often a dream will follow in which the other person will appear, and it may even be that the dream will draw to our conscious attention the possibilities of the relationship that would otherwise have passed us by. In any event the moment will almost always come when the other person will be recognized, and this will be manifested in a sudden awakening of *interest,* of attention. And this attention will be totally lacking when there is no karmic connection of any kind between the two persons. We meet dozens of new people every year during the most active period in our lives, but only a small percentage of these will be karmically connected with us. Sometimes there will be a short time during which we appear to be strongly connected with someone we meet. Then circumstances of life may separate us, sometimes for the rest of this incarnation. On looking back at this relationship we may recognize that either we did something important for the other during this short period, or he for us. Such a deed may have been a karmic debt from former lives that was paid during that short period when we were in touch. But only that debt had to be repaid, and its paying did not entail the consequence that we were also required to spend a large part of our lives together. This aspect of a relationship is often not understood, especially when an undertaking as serious as a marriage follows. But if the relationship is of this kind it may be that both partners quite quickly decide it was a mistake, and one or both decide they wish to put an end to it.

It may be that they are right. They met and each recognized subconsciously that there was a karmic link between them. Perhaps they were greatly attracted to one another, and they made the decision to unite in marriage. But this was not the relationship they had decided on before birth, and whatever the karma was between them it could have been resolved in a different way. In one of Steiner's Mystery Dramas; which are concerned with several successive lives of the most important characters, two of them had been brother and sister in a former incarnation and were greatly attracted to each other in the subsequent one. But that was the only connection; marriage in the second one would have led to disaster. When a karma between two persons is only temporary and yet they marry, it may be that each will very quickly tire of the other and regret the hasty marriage – or, just possibly and most unhappily, one will tire and the other will wish to continue. Even so, the second party may or may not genuinely wish to do so. It can also be that he or she will have extraneous reasons for not wishing to dissolve the marriage, reasons concerned with material considerations or religious scruples, or because of the well-being of the offspring of the marriage that might seem to dictate that, in spite of the differences between the couple, the marriage ought to be preserved.

It is of course quite impossible for any consultant to arrive at a definite judgement in such a case. But he should be aware of the very real possibility that each party to the marriage has fulfilled what was required by their karma together, and that the course of both their lives should now be changed for the further development of both. In some difficult cases it may even be that the children born of such a marriage needed precisely the parentage with which they were in fact provided, but that it was for their own higher good that they should not also be brought up by these parents (whom they had chosen solely for the physical characteristics they needed) or at least not by both of them. This too will be within the karma of the children and the possibility must be taken into consideration by the consultant. If then the marriage is dissolved the opportunity is opened up for both parties for a future in which a totally new and truly fruitful relationship can be established with partners with whom the rest of their lives can indeed be spent together in love and amity. Then the karmic relationship that had always been intended for them can be fulfilled. In later years both partners of the dissolved marriage may come to recognize fully what had been its true purpose, and at the same time to recognize what the link between them had been, and what the debt had been that was in the end repaid.

In a case such as the one we have been describing it is also possible to avoid making the mistake of believing that a relationship was intended to be permanent when it ought instead to have been for a limited time, and for limited purposes. If we are content simply to explore a relationship with the knowledge that it may not even be a karmic relationship at all, or that it is a limited one, then we may perhaps reach the point of recognizing its nature, and be able to part in amity or continue the relationship on a different basis from that on which it began. As a rule a certain amount of soul maturity is necessary for this, and one must especially have enough control over one's life of emotions to resist the pull they undoubtedly exercise over our judgement. Numerous relationships are possible in life, including between men and women of marriageable age, and wonderful friendships can be developed between those who are karmically linked and who have much to learn from each other if the effort is made, and above all if one learns to wait rather than, as too often in our impatient age, taking precipitate action that may ruin *all* the possibilities. New links of karma are also waiting to be forged, especially in the second half of life, and these may bear fruit of all kinds in another life.

We have hitherto been speaking of attractions on which probably the consultant's advice will be more frequently asked. But we are also karmically linked with our enemies and opponents who, like ourselves, have entered upon their incarnation with a debt toward us waiting to be paid. This does not mean that our enemy (or rival) in this life was necessarily an antagonist in a previous life. He may have been a friend whom we have wronged or who may have wronged us. Or he may have been someone who was linked with us by other ties, perhaps an uncaring or tyrannical parent, or even a judge who gave a wrong verdict in a lawsuit or condemned us wrongly in a criminal case in which we came before him. We resented his verdict, rightly or wrongly, and he may indeed have given it for improper reasons. The possibilities are endless. But the karmic link that may have existed over many lives is one that will manifest itself again in this one in an enmity, which, from an earthly point of view, may have no obvious reason or justification.

In such cases it is necessary for a resolution to be brought about some day, and one or both of us must make the effort if it is indeed ever to be resolved. The only way open to us as free human beings is to recognize the possibility that it is we who in an earlier life were responsible for what has now become a real enmity, and try to make compensation in this one. Above all we must try to avoid harbouring a grudge against our enemy. If another karmic compensation is necessary also in the next life there is nothing we can do about it in this one. But it may be possible for us to prevent it from being necessary by our attitude of total forgiveness this time, perhaps in the end even reconciling ourselves with him, and maybe, with the aid of higher powers, turning the evil he had done or is doing into a higher good. Such a deed will bear fruit for both of us after death, and perhaps next time he will be our friend and benefactor from the beginning.

In the same way that it is possible through the understanding of karma to turn our enmity to ultimate good it is possible to regard illness and suffering as opportunities to be used for our spiritual progress. Steiner explained on many occasions, and with a wealth of detail, not only how our entire physical organism is metamorphosed between incarnations (a fact that need not concern us here) but also how our qualities, good and bad alike, also undergo a similar metamorphosis. Certain diseases and organic weaknesses are likewise the visible expressions of failings in a former life, while beauty of form and figure in this life may be a consequence of suffering endured patiently in a former one. Many of Steiner's medical lectures were indeed concerned with diseases that come over into this life from previous ones. These are matters with which we are not greatly concerned in this book, but they suggest how such knowledge might make it possible for us to adopt a different attitude towards illness and suffering than is habitual to us. Some people are gifted with a strong constitution that makes them less susceptible to disease while others suffer from almost constant illness. Still others may be handicapped by deformities from the time of their birth onwards.

About these latter Steiner had much to say, and indeed initiated a new method of caring for them which is now practised in dozens of homes for retarded and handicapped children (these he called *Seelenpflegebedürftig:* children in-need-of-special-care-of-the-soul). Such incarnations may be results of past lives, and they can in certain cases be the result of a horror of the world as it now is, experienced by the incarnating soul just before birth. However, they may also be a preparation for another life of great importance and significance; whether this purpose will be fulfilled depends very greatly on the attitude of those persons whose task this time is to take care of them. Obviously there is a deep karmic tie between these children and those who look after them, just because in this life they are too helpless to look after themselves. It should always be remembered that the true selves of these children are not able to express themselves in the bodies they have constructed. But every night in sleep, when they are freed from their bodies, their own higher being is as active as that of any normal human being. Also they are unburdened by the sin and guilt in this life from which the ordinary conscious human being is never free. For this reason there can be a very close and loving relationship with those who look after them if these latter can come to understand what they are, and why they are as they are. They often respond well to every feeling and gesture of love and compassion, so that it can even be a special grace to have the task of caring for them. It may well be that in the next life when the deformed child will have metamorphosed his deformity he will become a leader of men, and it may become his task to look after those who previously cared for him. Steiner is said to have remarked that all the great initiate leaders of mankind have at some time or another been born with bodies that they could not effectively use. But in those apparently useless lives, spent without a normal waking-day consciousness, they learnt a special lesson that could later be made fruitful.

Most of us will have noticed that after we have overcome and recovered from an illness involving high fever we feel an excess of strength that we did not have before. This is a very simple example of the general rule that the overcoming of an illness has a beneficial effect, even though nothing may be visible in the physical organism. An illness that comes from a former earthly life was necessary for us to endure. If it was a karmic compensation for former deeds then once it is over we can pick up our life again without having to make the compensation again, and it may now become possible to perform deeds that no one would have expected of us. An outstanding historical example is that of the Roman emperor Augustus who was sickly all his youth and had constantly to fight illness, as well as his enemies, before he was able to win the absolute power he wielded in the second half of his life. This power he was then able to use to found the long-enduring Roman Empire; he lived to what was then a ripe old age without any further physical ailments of consequence. If, however, we constantly bemoan our ailments and make no inner progress we may have to continue to make compensation, sometimes for all our lives.

Nevertheless, it is also true that even if we are making spiritual progress we may not attain to health, and we may continue to suffer from illnesses all our lives. In such a case we may be preparing for a life of great importance and significance next time, and it should also never be forgotten that those who care for us during our illnesses are also compensating for acts of a previous life, or preparing for a next one, or both. Thus an opportunity is given to them to be of service, something that in different circumstances might well not have been possible. So the knowledge of karma ought above all to help us to understand and accept our illnesses, even including the burden we necessarily lay on others through them. But to complain of them is precisely the attitude that will take away the value they have for all of us, and negate the wisdom shown by those higher beings who chose the way of illness to make our spiritual progress possible.

It should be clear from all that has been said in this and previous chapters that what I have called spiritual progress is not by any means the prerogative only of those who pursue it directly through exercises, meditation, and perhaps the study of anthroposophy. We are all without exception on the same path, but we may have fallen behind, far behind, or we may be making no visible progress. Moreover we may be totally unconscious of the need to make any effort. This too may be the result of our karma; we may not in previous lives have done anything or experienced anything that would have led us to seek spiritual knowledge in our present life. So we do not meet it, and it does not come to meet us because even our experience in the spiritual worlds between death and rebirth was itself conditioned by former lives on earth.

It should not be thought that once we have discarded our bodies and become spiritual beings after death all the spiritual worlds are at once open to our gaze, and we are suddenly omniscient. In the spiritual worlds, as on earth, there are what we may think of as 'schools' where we are able to learn about higher spiritual beings and the work they do on earth. If we have learned there, in those schools, this knowledge will continue to live in our subconscious while we are in incarnation, and it will be easier for us here to come in touch with higher knowledge. As Rudolf Steiner wrote near the end of his life: "Only they can be anthroposophists who feel certain questions on the nature of man and the universe as an elemental need of life, just as one feels hunger and thirst".

Thus only those who have this hunger and thirst will be brought by their karma to those persons or those books that will give them the spiritual nourishment that in their subconscious they are seeking. The hunger and thirst arose in them because their previous earth lives led them to those regions of the spiritual worlds between death and rebirth where they could learn what they needed to know from higher beings, and from discarnate human beings, who are connected with them by karma and are on the same path – perhaps a little ahead of themselves. But it is true also that *all life* can be a preparation for spiritual knowledge and spiritual understanding, whether or not we may be conscious of our need for it. To live out fully the life with which we have been entrusted, and to do our utmost in those circumstances of life to which we have been led by our karma, is always a preparation for another life in which the opportunities will be different. And it is this knowledge that every anthroposophical consultant should always have in the forefront of his mind and heart when a new client knocks on his door with a request to speak to him – the great moment when a new opportunity is offered to him to be of service as he looks for the first time upon his new client and his controlled imagination once again begins to work.

Bibliographical note

No individual books or lecture cycles by Steiner cover very much of the material contained in this study. Certain cycles dealing with specific topics are referred to in the footnotes, and all those mentioned are also of general interest. The basic books *Theosophy* (1904) and *Occult Science: an Outline* (1909) published in many different editions and translations, contain in the most convenient form Steiner's teachings about the nature of man and the evolution of humanity, while *Knowledge of the Higher Worlds and its Attainment* (1904) deals in detail with the anthroposophical path of development. Nevertheless it may be best for the beginner to start with a very compact cycle given at the Theosophical Congress in Budapest in 1909 entitled *Rosicrucian Esotericism* (Spring Valley, New York: Anthroposophic Press, 1978), in which similar material is presented with exemplary brevity and clarity. Two books concerned with education throw much light on human nature as seen from the anthroposophical point of view. *The Education of the Child in the Light of Anthroposophy* was a fundamental lecture given by Steiner long before there was any prospect of his ideas being put into execution in the field of education. It was a public lecture given in the Architects' House in Berlin in January, 1907, and has been reprinted many times since in numerous languages, and contains for the first time a description of the seven year cycles in human development. Much more comprehensive and detailed is the course Steiner gave to the first group of hand picked teachers who were scheduled to teach in the first Waldorf School at Stuttgart in August, 1919 *The Study of Man* (London: Rudolf Steiner Press, 1981). Although the main purpose of this course was to instruct the prospective teachers, all the knowledge contained in it is valuable for psychologists. Two groups of lectures also given in the Architects' House in Berlin to a general but well informed public may also be recommended. These lectures have long been out of print but a new translation is now available. It is difficult to find elsewhere as much information about the human soul as is to be found in these lectures, which formerly bore the title *Paths of Experience* and *Metamorphoses of the Soul,* reprinted London 1984.

By contrast a group of lectures published under the title of *Psychoanalysis in the Light of Anthroposophy* (New York: Anthroposophic Press, 1946) given at different times in Dornach and Munich is not recommended for beginners in spite of the promise conveyed in its title. Although many subjects of great interest are touched upon in these lectures, a considerable amount of anthroposophical knowledge is needed to understand (and in places not be shocked by) them. A public lecture formerly published separately under the title *The Psychological Foundations of Anthroposophy* (now included in a collection called *Esoteric Development,* Anthroposophic Press, 1983) will be found rather difficult by most beginning students of anthroposophy, and indeed by many mature students who lack a good foundation in philosophy. The lecture was in fact given by Steiner in April, 1911 to an international Philosophical Congress in Bologna. Much more comprehensible are two introductory lectures given in Vienna in 1914 just before a deeply esoteric cycle called *The Inner Nature of Man and Life Between Death and Rebirth.* These two introductory lectures will be for the first time available in English in a new edition of this cycle to be published by Rudolf Steiner, Press.

Steiner spoke often and in very different contexts on the subject of conscience, but no individual book or cycle contains more than a small part of what he gave. The last two lectures of the cycle given to members in Berlin entitled *The Christ Impulse and the Development of the Ego Consciousness* (1910) are concerned with the birth of conscience (Anthroposophic Press, 1976), and there is a wonderful lecture on the mission of the Earth and the role of wonder, compassion and conscience to be found in the 1912 Berlin cycle *Earthly and Cosmic Man* that can be read with profit by anyone, though the cycle at present is out of print. How conscience is created can be studied in Lecture 8 of the late cycle *Anthroposophy: an Introduction* (Rudolf Steiner Press, 1983) mentioned already in the footnotes, and how it is possible for man freely to create his own morality is discussed in detail in the book *Philosophy of Freedom* also recommended in a footnote. Rudolf Steiner's last words on the subject of conscience may be found in an article written just before his death entitled "Memory and Conscience", included in *Anthroposophical Leading Thoughts* (Rudolf Steiner Press, 1973), page 201. This aphoristic but beautifully illuminating essay requires a considerable anthroposophical background if its full meaning is to be grasped.

On the subject of reincarnation and karma two groups of

lectures in addition to those mentioned in the footnotes should not be missed. These are: *Manifestations of Karma,* given in Hamburg in 1910 (Rudolf Steiner Press, 1976), and *Reincarnation and Karma: Their Significance in Modern Culture* (Vancouver: Steiner Book Centre, 1977). The first named deals with karma from many different points of view, while the second provides some fundamental information not easily found elsewhere. These lectures were given in Berlin and Stuttgart in 1912. Among the lectures to be found in the eight volumes entitled *Karmic Relationships* the first six lectures of Volume I constitute an excellent introduction to the subject of karma, and lectures 18 to 28 in Volume II are also concerned with karma in general rather than with the successive earth lives of different individualities, which form much of the material of most of the lectures in this series. The beautiful last three lectures given in Breslau in June 1924 also throw much light on certain aspects of karma some of which have been studied in this book (Vol. VII pages 96 to end).

I have purposely refrained from mentioning in this bibliographical note any works by anthroposophists other than Steiner. But I should wish to conclude with one unique book that has already been mentioned in the text. This is F.W. Zeylmans van Emmichoven, *The Anthroposophical Understanding of the Soul,* a work that brings together not only what Steiner tells us about the soul but also much that has been discovered by recent psychologists, the whole thoroughly assimilated by a highly developed practising anthroposophical psychologist who founded his own clinic in the Hague and was the head of the Anthroposophical Society in Holland from its founding to his death in 1961. The book is not easy but well repays serious study.

COCKBURN
43550

JERICHO ROAD

CLAUD COCKBURN

CASSELL · LONDON

CASSELL & COMPANY LTD
35 Red Lion Square, London WC1R 4SG
Sydney Auckland Toronto
Johannesburg

First published 1974

ISBN 0 304 29322 9

Printed in Great Britain by
Northumberland Press Ltd.,
Gateshead
F. 1173

CHAPTER ONE

The scream came and went so fast it might have been imagined, or been just a harsh throb inside a man's own head. Equally, it was so violently clear it must have been what it seemed to be, a scream from outside. In that shapeless place it could have come from anywhere: from in front, from left or right, or even from behind.

They said of this stretch of country that when God made it, he laughed.

There was no way of measuring anything by comparison with anything else. An object could be a boulder near the track or a big stony hill far off. The scream, too, could be from near or far.

Rigid from the neck down, the rider reined in, stared ahead, turned his head left and right, cautiously, as though by seeing something he risked to provoke it into deadly action. There are snakes which might lie harmless but will go for a man if they see him staring at them.

A regret came like a belch. Why not have listened carefully to that damned inn-keeper at that last inn on this route. Mortally dangerous, he said, to go further on this road 'just at the present time'.

That inn had a reputation among travelling men, though not a place they stayed at. Why not? Nobody said why not, except that it was a peculiar class of place. So who stayed there? A peculiar class of people. It was spoken about as the Inn of the Knower. This inn-keeper gave himself out to be one of the sect called The Knowers. What did they know? Answer: the Unknown God. Known to them, their talkers said, and at the same time unknown, too. The Alien God, they said. Now you see it, now you don't. The Knower had a woman at the Inn. Well, and so? So what? A very peculiar class of woman.

Could be the man knew something: about dangers on this

road, for instance. But then why so cloudy, murky in his talk? Why not spell it out in a way to convince a man with work to be done? One that had to size things up in a level-headed manner. Why such jabber, jargon and mystification? The manner of a charlatan. A level-headed man could sum him up and dismiss him as such.

As an inn-keeper he had crude motives for delaying travellers; force them to pay money for food and lodging until he could assure them (he pretended to be able to do so at the proper time) that the route was safe. A common crook that any experienced traveller could see through with half an eye. He had invented dangers for the good of his business.

But now there was this scream. It gave a harsh kind of reality to that inn-keeper's wild, crooked, flesh-creeping line of talk. A man from the East, probably a Babylonian. In fact a ridiculously typical example of that breed. Such fellows could be met with everywhere. Malicious jugglers. Among level-headed men they were a sour joke.

But just how level-headed is this level-headed one, out in the middle of God's joke? Delayed in the city, not wakened at the proper time because the lazy whore he spent the night with had not roused him as promised, he had started a long while after dawn and tried to make up time. Mistakes never come singly, one breeds another. As a result, he pushed his beast too hard. So that when he came to the last inn, on this route which was new to him, he saw that he would have to rest the mule for an hour or more. Making the best of it, he would rest himself, too, with a little food and drink and a short doze in the shaded courtyard.

So now he was here on the road, scared. He should have told that fast-speaking charlatan to mind his own business and let a tired man doze. But right at the outset there was a small hitch. At the end of his first bout of patter the fellow said, 'If you want my name, it's Simon.'

Not at all an uncommon name, though in the case of this man so obviously from the East, certainly false. But the traveller's dozy mind went a little bit off the track at this point because at that moment he had been brooding, furiously and contemptuously, on the subject of his senior partner back in Sachem, whose name was Simon too. In his snoozy state he was briefly amused by the meaningless fact that this mountebank inn-keeper should share a name with sober-sided, square-bottomed prig-mouthed Simon of Sachem, who would have snuffled out of his nose at this man as at a talking cockroach. 'Such people,' Simon of Sachem would have said, snuffling as though the Lord God had appointed him to look people over and give them their proper rating, 'are up to no good. You've only to look at their eyes. Common crooks. Or,' he would add heavily, 'worse.' In Simon of Sachem's estimation, there was always something worse for people to be.

The distraction of these thoughts, maybe the smile that went with them, killed any chance to send the inn-keeper off and gave him the opportunity to sit down and proceed with his conversation if he insisted, which he did.

What he said next was an annoyance.

'You don't know me,' he said, 'never been down this way before, have you? But I've heard of you. Back in your home town they call you Hop. Grasshopper. Always on the jump. Buy and sell, buy and sell. Whatsoever may chance to be available for the purpose.'

True enough, such was his nickname among his fellow citizens: a recognition of energy, being on the move, going after money where the money was. But used by this stranger it seemed an intrusion, an impertinence. The man Hop, the Grasshopper, half closed his eyes. But Simon the Babylonian was away now on a stream of the sort of talk to be expected from such a man. It moved through references to troubled times, lack of confidence, incidence of crime, possibilities of rebellion and civil war. It babbled on to observations on the increasing number of prophets roaming the land. Some mad, some bad and some, said the inn-keeper, perhaps neither. Who, he asked, as though this were a fresh and profound question, really knew?

The talk went on and on and somewhere along the line Hop, who was sometimes also called Rat because they said he could sense things through the tips of his whiskers, had a whisker-tip sensation that this chatter, and the man who chattered, were going to turn into something different from the chatter and the chatterers about this kind of thing to be heard in every inn and caravanserai up and down the country.

And it was so. The Babylonian did change his tone. Not just his tone of voice, but his gestures, the way he sat on the bench, the look, even, so it seemed, the shape of his eyes. Hop thought of frogs and other creatures that puff themselves up. On this newly puffed up creature, the false-friendly smile of the inn-keeper turned from servility into a sneer and leer meaning 'I'm bigger than you are'.

He came out with some extravagant verbiage; seemed to be speaking familiarly of God, the Universe and that entire class of area and topic. He puffed himself and leaned towards Hop, boring at him with his eyes. He said:

'Take a man of your cast of character, lineaments and processes of mind. Knows his business, is familiar with his area of operation. Buys and sells to advantage. They are wont to call you not only Hop, but Rat. I am correct? Yet suppose a person, as it might be myself, put forward to you some truly novel, unheard-of thing. Such a thing could not be encompassed within the confines of your understanding.'

Hop shrugged.

'Not a conjuring trick, Grasshopper. Not even a tree—that tree there—to be shown suddenly withering under the power of my inimical thought. You, with your processes of mind, would seek to pierce the nature of the conjuring trick. In the withering of the tree you would see only the power of your God, the God of your world, passing through me like the lightning, to bring about the blasting of that same tree. But suppose I were to tell you something that would really make you jump. Suppose I were to tell you that I am not an instrument of your God, but a part of the power that was before there was a God? The illimitable power, the unfathomable Silence?'

'Silence? What silence?'

'The silence that was before everything and is beyond everything.'

'I'm listening to the silence.'

'And you know, from your own area of operation, you know the country's like milk in the pan before it boils. Bubbles here, bubbles there. People waiting. And suppose,' he seemed to swell more than ever, 'suppose I told you that I, part of the great power and the old silence, am here to be and to become what they all are waiting for? The way on? The newcomer? The saviour? Part and parcel of the Unknown God?' He tapped sharply with his foot.

'You jump as I say it. I saw you jump right there on your backside. You wouldn't believe it, would you now? Not this low publican, you'd say to yourself. Between one breath and another you'd have five hundred and fifty-five reasons for not believing any such thing.'

Hop knew that he had stirred a little, and there certainly were five hundred and fifty-five reasons. He remembered how he had sometimes teased the other Simon, Simon of Sachem, with religious speculations, pretending, for the sake of making Simon snuffle, to believe in all kinds of outrageous things, or at least to believe that everything is an open question, anything can be true. Now the Babylonian was playing the same trick on him. Puffed up to tease.

He said nothing, looking at the pattern of cracks in the mud of the courtyard just beyond his feet. It was as though the silence had been the pause between two acts in a show. For the Babylonian suddenly clapped his hands, like the manager of a troupe of performers calling for the new act.

On the signal, there came through the curtain at the side of the yard a young woman; big, handsome, sluttish. Tough-skinned as a wildcat, and proud of it. Coming nearer through the stagnant air she stank somewhat of scent, sweat and flesh. She stood in front of them, looking up and over into nowhere, as if to be inspected or await further orders. Maybe she was supposed to dance.

The Babylonian said, 'Shall I tell you about this one?'

He put his hand on her buttock like a dealer showing off an animal. Looking at her, what Hop felt was resentment at the way things happened. The whore all night, and now he was tired and in a hurry too. This one ought to have happened first.

'A woman, you say,' said the Babylonian. 'A loose woman, you say. A lewd low whore you say.'

Hop growled in his throat; shagged out and randy too.

'And,' said the Babylonian, 'you would not be faulty in your judgment. You would not err in your appraisal. A woman I picked out of the lowest brothel in the city of Tyre. A Greek whore. You ask me why?'

Hop shrugged angrily.

'Because amid the lowest is the highest. You know, you have heard tell, of the Thought of the Unknown God? Of how that Thought, though still one with the Unknown, yet was separated and made flesh and sent on a long, long journey through this world? You have heard of that thing?'

'I've heard preachers preaching. I know the pattern.'

'And the Thought was forced to mingle with the evil Archons, rulers of this world. And the Thought was made a woman. She was many women. She was Helena, the woman the Greeks and Trojans fought over in that long and terrible war, famed in legend. And she was the lowest of women. I knew it. So where to look for her? In a whorehouse. And where are the lowest whorehouses in all this area and region? In the city of Tyre. And there I found her. And I brought her here, and she is here with me. A part of me, yet separate. A Greek whore.'

Hop realized what was familiar about the way the young woman stood. The star turn in any whorehouse, bringing in the best money. No need to go to Tyre to see that. He said so.

The Babylonian muttered something and the woman went away through the curtain again as though she had completed her dance, or whatever act it was that she was billed to perform. The puffed-up frog seemed to let himself down to natural size. His sneer shrank to a nearly obsequious smile. And he then said what he said about the dangers of the road. He was speaking not, as earlier, of the general situation in the country, but of dangers now, on this road between here and there. He spoke of bandits, revolutionaries, murderers. A very dangerous road to travel 'just at the present time'. The thing to do was to wait a day or two, or three, then proceed when 'things have settled down a bit'. In the meantime, a man could rest here at the inn. The woman, he said, making an obscene noise in his throat, would also be available to him. 'It is part of her fate,' said the Babylonian.

The body-smell the woman had left in the stagnant air was annoying. Worse was to be taken for a fool, a sucker, by this pimp who had hit on the notion of using a lot of religious jargon to wrap the meat in. The situation required no use of rat-whiskers to be understood. Hop made a decision. He was quite insufficiently rested, and after less than an hour in that place the mule was no doubt insufficiently rested too. Still, he demanded that it be got ready, and presently he was astride and headed south. The Babylonian stood in the gate of the inn, watching him go. His last words were, 'You see. You believe nothing. Even when you have truth under your nose you believe nothing.'

'What you give me under my nose is an all-round stink,' said Hop, who had meant to say nothing, but by now was too indignant to keep silence.

'Things will go badly with you,' said the Babylonian. 'You are in danger. The route is dangerous.'

Hop said, 'I've work to do,' and jogged forward.

And now, out of the nowhere which was everywhere, came this scream.

After the terrified pause while he looked so cautiously about him, and memories of that inn-keeper rushed through his head, he said loudly, a kind of magic incantation in the empty desert, 'I have work to do.'

The thing to do now was to get the mule into action, go ahead, look straight ahead, not peer left and right. For what might one not see? And what could one do if something were seen? Best not to provoke the snake. In this way he jogged over a hump in the road and saw by the side of the road the sprawled naked body of a man, with blood on it.

Hop reined in again and sat there looking. A youngish, muscular man with a lot of fresh-looking blood on him. He might be dead. By peering at him from his mule-seat, Hop hoped to make sure that he was dead. There would be nothing more to be done, and Hop could jog ahead, just hoping that the same thing was not going to happen to himself over the next hump or the next after that or the next on this road.

While he was hoping this might be so, from the dead-looking mouth and throat came, for the second time, that same scream. It appeared this was the only effort, or sign of life, the man was capable of. He made it and then continued to lie there for dead.

To any rat's whiskers, the scream therefore presented itself as some sort of signal. For instance, a signal to people lurking in the scrub just out of sight that the bait they had planted there—a man shamming dead—had hooked a fish; a fat fish of a travelling man, with his good mule and good clothes and some cash money and his samples, valuable samples perhaps, in his saddle bags. He would be armed, too. Armed and mounted he might have a chance of escape, or at least of killing one or more attackers. But if he could be lured off that mule on to his two feet he would be done for.

Hop hoped, more forcibly than ever, that the man was dead. In that case the second scream would have been no signal but rather in the nature of a death rattle. And there would be no possible reason for entertaining any thought of dismounting. The proper thing to do was to count up to thirteen. If the man still lay there, a dead dog, then it would be reasonable to jog on, with the knife ready and eyes alert. He started to count, praying at the same time that the man should be dead. He found himself hurrying the count. But that sort of trickery could be an offence to God. And how expect much from a prayer to a God you are tricking? To make sure he was doing nothing of that kind, and also because he was pretty sure that the man was genuinely dead and not a bit of live bait dangled there by his fellow-robbers, he went back to the beginning of his counting, started all over with One, pause, Two.

He got to Eleven. During the pause, left to please God, between Eleven and Twelve, the naked man's wrist moved and his eyes flickered. Hop swore aloud and cursed that man who by rights should have been a corpse, to be left properly and prudently to vultures.

Without looking towards the scrub, where the light was making the air do dizzy dances of what might be real figures or imaginary ones, Hop dismounted and walked over to the side of the road. And now, as though having to dismount were not enough, it was going to be necessary to make himself even more helplessly vulnerable by bending over this abominably unchancey creature to see what actually ailed him. He did so, looking him over from head to foot. He noted that the man's sexual parts had not been mutilated. His fear, and his anger at this probable shammer, increased. From what he had heard in his many travels, genuine robbers would have mutilated him, as a sign of their victory and their contempt for the victim.

Genuine robbers would probably have shat on him too. It was a well known ritual. Eagerly but hopelessly he looked for any sign of that having been done. But the man was dirty only with blood and dust; there was no excrement.

In the little time while Hop noted these facts, the man by the road opened his eyes, shut them, blinked, and opened them again wide. Coming out of that dead face, the light in the eyes was shockingly, menacingly wild and lively. Also the man's mouth now began to move and twist in what could have been either a twist of pain or an ugly grin. The eyes and mouth together seemed to be saying as clear as the snap of a trap that this was a dirty trick and Hop its silly victim. His nerves cracking at the thought of the vile, humiliating trickery, and the danger of death he was in, he lashed out with his heavy sandal and kicked the man just below the ribs. He said aloud, 'God damn you, if you're shamming that'll teach you. And I can kill you before your friends get here.'

The man squirmed a little from the kick, but otherwise only continued to stare, blink, stare, and twist his mouth about. Hop was now nearly shouting, partly to give himself courage, partly to hear himself telling himself that this was his fate. He had to deal with this thing he was in, whatever it was, rather than cut and run, try to get back on that safe mule and jog on. Jog on was not what he must now do.

With that thought, he actually kneeled down in the dust beside the naked body and began to examine the wounds. At this point he received a reward. The injuries to flesh and bone, though none of them, he thought likely to be fatal, were such as to convince him that nobody in his right senses would have allowed himself to be beaten up by his associates to that extent just for the sake of luring unsuspecting travellers to be robbed. So it was no trick after all, and he had not been made a fool of.

Possible, of course, that the people who had attacked this young man might still be lurking out there in the scrub. But he thought not. Once it was certain that the thing was no plant, then it was more likely that this attack had been a single quick operation, and the operators were by now miles away with what small booty they might have got: it would seem to have been small because there were no animal tracks around in the dust, which would indicate that the young man had been travelling on foot. Why, in that harsh bit of land, God and the man himself alone knew.

As a man who travelled almost continuously on his business in areas which were often dangerous, where at any time you could suffer some sort of physical injury such as a bad fall, a kick from a mule, a stab from a knife, he carried with him simple essentials for dealing with that kind of thing until you could get yourself, or your friend, to a physician.

He went across to where the mule stood, got his medicaments and bandages out of his saddle bag, returned, and started to dress the wounds of the young man, and cautiously to strap up his ribs, which he had probed and believed to be either cracked or broken. He was afraid to probe much for fear of driving spikes into the man's heart and killing him after all. At small intervals while he worked he gave the victim liquor—wine from one flask, and from another flask tots of stronger stuff they made back home in Samaria.

After what seemed a long time at the work, he observed the man and thought the time had come when it was reasonable to say, 'Can you get up now if I help you?' The man made a trial flexing of his muscles, and pulled his feet up slowly under his knees.

'I think so.'

'You'll have to help. You're heavier than I am.'

The young man remained for a long bit of time so passive that Hop thought the whole thing had been futile, that the man had relapsed and died. Then the naked figure literally pulled itself together.

'Stand up,' the man said, 'so when I push myself on to my feet I can reach for your shoulders right away.'

Hop stood up, turned his back and braced himself.

He was aware of some kind of physical convulsion behind him, and then of a heavy weight dragging at his shoulders.

'All right?'

'Let's move,' said a voice in his ear.

Two pair of feet shuffled and staggered across the road to the mule. Once by its side, it was a long business getting the wounded stranger into the saddle. Fortunately the powerful muscles of his thighs and calves had, it was evident, suffered no injury or weakening. He sat on the mule like one of the naked statues the Greeks made. Hop took off his hooded outer cloak, his principal protection against the sun, and handed it up. The man silently clutched at it and managed to settle it round his shoulders and head.

'Can you hold on when we move?'

'Yes.'

Leading the mule forward, Hop, without his cloak, and only

a scarf round his head, was in discomfort from the sun. Worse was the pain in his feet. The sandals he had on were not meant for walking on the stony road.

The man on the mule said, 'Where are we going?'

Hop said, 'Jericho, I hope.'

'How far? How long?'

'Far enough,' Hop said. 'And long enough at this pace.'

CHAPTER TWO

They looked down on the town and Hop said, loudly to deaden the pain of his feet and the heat, 'What a hell hole.'

The man on the mule said nothing. Perhaps it was all he could do to keep in the saddle, with nothing left over for talk. Hop furiously continued his side of this dialogue of which the other side was not there.

'You don't think so? I can tell from here. They say it's the oldest city in the country and, by God! just looking at it from here I can believe it. Look at those trees they've let grow so high they can't shade anyone. Proof of old age. What bastards. Look at those roofs with the dust blowing off them. Why don't they lay that dust with water? Just content to have such a damned old town.'

His voice rose to a high pitch and the man on the mule kept on saying nothing, perhaps not even seeing the civic panorama ahead and below.

'The inn's going to be a hell hole too, you can bet on that,' Hop said malevolently.

But this was not the case. Somewhere near the city centre the great door of the inn opened into an archway beyond which could be seen a spacious courtyard shaded with sweet-smelling shrubs. Fountains played there. From a dark interior on one side of the arch, a man first looked out, then waddled out, his arms stretched wide in welcome. His voice was a warm welcome.

'Hop! *You* here? Sight for sore eyes.'

Hop, holding the mule's bridle, turned awkwardly, tottering on his sore feet.

'Joshua!' It came out of his dry throat as a croak.

This was Joshua of Jerusalem, formerly inn-keeper there, much esteemed by travelling men from far and near, and now, it turned out in quick conversation with Hop, proprietor of this establishment in Jericho. They talked and each put an arm round the other's shoulder. Hop, still holding the bridle with his other hand, tottered again.

'My poor friend,' said Joshua. 'You're in a bad way. How come? And who's this?'

For the tenth time his eyes flickered up at the young man on the mule, sitting there like a statue. Hop babbled words, seemingly too happy to have found a friend in the hell-hole to bother about whether he made himself clear or not. But he did manage to get out some kind of sketch of how the man on the mule came to be there.

'And what I want,' he said, 'what he needs, don't you see Joshua, is a place to lie down. Rest up.'

'That's of course. And you too.'

Joshua looked more carefully at the man on the mule. He said, 'He has a name? I'll have to register him. For the police, as you know. Very strict these days.'

'I don't know his name.'

'No. How could you, given the circumstances?'

Hop too now gazed at the silent figure. Evidently he felt a need to justify the man's rude indifference, which could give the impression that the fellow was waiting haughtily for servitors to get busy and minister to his needs.

Hop said, 'He's had a shock. We have to look after him. You have a little while before you have to report to the police. Before that we'll probably be able to get his particulars.'

Joshua said, 'Of course.'

That special 'of course' was a phrase which had endeared him to many in Jerusalem. He took as matters of course situations, requests, demands, frightful problems which other men, other inn-keepers were likely to peer at, ask questions about, refuse to act on.

Together they got the man off the mule and half carried him to a small, barely furnished interior room, not looking on to the courtyard.

'No use,' Joshua said, 'drawing attention to him before we know who he is.'

In a larger room, opening on to a view of the shrubs and the fountains, Hop ate, drank, rested his feet and gossiped with Joshua. Then he slept. Towards evening, Joshua roused him. He said, 'Our young friend seems to be coming out of his daze. I can delay reporting him until midnight. But some inspector comes snooping, we'd better have something ready to tell him. Get everything in order as per regulations.'

Hop accompanied him to the young man's little room. The stranger lay on his back with his hands behind his head. He turned his head very slightly to look at them out of his wild, lively eyes, which now had an expression that was nearly insolent. His whole attitude as he lay there managed to suggest that he was doing them a favour by allowing them to disturb his rest and his thoughts. They explained that, under the regulations imposed on inn-keepers, they had to know his name and where he came from. The stranger made a small contemptuous shrug, and pouted with his rather thick lips. After a pause, he said, 'Call me Alpha.'

'If that's the way you want it,' Joshua said. 'Is it supposed to tell me you're from up the coast? Laodicea? Antioch?' He said to Hop, 'A lot of Greeks from those parts come through Jerusalem and this place. Mostly they're going to the Greek colony in Alexandria.'

The man who called himself Alpha said impudently, 'It's not supposed to tell you anything. Not anything at all. And I'm not "from" anywhere. Not the way you mean.'

Hop twitched and half clenched a fist. Joshua sighed.

'All right, all right. But I have to put down something.'

Alpha said, 'So go ahead and put down what you said. Proceeding from Antioch to Alexandria. D'you want me to prove it?'

'I don't,' said Joshua, 'ask you to prove that it is so. I want you to tell me that no one can prove that it isn't so.'

'All right on that,' said Alpha. 'Be easy in your mind.'

On this he actually closed his eyes, indicating that the interview so graciously granted was now at an end.

On the way back to Joshua's place in the big rooms under the arch, Joshua expressed outrage on behalf of Hop. 'What a son-of-a-bitch. You saved his life. And he looks at you as though he had a right to have you do that. You could have let him die there on the road. Might have been a good job too.'

For his part, Hop expressed outrage on behalf of Joshua. 'No harm to me. I don't expect anything. But what about you? You take this naked bastard in and he doesn't puff an extra breath to help you with the registration. No co-operation at all. What a bastard, come to think of it.'

'There may be no trouble,' said Joshua. 'Or no worse trouble than usual.'

'Here's hoping. If it's no worse than usual it'll be bad enough.'

They drank and talked. Hop said, 'You know, I've got to be up before first light. This is new territory for us. My business can take me eight, nine, ten days.'

Joshua said, 'You'll do good business out there with the farmers and ranchers and maybe some of the little business fellows in the villages. If those people out there die young it's on account of over-eating. That's where the money is. Anyway you'll be well out of this greasy death-trap.'

'How d'you mean, "death-trap"?'

Joshua considered. He said, 'I didn't mean it. I have a nice place here. I make a good living. Look at the layout of the place. Fountains and so on. Better than my place in Jerusalem. Just once in a while it gets on my nerves. Forget what I said. And,' he suddenly sharpened his tone, 'don't tell anyone else I said what I just said about the greasy and so on and so on.'

'I see. Yes naturally. Who d'you take me for? I wasn't born yesterday.'

Joshua laughed. 'The way things are going a person would need to be born tomorrow to keep ahead of the situation.'

'I've been noticing that for years. Now listen. I have to get some sleep. Like I tell you, I'll be away a bit over a week, take or leave a day or two according as how the orders come in. So keep my room for me, so it's ready when I get back. And about this Greek, I'll pay in advance for him.'

'You needn't do that. You'll be back.'

'Troubled times, Joshua, very troubled times. Suppose I don't get back. Knocked on the head somewhere in these happy valleys. No sense putting you to a loss on his account. Figure out what it'll cost to board him for, say, eight days.'

Joshua figured, and Hop handed over the money.

'Let him have what he wants, and if it comes to more than that I'll settle it as and when I get back. He'll probably be gone by then. Off to Alexandria, if that's where he's really going.'

'If,' said Joshua.

In the morning dusk he was on hand to wish Hop good luck. Apparently forgetting what he had said earlier about 'good business' and so on, he added, 'I expect you'll need it.' The remark, pointless or pointed, hung in the air between them. In that time and place it was the kind of thing people said automatically, instinctively; a kind of tribute to troubled times, and perhaps a talisman against dangers lurking everywhere.

Hop was just about to jog off when he turned to Joshua and asked him on which days the mail courier left for Jerusalem. Joshua told him.

'In that case,' said Hop, 'I have to be back within five days. I have to send a report to my partner up in Sachem. If I don't, he'll start creating and making general stink. He's capable of telling everyone I've absconded.'

'What a damn fool,' said Joshua.

'Just normal,' said Hop. 'Nothing out of the way. Man has to live with damn fools. Point is they're usually more trouble than villains.'

He went jogging off under the high trees whose leafy tops were now almost lost in the dawn haze and later would be useless as shade. Headed out into the country he was aware of his rat-whiskers becoming sensitive. A new territory, new people, new business. And everywhere politics. Simon of Sachem was for ever declaring he had no interest in politics. He would repeat till you snored that 'politics' was just an interference with business. If you woke up and asked him just what he meant by that he would disclose his meaning which was that governments and police forces and such should devote themselves to maintaining a state of affairs where decent businessmen could get on with their business. People who interfered with sound business should be jailed, stoned, or crucified, according to the degree of their offence. Just at the present time, Simon considered, prophets and soothsayers, hallucinating people with disturbing talk and visions, should be the first to be penalized. They were worse, he said, than the professional criminals, but there were always corrupt politicians willing to protect them, and the criminals too. That was why there were more criminals than ever before. If you said to Simon that there always had been a lot of prophets, visionaries, charlatans and criminals, Simon would say, 'Nothing like what it's like today.' He would snuffle on and on about some period, barely out of sight and seemingly within his living memory, when these things had been otherwise than they were today.

It seemed to Hop, more Rat than Grasshopper now, that, say whatever you like about differences of geography and religion, the people of the Jericho environs mainly saw eye to eye with Simon of Sachem. There were times during those days when he had to shake himself to remember that the man he was talking to now was not the same man he had been talking to yesterday. All right. So he sincerely agreed with a lot of what these nearly identical people said. But it was hearing the stuff—statements, pronouncements—over and over again, and in the interests of business having over and over again to come out with his own 'Yes, indeed' and 'that's damn true', which at the end of a hot day left him exhausted.

It was at the end of just such a day that he came to a village near the end of his list of calls to be made. A rich little village, and he had the name of the richest man in or near it, a big fruit-farmer who once or twice had bought, through a middleman in Jerusalem, products of the business in Sachem, and was now to be approached direct. Hop planned to pride into the village, stop for a half hour at the inn to rest himself and the mule, and ask the way to the big farm which he understood was a mile or more distant from there. The inn would be a miserable place, and he took it for granted that he would be invited to spend the night at the farm.

That is to say, he took that for granted until about a half-hour after dismounting at the inn. Within that space of time he knew that he was probably not going to carry out that plan, might never do business with that prospective customer.

If he had been asked about it he would have said that almost as soon as he was inside that inn he felt that this was a place were something nasty either had just happened or was just going to happen. Both notions turned out to be in a general way true. A half dozen men slouched in the shabby courtyard stopped talking as he came in. Their responses to his civil greeting were more like grunts. It seemed they needed all their energy for their eyes to look him over with. He drank wine and ate bread and dates. He could nearly feel them watching each gulp, watching his jaws munch.

When he had finished he asked what was the way to the farm he was bound for. After a little pause, one of the men said, to the others rather than to him, 'He means Zeb's place.'

'Big place a mile or so out of here,' Hop said.

'That's right,' said the man, 'Zeb's place.' He lolled against the wall, looking at Hop with his eyes half closed. In the inertia of the yard where these men lolled, the only liveliness was in the antics of a small boy who had come out to stare at the stranger and was now playing with some filth in a corner, but listening too.

In the rudely hostile silence Hop's voice changed and became harsh.

'So how do I get there? Which path from here?'

One of the men said, after another pause like an insult, 'If I was you, *stranger,* I wouldn't go there at all. Not at all.'

Another said, 'Zeb don't take to strangers. Not just at the present time.'

'And why not?'

The men turned their heads slowly to look at one another, slowly and knowingly. One said, 'The stranger's asking why not.'

'Well?' said Hop sharply. 'Why not?'

The small boy was staring with his eyes bulging darkly. Now it was as though Hop's question, or the tone it was asked in, had pulled a trigger in the boy. He gave out with a kind of shrill bark. He said, 'Because they killed a man up there today. They killed a strange man that went snooping around where he wasn't wanted. He got what was coming to him that man did, stranger. Yes he did.'

For a second he left his mouth gaping, petrified by his own impudent audacity. One of the men started to lumber up off his behind with his hand raised threateningly. The boy had bolted out of sight before the man could get fully to his feet.

He sat down again heavily. They all looked at Hop. One said, 'Well, stranger. You heard. What's that they say about out of the mouths of babes and suchlike?'

They made a sickening appearance, stupidly, confidently threatening, not bothering to talk straight or move themselves. It was like being casually spat on. Also, the rat's whisker suggested, just to sit there and take it could possibly be dangerous, an encouragement to their evil notions. Hop got to his feet.

He said, 'Friends, I'm not just any kind of a stranger. I'm here on business. I expect to do business with your man Zeb.'

He glared at one jellyfish face after another and went marching out to the street where the mule was tethered. Wondering which of two paths to take, he recalled an unconscious jerk of the head one of the men had made when he first spoke of 'Zeb's place', and decided to take his direction from that.

'Jog,' he said to the mule.

The path went gently upwards across barren ground. Then ahead he saw the road blocked by wattles and brushwood which could have been a gate or a barricade, with a wall of rough stone extending from either side of it. From a hump of land just beyond the wall, where the path up out of the village could be overlooked, four men were coming down to the barricaded gap in the wall. One, an old bull of a man carrying an iron pike, forced his way like a bull through the brushwood barricade and stood in front of it. The other three, two carrying clubs and one a sickle, remained behind it.

The big old man leaned on his pike. He looked relaxed and yet, from the way he held himself, ready to spring too. At a hundred yards' distance the mule stopped.

'Jog,' said Hop.

The mule moved forward slowly. Hop called out a greeting. There was no answer. The big man's face was taut with a savage, sneering grin or grimace. The rat's whiskers signalled suddenly that this man was going to stand absolutely still and silent like that, waiting for Hop to come very close and lean over to talk to him and then he would lunge with the pike. Hop reined in the mule, which not only stopped, but backed a little away.

Raising his voice Hop said, 'Are you farmer Zebedee?'

The big man, his eyes now watching Hop like a wrestler's eyes, gave what could just pass for a nod.

Pulling gently on the bridle, Hop got the mule turned sideways on the path. Like that, if the man rushed him he would have space and time to get headed away and run for it. Then he spoke carefully, explaining who he was and his business.

The big old man listened, not moving, not saying anything. 'So I thought,' said Hop, 'I'd just come out here and find out whether there's anything we supply that you need. I thought I could look around the place and get an idea.'

At that there was a noise from the big man's throat as though he were straining to retch out words that were choking him and he could hardly spew out. They came, at first unintelligibly. The first that Hop could make out were, 'Look around! Look around he says!' The thought so expressed caused the sense of whatever the man was saying next to be engulfed in a vomit of words. He held the pike up and shook it and his body was shaking all over. The three men with the clubs were watching him and watching Hop.

The old man had his words under control now, and they came out in a steady, violent drone. It was about Hop, at first; the stranger and spy trying to get in and look around. Then about that other stranger who had been there that day. Hop saw the men with the clubs and the sickle looked at one another when that other stranger was mentioned.

As if he knew that Hop knew what had happened to that other stranger, the old man's drone vibrated with new violence: he was the advocate for the defence of just actions, unjustly misunderstood. What did anyone, any outsider from Jericho, or God knew where, know about how things were with a fruit farmer whose father before him had built up this farm and he himself had doubled its size and crop, and now was menaced horribly by bandits, tax-collectors, no account landless swine with preachers preaching revolt, preaching grab, getting ready to murder all the farmers in the country and take over?

Madly, the shaking pike calling heaven to witness, this old man was spitting out with curses his story of his life, his heart's blood, it seemed, rushing to his brain and boiling there. His words poured from a deep storage tank of hatreds. Hop sat there for a while, looking gloomily ahead of him between the twitching ears of the mule. Then he turned the animal in the direction of the village and said, 'Jog.' The mule jogged fast, perhaps scared or bothered by the furious voice coming after them.

Ten miles from Jericho, the sun down, and no moon. The inn was quiet. Two of the men who had been in the yard were on the flat roof, taking the late evening air. Only the proprietor was dozing in the courtyard. He made no comment on Hop's quick return from 'Zeb's place'. Perhaps he had all along taken it for granted. Perhaps he made it his business never to comment on anything. He showed Hop where to stall the mule, and the little room looking on to the courtyard where he could sleep. The stew he brought for supper was good, a thing which surprised Hop, who had by now concluded that everything about this hamlet was about as vile as it could be. The wine was neither better nor worse than was to be expected in such a place. Hop ate and drank slowly, sat for a while watching the stars come out and writing off whatever profits might have been anticipated from business at 'Zeb's place', and went to lie down in the little room. He kept his rat's whiskers, so to speak, outside the cloak he wrapped himself in. The other stranger had been killed. On the other hand, that other one had been killed snooping around right inside the old man's fruit farm. Hop had done nothing so dangerous. He slept lightly.

In the dead of the night some noise other than the noise of night insects out there in the scrub wakened him. He heard the mule stamp twice in its stall. There was another sound, possibly a pariah dog scuffing at a rubbish heap. He dozed again, and his doze was pierced and torn by a high whinnying yell or howl of terror and agony. It was the mule for sure. Hop jumped from the bunk, went fast to the door, checked himself, peering this way and that in the starlight and loosening the great knife at his belt. The screams of the mule were a pain in the ear drums. Nothing moved in the courtyard. Hop went across it quickly pausing again before going out from under the short low passage leading to the patch of wasteland where the stable was. The screams came, stopped and came again in a searing incantation.

The mule had sunk half down on the left side of its rump, its hind legs sprawled sideways. Its front legs were still standing, the feet drumming feebly and pawing at the ground. Its head was strained so far back that muzzle, neck and back were in a line all the way back to the bloody ground at the back, the blood coming from the slashing of the sinews of the hough of both legs, where the animal had been hamstrung, seemingly with a sickle.

Hop drew his heavy-bladed, razor-sharp knife, and slashed with all his force at the tensed throat, twice along the same line. The blood gushed, drowning the screams in a bubble of moans, and the whole front part of the mule fell heavily on the earth. As Hop turned and started to go, a last jet of blood gushed.

Stepping stealthily, he got out of the stable and round it. There was nothing to be heard but the insect sounds and the careful padding of his own feet.

He took a line through the scrub which he reckoned would bring him to the Jericho track a mile or so from the inn. After half a mile of fast going, with several stops to look and listen, he was sure there was no pursuit. There might still be an ambush. But why that, when it would have been easy to set on him by the stable? Maybe they thought that to kill two men in their territory in a single day and night could risk to bring the gendarmes down on them. They could calculate that one man killed and another man's mule hamstrung were warning enough to strangers to keep out.

He got on to the track and the going should have been easy. And he wanted to go fast because today was the day when the postal courier left Jericho for Sachem and he had to get his report to Simon into the postbag. He recalled bitterly how he had expected to look around 'Zeb's place' in the cool of the evening, talk business with Zeb, get a comfortable night's rest at the fruit farm, and start riding at first light. It was a good track and the mule could have got him to Jericho in good time. No rest. No business. No mule. If his feet had been in good shape he could still have made it comfortably. But they were still tender, with small cuts not properly healed, after that painful trudge on the Jerusalem to Jericho after he had picked up the man by the roadside. He cursed the man who called himself Alpha—not as a person, but for being there, half dead, just at that time, thereby causing trouble and inconvenience which seemed to be going on and on. On his account Hop was being reduced to stumbling along this track at about half a man's normal walking speed, and even at that pace suffering pain in his feet all the time.

To help himself along he sang verses from an obscene song. His voice was powerful and he much liked to sing. But except in taverns late at night when people were fuddled, he got little chance to sing when people were around. They said he had no sense of tune and beat. Still less could he let his voice go when they were chanting the sacred hymns at religious ceremonies. Simon of Sachem, whose snuffling voice could not chant so much as a bar, saw fit to sneer at Hop's voice and prophesy that his uncouth noises would get them turned out of the religious community, with consequent grave loss of business.

Recalling this, and also because his mood became sombrely sad as he trudged under the stars, Hop changed from one sort of song to quite another. He remembered a sort of song which had once been a solemn psalm and then had somehow got translated into a dolorous kind of marching song.

'What can I do?' said Great Man Moses ... ayah ... ayah
'My war is lost ... ayah ... ayah
'Who lost it? Who lost it?
'Adam lost the war,' said Great Man Moses
'Adam lost the war ... ay ... ay ... ah.'

Even marching troops could not sing all night, still less a man walking painfully alone. He brooded furiously on his dismal state, the state of the country and finally the aloof, unco-operative, often apparently downright hostile attitude of God which the priests explained as being fully justified by the sinfulness of man but which Hop under present conditions considered unfair, childishly so. Light-headed with weariness and rage he looked up at the stars and the thought came to him that you couldn't even spit at them without the spit falling back on you. Typical of the situation of a human being on this earth. 'God,' he croaked, 'if you can't help why can't you leave us alone? Clear right out and let us get on with things without you messing us about.'

Then it was dawn and sunrise and the glare of the sun made his temper worse. But by the time he looked down on Jericho, hazy under its palm trees, he was numb to everything except the knowledge that he had come to journey's end, that very soon now he would be stumbling up to the door of Joshua's place, and he would eat and drink and rest his feet and get his report to Simon of Sachem done, unless that postal courier had already gone.

Sarah, his wife, would get the news from Simon. On getting the report, Simon would rush round to her to announce that, after all, and to his amazement, Hop had not absconded with the firm's money, abandoning also the wife of his bosom. He would indicate that it was, after all, just the sort of thing that might have happened. And Sarah would laugh in his face. Thinking about Sarah, Hop thought that the thing he would most like to happen to him now would be to be home again and hear Sarah laughing.

There were few people about in the streets. Some of them overtook him on the street and then turned to stare at him. He cursed them under his breath. He was only a few hundred yards from the inn when he was aware of a man walking briskly up from behind and calling out to him, 'Just a minute there.'

He stopped wearily and, turning, saw a man with the insignia of the Civil Police Corps.

The man addressed him by his full name as written in Joshua's register. 'That's me,' Hop said.

'I'll have to ask you,' said the policeman, civil-spoken and harsh-toned, 'to come with me to Headquarters. The Chief wants to see you.'

'Is it far? I don't want to have to walk far. I'm all in.'

'Not very far,' the policeman said.

CHAPTER THREE

Not very far; but once inside, it seemed a person had come a long way. A long way from Samaria, and Joshua's inn, and even the streets of Jericho.

This was very different from the police station at Sachem, often familiarly visited by Hop on routine matters such as permits, travel papers. This was bigger, naturally. More active, of course. But it was more than bigger and busier: more alien. Uniformed men, plain clothes men, continuously on the move: up to something urgent you would have told from their looks and their walk; urgent, and secret too.

'It was like,' Hop told Joshua later, 'being on the inside of a wasps' nest.'

He said to the policeman who had brought him there: 'I'm all in. Get me something to eat and drink. I can't talk to anyone the way I feel.'

Presently a boy brought him a platter with water, wine, bread and fruit. A police officer, very young, very jaunty, followed the boy. Looking down at Hop he said, 'Treat our place as an hotel. We strive to please.'

When Hop only nodded and began to eat and drink the officer said: 'We like our clients to be in good shape. More use that way to Mr J. Likes to see them come in full of health and spirits. Naturally, the way they go out, that's a different matter.' He smiled unpleasantly.

'Mr J.?'

The officer put his head back a little and half closed his eyes. He looked down with a look both haughty and suddenly suspicious.

'You don't know who I mean? You're that much of a stranger?'

'First time in Jericho.'

'Is that really so?'

He asked it in a tone suggesting that perhaps it was not really so.

Hop said, 'You're from Jericho yourself?'

The officer smiled, looking more haughty and jaunty than before.

'I certainly am,' he said. He added, as though the stranger had committed a stupidity: 'You'll learn to know a Jericho officer when you see him.'

What then was special about Jericho police officers? This brash look? This sarcastic, jaunty, obscurely threatening manner?

Hop said, 'Any idea why I've been brought here? I'm a busy man.'

'Not too busy to see us. We're very busy men too. Work for all at a time like this.'

'Anything special about the time?'

'Why ask me? You go about. You travel the country. You see things. And you ask what's special?'

A voice called sharply from somewhere just out of sight.

The officer looked over his shoulder and said to Hop, 'He's ready for you. Best get moving.'

He accompanied Hop to a room where was seated a man with a face like a block of wood that someone had drawn features on with rough charcoal.

'This is the man Superintendent,' the officer said, and left the two of them alone.

The Superintendent established a fact: that some days previously Hop had picked up a man lying beaten and naked beside the Jerusalem–Jericho road and brought him to Jericho.

Question: 'How did you know the fellow wasn't a plant?'

Answer: 'I didn't. I didn't know that he wasn't.'

Question: 'Did you not? I mean it would have been the natural normal thing for you to think. The man lies there, screams, traveller stops, gets down on the roadway, the gang jumps out of the bushes, loots him, kills him maybe. It happens.'

Answer: 'I know it happens. I wasn't born yesterday. I tell you I didn't know, how could I? whether he was a plant or not. I just knew he seemed to be in very great pain and screamed twice—I suppose for help.'

Question: 'But if he *had* been a plant he'd have done just that, wouldn't he.'

Answer: 'I took a chance.'

Question: 'Was it really a chance?'

Answer: 'What d'you mean by that?'

Question: 'Might you not have known a bit more about the circumstances than you've told me?'

Answer: 'What the hell could I have known?'

Question: 'Doesn't it strike you as a bit odd that a man like you, a *respectable* traveller, with a lot of urgent and legitimate business to do, no doubt, should have taken a chance like that?'

Answer (suddenly shouted furiously): 'So everyone can die in a ditch by God so long as everything's done in due order? Is that it? You cops should die screaming in ditches while someone treks up to heaven or wherever to ask the Lord God are you the type of citizen that ought to be kept alive? That'll be the day and may I be there to see it.'

Hop had jumped to his feet to make this utterance, gesticulating violently as he did so. But before the other could order him to sit down, or possibly shout for help, Hop sat down, breathing heavily. After a brief pause:

Question: 'Once you'd brought this man into town, why didn't you notify official quarters?'

Answer: 'I thought the inn notified the police of registrations.'

Question: 'Didn't it occur to you, in these particular circumstances, to notify the health authorities? Don't you appreciate that Jericho has the best health record in the country? How can we keep that up if irresponsible people bring sick people into town and plant them in inns without a word to the proper quarters? Suppose everyone acted like that.'

Answer: 'D'you mean the area is so badly policed that people are found half dead by the roadside twice a week? Is that standard for Jericho and district?'

The Superintendent returned suddenly to the original point.

'So you deny, formally and categorically and in so many words that you had any previous contact with or knowledge of this individual found by you at the roadside?'

He spoke as though he were reading from some invisible manual of interrogation written on the wall behind Hop's head.

'Great God,' said Hop, 'how could I?' He stared at the man in astonishment at the kind of ideas which could enter these people's heads.

The Superintendent shrugged slightly. The small gesture, breaking his previous total immobility, was as startling as a sudden wave of his arm.

'There might be ways,' he said, speaking as though to himself. He fell silent, looking concentratedly at his hands folded on his knees. Hop started to say something, but the other interrupted him by clapping his hands loudly together and calling out some name. The young officer appeared in the office.

The interrogator said, 'The Chief will want to see this man. I'm going now to have a word with him. Take this man to the waiting room and stay with him until he's sent for.'

In the waiting room Hop asked:

'What now?'

His off-hand, semi-confidential manner suddenly transformed, the officer said, 'I'm not here to answer questions.'

At that, Hop became aware that across a corridor opposite the waiting room a door was open, a curtain had been a little parted. From behind it someone was looking at him.

The officer remained austerely silent. Hop continued to stare across the corridor. Then a voice from somewhere behind the curtain called, 'All right, officer.'

The officer led him into the room behind the curtain and left him.

It was a room like the Superintendent's, and the Superintendent was standing in it. But the seated man was not at all like: in fact seemingly was the opposite of the Superintendent at every point. He was young; his face handsome, mobile and very dark. He wore civilian clothes of a cut and colours that gave the impression of being an expensive fancy-dress, or a disguise. He was apparently concluding a consultation with the Superintendent. He talked volubly and laughed often. His gestures were continuous and elegant: his flow of words likewise. He did not bother to halt the flow or lower his voice as Hop entered, except to signal to him to be seated.

'No, no. If there's anything in this, we'll keep it all for ourselves just as long as we can. Our little bit of manna from Heaven. No reason in the world to let the Men in Black or the lads from Tiber-side get any credit if we can help it.'

These references (fully understood by Hop) to the Sanhedrin Police Corps, and the Roman Military Police, respectively, seemed to shock the Superintendent who actually shook his head slightly and pulled his mouth into a disapproving shape.

'All right, all right,' said the other, 'leave it all to me, leave it to your young uncle. If there's blame to be taken afterwards, uncle will take it.'

The Superintendent left the room, and the Chief smiled gaily at Hop. 'Make yourself comfortable. Rest yourself. You've had a tiring day, or night.'

Hop shifted slightly on the couch.

The Chief continued to smile at him and said, 'So you're the Samaritan. From Sachem, I see by your papers.'

Hop told Joshua later, that, 'When he started on that tack I could feel belly-muscles beginning to act up.' He had often noticed, Hop said to Joshua, that when Judaeans started talking about a given man as a Samaritan instead of just as a man, or a trader or whatever, there was always one of two reasons for it. Either the person talking was keenly, maybe fanatically religious, seeing Samaritans as dangerous heretics the way the Samaritan religious people saw the Judaeans, or else the reason was something to do with politics.

'When there's political trouble around,' he said to Joshua, 'discontent, agitation, subversion or what the hell, first thing a lot of people do is start a game of Hunt the Samaritan. Either we Samaritans are behind whatever the trouble is, or if we aren't behind it already, we're getting all set to aid and abet it.'

Looking at the Chief, Hop felt he could bet that this man was no fanatic for any version of the true interpretation of Holy Writ. It followed that there was something political in the works. There was. The Chief was saying, 'Naturally, as you'll of course appreciate, it would be of interest to me to know, quite generally and roughly you understand, something of your political affiliations. If any, of course, if any.'

Hop said that he had no political affiliations. He said he hardly knew one political party or political group from another. Recalling the kind of thing Simon of Sachem said, he declared that in his opinion all politics was a racket and a swindle. All those fellows were simply out for what they could get.

'Quite so,' said the Chief, 'quite so. A perfectly tenable attitude. We are all of us to some extent victims of the politicians. We officials and civil servants no less than you business men.

'And not the least exasperating factor in our situation,' he added, smiling suddenly and brilliantly, 'as I have often had occasion to note, is that every subversive and criminal revolutionary when caught always starts by denying that he has the least interest in politics and vehemently asserting that so far as he is concerned politics is just a racket and a swindle and can go to the devil. It's a damn nuisance, don't you find? But of course you won't have had the disagreeably frequent contacts with such people that I am forced to experience.'

Hop held himself very still on the couch. Whiff of an unknown danger?

'Though when I say "criminal",' the Chief continued, 'I should add that I would be the last to deny that some of such people are what, in a general, not perhaps very precise or illuminating way of speaking, is termed "sincere". Whether this quality makes them more or less dangerous to the State is a matter I have often heard discussed by experts more qualified to judge than I am. In my,' he fluttered his hand, 'admittedly limited experience which, all the same, must of course be a great deal more extensive than your own, some of those who are what is called "sincere" are also criminals in the most ordinary sense of the word. They steal. They murder for profit. And nobody is ever, or hardly ever, sure when a given man is robbing and murdering in aid of his own pocket or to finance some political activity in which, as he says, he "believes". Or take miracle-workers. Many of them may be taking subsidies from conspirators in the shadows, so to speak, who use these persons to attract a following, influence crowds, create—don't you see, for instance—possibilities of riot.

'I need not remind you,' the voice went on, 'that there have been occasions, quite recent occasions, when the authorities, thinking such people harmless, failed to check their activities in time. I myself was very young then but you will certainly recall clearly the time when the Palace of King Herod was besieged by the mob in Jerusalem. The streets ran, as the saying goes, with blood. And that was no saying. And you will remember that no less than two thousand persons—*two thousand*—had to be crucified afterwards. I've been told that their howls of agony, hundreds of them howling all together as the nails were hammered in, could be heard for miles.'

'I was in Samaria at the time,' Hop said.

'You were fortunate. Samaria was the place of peace in, so to speak, the middle of those pools of blood. For as you'll of course recall, there was just to the north of your country, in Galilee, at almost the same time that disastrous—nearly disastrous I should say—revolt of Judas the Galilean. His father, as you may remember, had been crucified on the fully justified order of the late King.'

'I remember something of the sort.'

'The interest of the past is, of course, sometimes enhanced if it has some bearing on the present. Just to take an instance, we all know, don't we? that the defeated forces of Judas the Galilean reorganized themselves. They exist, very much so one may think, at this very day—we call them the Zealots or the Rebels, and our Roman friends in their more simple terms describe them as "Sicarii", "the dagger men" or "the assassins".

'You'll appreciate that if I let all these thoughts run through my mind now, if I risk to bore you with them, it is simply because here in Jericho—this happy city which I am sure our friend next door has told you has the best health record in the country—we are confronted with certain special problems. Here, in what some of the leading citizens like to think of as our "garden city" we simply cannot afford,' the chief paused and looked up at the roof of the room, 'to be,' he looked round at the walls, 'careless. Or, how shall I put it? gentle.'

Hop, quite in control of his temper now, saw fit to make a deliberate explosion.

'What in God's name,' he said, 'is the use of all this rigmarole? You are threatening me. You are trying to frighten me. Well let me tell you, my good sir, it won't wash. The hell with you and your threats. And as you seem to be a half-ways intelligent man, let me point out to you that whatever you do to me you'll be none the better off, you'll get no credit for your Civil Police Corps, because I just don't know anything? Can you understand there can be a man who doesn't *know or care* a single goddamn thing about all the sort of stuff you've been talking about. Except, of course, when political trouble's bad for business.'

The Chief made a soothing, patting gesture with his hand. 'Yes, yes,' he said. 'That's of course. If I may say so, your irritation at any suggestion whatever that you might have any special knowledge of such people does you credit. Believe me, to be in the position of even seeming to make such a suggestion is embarrassing to me. But you'll appreciate,' he said, 'you surely must appreciate that when one finds a stranger, quite incidentally a Samaritan, with what we bloody cops would call excellent "cover" as a businessman, more or less smuggling into the city a certain man, real name unknown, found in suspicious circumstances beside the Jerusalem road, one wonders. It's one's tiresome duty to wonder. One asks oneself certain questions. It's, how shall I say? automatic.'

Hop said, 'I still find it amazing, to be the object of such questions. It's . . . grotesque. I've no connection whatever with this certain man beyond finding him half dead and bringing him, not "smuggling" him, into town. I've hardly had twenty words with him. He wasn't, when I last saw him five days ago, in any condition to talk. All he could say was that he came from somewhere up north, Laodicea I think or Antioch, and he was going down from Jerusalem to Jericho when he was attacked by thieves.'

'That's perfectly clear. Still, I'm afraid you'll have to bear with me while I go through just a bit more of police routine.' He suddenly handed across to Hop what seemed to be a list of names, about twenty of them, with different small markings after each, some kind of code. 'How many of these do you know of?' he asked.

There was an interruption. An enormous dog pushed its cruel-seeming head and its fore-quarters through the door-curtain. Looking at the Chief and the dog in the same half-second, Hop saw the man's face twisted by a rictus of anger, and a flash of panic in his eyes. The dog was tensing itself. Its eyes were fixed on Hop as on a target.

The Chief spoke, vibrantly, two unintelligible words. The dog's eyes swivelled round to him. Its muscular bulk quivered. Its tongue came out and licked the outside of its mouth. The Chief spoke again. Without turning or taking its eyes off the Chief the dog backed slowly, like a huge man performing with precision the steps of a dance. Then a scared voice was heard calling in the corridor. The footsteps of the dog and a man could be heard going away together.

The Chief raised his voice and called. The young officer appeared and stood expectantly. Without raising his voice much above a whisper, the Chief cursed him venomously. How had the dog got loose? What had the handler been up to? That handler was to be flogged. He was to be forbidden all contact with the police dogs. The dog's trainer was to report in half an hour. He cursed the officer again for dereliction of duty. The officer withdrew, trembling.

The Chief massaged his dark face gently with both hands and smiled gravely at Hop.

'You have my apologies,' he said. 'I really am ashamed that such a thing could happen. Those dogs are supposed to be under total and immediate control, always. Rigorous and intelligent training, continual supervision and control. With it—an indispensable addition to our resources. Without it—a menace.'

Hop said, 'You seemed to have it under control all right.'

'I've been through the training course for the trainers. At first I couldn't believe what was told me about the potentialities of dogs; truly trained dogs. Now I know. A remarkable weapon.'

'I didn't know the police used them.'

'We in Jericho are the first to do so. The others ... either they can't believe how the dogs can be so trained, or they haven't the imagination to understand their unique uses.'

'Such as?'

'In all cases of what I call "individual confrontation". No use against a big mob, for instance. Or against a number of men trained to act together. But against a man, or a few men. They introduce you see,' he fluttered his hands in an explanatory gesture, 'the element of the unpredictable. Unpredictable, that is to all but the trainers and handlers. To the criminal this purposeful animal seems not just *non*-human but in some sense *super*-human.'

He seemed to brood, and then added, 'There is also—by way, you know, of a little bonus—what I may call the sexual factor.'

'How?'

'The balls,' said the Chief simply. 'A man's awareness of the exposed position of his balls in relation to a dog. A dog which can be trained to go, specifically, for the sexual organs. It produces a fear much worse than fear of a cracked skull. Particularly,' he smiled, 'on lusty young men with women on their minds.'

Hop said, 'So you feel that in Jericho, at least, you have the criminals under control?'

The Chief leaned back, sighing. 'Alas,' he said, 'there is no totally reliable recipe for that. Some of the criminals and villains are just as clever as we are. Naturally. They are thinking men, too. They have learned from us about the dogs. They found the district, down there in the south, where we get them. They bribed one of our trainers with really big money. He was detected and executed. But he had taught them all the tricks. As they say, to every attack there is a defence.'

He sighed again and said, 'But you were going to look through that list.' Hop looked at the names. In the sense of having met or talked with them, he knew none. There were several whose doings as gangsters or agitators or supposed spies, spying for the Egyptians or Syrians or others, were so commonly talked of up and down the country that a man would have to be a deaf hermit not to have heard of them. A travelling man of business who pretended such ignorance would be liable to be nailed as a liar. Hop pointed to the fourth name on the list and said yes, he had heard of *him*. The Chief nodded and then got up and came over to stand behind him, reading over his shoulder, pointing with his finger. What about that one? And that one? At about the eighth name, the Chief said, 'What about this Essene? At least, this little code mark indicates that our industrious and omniscient Secret Service believes him to be a member of the Essene sect. Hails from Galilee like the late Judas we were talking about just now. He's been raising a lot of hell up there and all over the place. He was in your neck of the woods, in Samaria quite a while.'

'Yes, I've certainly heard of him. Can't say I know anything much about him. Not beyond the tales every travelling man hears about such people.'

'As a man,' said the Chief, 'who, as you say is forced to be interested in politics when politics becomes bad for business, you might find this Essene, if he is an Essene, worth studying. Not long ago he was actually here in Jericho for a few days. Naturally we kept a close eye on him. Not at all the type of character our leading citizens welcome in their midst. Some of them came here and complained pretty vigorously of what they called police laxity because we had let him enter the city at all. In point of fact they were wrong, because he did his precious reputation a good deal of harm while he was here. If I may say so without undue complacency, I had foreseen something of the kind. Studying his record I had reached the conclusion that he was an excellent example of the type of person we were talking of earlier—partly sincere believer in some cause or other, partly criminal with a sharp eye to the main chance.'

'I didn't know he'd been here,' Hop said defensively, thinking some new allegation was being made or hinted. 'I haven't been here long enough to hear any local gossip. I've never been in Jericho before in my life.'

'Well what happened,' said the Chief, 'was that he came strolling into town with his little gang of devotees or disciples or strong-arm men or whatever they are, and of course our poorer, less fortunate citizens had heard all sorts of rumours about how he was all against the rich, in favour of general expropriation and so on and so forth. They turned out in force to have a look at him and hear what he had to say. There were a lot of sick people, too; lame people and blind people, hoping for some miracle cure.'

'I thought Jericho had such a fine record of public health.'

The Chief smiled appreciatively. 'We have. But even our excellent health officials can't, unfortunately, perform miracles. As I was saying, there was a big crowd and naturally there was a good deal of pressure on us to break it up as an unlawful assembly and arrest the fellow for incitement to riot or something of the kind. I was taking a bit of a chance, but my instinct told me to let the man have a little more rope.

'My instinct, a feeling about Jericho.

'Though I say it, the fellow obligingly proved me right. What happened was that while this mob was pushing and shoving round him, there appeared on the scene a wee man, but a damned prominent citizen, called Zacchaeus. A tax-farmer. Lives on the difference between what he pays Government for the concession and what he actually raises in taxes. And believe me, my friend, that's plenty. In fact the fellow's as rich as Croesus and as crooked as they come. I don't know just what got into him that day, but whatever it was he seems to have got to brooding on his misspent days and what might happen to him at his latter end.

'Apparently he had some crazy idea that if he could conciliate this Essene, the Essene would put in a good word for him with the powers above or the powers beyond or whatever. But being a runt-sized little old fellow-me-lad, he can't see the Essene or, more important, catch his eye, without climbing up into a tree so he can look over the people's heads. Well as you may imagine the sight of little Moneybags acting like a pot-bellied monkey up that tree draws plenty of attention from the crowd. Half of them of course hold him directly responsible for their indigent condition. Boo-ing and cat-calling break out. And some of them are just waiting for a word from the Essene to go get that notable example of the nefarious rich and shake him out of his tree and take him apart.

'What's the general amazement and dismay when they see Moneybags making signs to the Essene with the hand that isn't occupied with a life or death grip on that branch, and the Essene, instead of denouncing him in the expected manner, hails him in very friendly fashion and tells him to hurry on down because he, the Essene, proposes to invite himself to dinner with the tax-man that very day.

'So Zacchaeus, all of a happy shake as you may imagine, comes shinning down the tree, and he and the Essene more or less fall into one another's arms. The crowd's too stunned by the sight to do anything just then, but later, while the Essene and his gang are living it up at the taxman's place, the mood of that confluence of under-privileged citizens turned very very nastily against the Essene. My observers who were there to make mental notes reported a list of really sulphurous observations on the subject of the Essene, including threats to stone him on sight.

'Of course nothing came of it. The Essene spent the night safe at Moneybags' place, and got out of town early next day. I don't say that a little word of warning I caused to be conveyed to him, to the effect you understand that the police might not be able to guarantee his safety if he lingered in Jericho, may not have speeded his going.

'I never was able to get an exact figure of what Zacchaeus paid him for saving his soul or whatever he was supposed to have done, but I imagine it was plenty. But it is a fact, and I mention this because it gives you a line on the shrewdness of that Essene, and is one of the reasons why we keep a very careful watch on him, before he left he got Zacchaeus to promise to make a huge donation to the poor and to promise that in cases where he had extorted money from people by falsely accusing them of tax evasion he would pay them back four times the amount he had extorted. You see the ingenuity of the Essene's ploy. Zacchaeus had to pay out what amounted to mob blackmail. On the other hand the mob, the poor, were going to feel that maybe they had misjudged that holy man, and that by subtle means he had after all got them a big handout from Moneybags. A damn clever fellow, the Essene. I admit I had to admire him, unofficially of course.'

'Quite a story,' said Hop cautiously.

'Instructive, is it not?' said the Chief, moving away from the couch and starting to pace about the room. 'I have told it to you at what I hope you will not think tedious length because I do feel, my instinct tells me, that intelligent and respectable business men like yourself by getting to know rather more than you, as you tell me, do about these gentry can from time to time perform valuable services to the State, indeed to that whole fabric of order and security upon which, in the last analysis, the prosperity of business depends.'

'I must say,' said Hop sincerely, 'I find it pretty difficult to get much idea of how their minds work. I mean the minds of these agitators, criminals, etcetera. I think I'll keep on doing my best to steer clear of the whole mess.'

'You'll forgive me, I'm sure,' said the Chief, walking

towards a corner of the room and turning to walk back again, 'for saying that in my opinion that is a somewhat short-sighted view. I cannot feel it's in your own interests to take such an attitude. Obviously information gathered about such people is of interest to us. And then, you know, supposing that a person such as yourself were at any time to find himself in some little difficulty with the authorities, some red tape nuisance, you know, the fact that he had co-operated with us in connection with matters arising at one time or another would naturally give him certain advantages which would otherwise be ... well, how shall I say? not by any means at his disposal.'

He re-seated himself carefully, giving Hop the impression that the interview was about to be terminated, perhaps still in time for him to get his report into the post bag. The Chief said:

'By the way, can you tell me as a matter of interest why the back of your cloak, just below the shoulder-blade, is soaked in newly dried blood?'

CHAPTER FOUR

Hop sat rigid, totally amazed. He tried to crane his neck to take a look at his own shoulder blade. Becoming aware that this action was not only futile but was twisting him into ludicrous and humiliating postures, he loosened the cloak, dragging part of the back round to the front. There was the bloodstain, a foot or so from top to bottom, very dark at the top, fading to brown at the bottom.

He stared and said, 'I just don't know.'

The Chief coughed faintly and said nothing.

Hop went on staring at the stain and trying to remember. Then he exclaimed, 'My mule!'

'Your what?' asked the Chief.

'My mule,' repeated Hop. 'I had to cut its throat. The blood must have got on my back without my knowing. I was in a hurry to get away.'

'Evidently,' said the Chief. 'But if I may say so the circumstances are not entirely clear. It's a trivial point, no doubt, but, as a matter of interest, just why did you cut your mule's throat? One doesn't do that every day, and on this occasion it seems to have forced you to take a long and exhausting walk from wherever it was you were. We might, in fact, start with that point. Where exactly were you?'

'By God,' said Hop, his rage of the night welling back into him. 'I'll tell you about that. Now maybe you'll learn something about criminals, murderers, etcetera, operating under the noses of your damned police corps.'

He told furiously of his visit to the village, his visit to 'Zeb's place', his reception there, of the open admission in the village that a stranger, apparently just because he was a stranger, had been murdered there that very day, or during the night before, of the ham-stringing of the mule.

'How d'you like it now, Chief?' he asked sarcastically.

'Of course,' said the Chief, 'that village and the farms around are not, strictly speaking—are not, in fact, at all—within my jurisdiction, which extends only to the city boundaries.'

'So you wash your hands of whatever happens there. Murder. Outside your jurisdiction. You aren't interested.'

'I didn't say that,' said the Chief. 'Naturally I'm interested. Very much so, in fact.' He paused, looking up at the roof. Then he said, 'Could you recall a little more fully the gist of the harangue which you describe the farmer as making?'

Hop did so to the best of his recollection. The impact of the old man's words had been such that it was easier to remember than forget them.

The Chief said, 'He mentioned landless swine, preachers preaching revolt.... Something about getting ready to murder all the farmers in the country and take over?'

'That was about it.'

The Chief again contemplated the roof, this time for a full quarter-minute. Then he said, 'May I take it that in the course of your travels in your pursuit of business, you've heard the name Barabbas?'

'Of course I have,' said Hop with some indignation. 'Who hasn't? D'you think I'm deaf, or stupid or something?'

'Neither, neither,' said the Chief smoothly. 'I assure you I don't take you for anything of the kind. Quite the contrary. My point is, quite simply that the terms the old man used are just the terms that people, certainly people in his position, commonly apply to the followers of Barabbas. Therefore it is possible that they are operating.... You follow my reasoning?'

'But Barabbas is supposed to be in jail in Jerusalem.'

'I know, I know. A stupid business. The people there picked him up. A ham-handed thing to do in the first place. If I'd been in charge I'd have let him run loose, waited and watched him till I could have put my hand on the leadership of the gang. But those clots in Jerusalem mess everything up. First they arrest him. Then they get cold feet. Think he's too hot to hold. They're scared of the mob up there that thinks he's a hero, a saviour, going to lead a revolt or something of the kind. So they turn him over to the Roman military. Though what those Tiberians really know about what goes on here you could put, as the saying goes, in a pig's ear.'

Hop said, 'Still and all, there doesn't seem much to go on. I mean just because that old brute of a farmer talked the way he did. Not much to prove that the stranger was anything to do with Barabbas.'

'Nothing at all to *prove* it,' said the Chief.

The dialogue continued.

Hop: 'After all, that farmer's pretty nearly a confessed murderer. But you seem to be treating the man who got murdered as the villain.'

Chief: 'The farmer? A killer, obviously. Murderer if you like. But would he have killed just any stranger?'

Hop: 'I don't understand.'

Chief: 'I mean if the man had been just any stray stranger, wouldn't he more likely have had him chased off his land? Beaten up, perhaps, and then chased off. But suppose the old man and his work people had some reason to think he was a scout or something for the Barabbas gang? That would have been a bit different, wouldn't it?'

Hop: 'Could be. It's just a guess, though. And I'd say that fellow, and the louts he had with him with their clubs and the sickle—I bet that was the sickle that did for my mule—they'd have been quite up to killing anyone they didn't like the looks of.'

Chief: 'Another point. I'm thinking of what you tell me about the attitude of the villagers to yourself. And then the way the old man burst out at you like that right away. A respectable-looking businessman on his mule. You'd think he'd at least have questioned you.'

Hop: 'These backwoodsmen. What with the state of the country they're always on about—they hear rumours, they get the jumps. They think every new face is an enemy.'

Chief: 'Of course. It could be like that. On the other hand let's look at it this way. Suppose, it's reasonable to suppose, they'd heard something about the episode you were involved in on the Jerusalem road. News of a thing like that gets about. There'd been four days or so for it to reach them.'

Hop: 'So what?'

Chief: 'Well, just suppose they knew, or believed, that the man by the roadside was one of Barabbas's people; or mixed up with them in some way. The way they get the story, this man is mysteriously picked up by a stranger, a Samaritan, and taken to Jericho. Soon after that they catch this trespasser, marauder or whatever he is on their land and see some reason to kill him. And later on the same day this same Samaritan on the mule turns up at the village, gets the story of that killing, and seems to want to look around the farm. You can see how their minds might work on a thing like that.'

Hop: 'I suppose so. People like that put two and two together and make nine. And that's enough to murder someone for, or hamstring a man's mule. What bloody-minded, ignorant pigs.'

He said this with vehement finality, taking it for granted that the Chief would heartily agree with him. To his astonishment and then to his angry dismay he saw that the Chief was again silently contemplating the roof. His attitude of aloof attention somehow suggested that he was simply considering two equal sides to a problem. The villagers could have thought *this*, and Hop was saying *that*, and the Chief had maddeningly the air of a man quite undecided as to which view of the events might be true.

'You must see if they believe that they'll believe anything,' Hop said.

'They've probably had a lot of wild things happen to them. They could think it safer to believe the worst rather than take anything on trust.'

'They could think that, I suppose,' said Hop. 'But,' he broke out in angry desperation, 'that's no good reason for anyone else to think it. Is it now, I ask you?'

Seeming to ignore this, the Chief said, 'What I would advise, if I may say so, is that you should make it your business, your quite urgent business in fact, to get to know rather more than you tell me you do about that young man from the roadside. You might learn something of his contacts, associates, political affiliations, if any. If any, of course.'

Hop snorted and shrugged despairingly.

'Anything of interest, and my instinct tells me there will be matters of interest, you can report to me. Not tomorrow. Say next day.'

'But I've no more business here. I'm leaving for Jerusalem tomorrow.'

'I'm anxious to explain to you that you *have* business here. You simply must not think of leaving town tomorrow, or even the next day. Quite frankly, we couldn't—as responsible officials—allow you to do so.'

'Damn you. I've got work to do.'

'So, as you see, have I.'

'For all I know the man's probably gone by now. What am I supposed to do about that? Get arrested, I suppose, for not giving up my business in the country and sticking around here watching him instead. Or he may have been even worse hurt than I thought. He may be dead by now.'

He stood up, shaking with indignation. The Chief rose too. He put a hand on Hop's shoulder and gave a happy little laugh.

'No, no,' he said, patting the shoulder. 'He's not left town. He's not dead either. Not even dying. Quite the contrary. I can promise you that. I think you'll find your young—how shall I say?—protégé in excellent form.'

On the way to Joshua's inn, Hop was resenting and hating that devious Chief so much that he found himself feeling positively sympathetic to the young man from the roadside. No question that fellow was in serious trouble. All his papers, stolen, for a start—assuming he ever had any. No papers at all were a lot worse even than Samaritan papers. His mind, inflamed by the sly hints and threats of the Chief, made ugly pictures of what they might do to the young man: scourges, stoning to death, nails hammering his hands on to the wood.

'And I,' he said bitterly to Joshua a little later, 'thought I was saving his life.'

Joshua had come hurrying out to meet him under the archway of the inn, just as he had all those five days ago. Joshua said, not asking a question, but stating a fact, 'Trouble.'

When they were resting comfortably on the veranda of Joshua's room, smelling the balsam from the garden court, Joshua said, 'Tell me first what's happened. Then I'll tell you.'

'Trouble for you too?'

Joshua fluttered his hands. 'Can be. Smells like it.'

Hop told him of his trip in the country, the murderous farm, the loss of the mule, his trek back and the interrogation at police Headquarters.

'So you see,' he concluded sourly, 'I'm not to be allowed to be a businessman. I'm ordered to be a police spy.'

Joshua sat looking gloomily out at the garden. Hop said, 'Well? So what's been with you in the meantime?'

Well, he had notified the local police precinct of the new arrivals. A few hours later a couple of detectives had come round, asking questions about 'this Samaritan' and 'this man who calls himself just Alpha'. They had wanted to see Alpha. They were told he was ill. They insisted. Joshua had gone with them. Alpha had been as arrogantly surly as he had been when Hop and Joshua first talked with him. Joshua had expected the detectives to get rough with him.

'But it looked as though they had some special instructions about that. They didn't lay a hand on him. They didn't even shout the way they normally do. Just went away without having got anywhere. That bothered me. It bothered me a lot.'

Next thing that happened was that Alpha sent word to Joshua that he wanted to move to a better room, one of the best over there on the other side of the garden. 'He knew, because the maidservant or someone had told him, that you'd told me to "let him have what he wants". So he wanted a better room, said it would be good for his health. He sort of leered at me and said he didn't suppose I wanted him to die on me? I told him I wouldn't give a damn, the way I felt about him and all the trouble he was causing. And he said, "But think what a big disappointment that would be to our mutual friend, after all the trouble he took to save my life." '

Joshua had mulled the thing over, and concluded that, given the general uncertainty surrounding this young man, and the fact that the police had some special interest in him, the best thing to do, in the interests of avoiding more trouble than was necessary, was to let him have the better room.

'If you think I was a damn fool,' said Joshua, 'I won't charge you the extra.'

'Hell,' said Hop, 'you were perfectly right.'

'There's more to come,' Joshua said apologetically. 'He found some way—through one of the servants I suppose—of sending out for a girl. Two girls as a matter of fact. Said they were something else he "wanted" and that you'd expect him to have. They're down on the bill too.'

Hop laughed suddenly. 'So it's funny?' Joshua asked.

'Hell, you have to admit the man has a nerve.'

'It's one way of looking at it.'

'Can you think of a better?'

'Maybe not. All the same.'

'All the same, what? You'd rather I cried and tore my hair over it?'

'Not that. But look. It could be that somehow, just because you took that chance when you picked him up off the roadside, you feel pretty special about him. Like when a person picks up a bit of lost jewellery, a bangle or something in the street. He half knows it's a phoney. But just because he found it, he wants to believe it's sound metal. Seems to me if you get to thinking that way about a person you know damn all about, you could be headed for trouble.'

Hop brooded. He said, 'Well, whatever about that, I'd better go see him right away. *He's* in trouble, that's for sure. Did the police come back again?'

'Once. I went with them again, to his new room. Very short visit. No results, and still no rough stuff. Then they went politely away. I didn't like the look of it a bit.'

'I'll talk to him. He may as well know what the police are thinking, damn them. He ought to know.'

'There you go again,' said Joshua.

On the veranda at the far end of the sweet-scented garden, Hop heard music; someone beyond the curtain at the back of the veranda strumming on strings, and a woman singing a sexy song; a good song but one sung so often in all places of entertainment up and down the country that a travelling-man was sick of the sound of it. However, the present singer was putting in some dirtier words than the song had to begin with, and this freshened it somewhat.

Hop called out. The singing stopped, but nobody answered. He pushed his way through the curtain. He brushed against a girl, the one with the instrument. She stood back a little and he noted that she wore the rig-out of the local whores. Coming out of the strong sunlight, he at first had difficulty in distinguishing figures in the dim room. There was another girl squatting by a bed against the opposite wall, and a half-naked young man, a stranger, looked up at him without interest from a low couch he was lounging on. Stepping forward a pace or two, Hop saw Alpha lying naked on the bed with a corner of bedcloth across his middle. Hop recognized him chiefly by the muscles of his shoulders, chest and arms. He had plenty of time to observe those muscles while trudging beside him into Jericho, keeping an eye on him all the time in case he was going to get faint from his wounds and start to slip off the mule.

Now, after peering closer, he could see, behind the clean, almost sleek face he was looking at, the twisted face, filthy with blood and dust he had first seen on the Jerusalem road.

The room smelt strongly and agreeably of hemp. There was a small brazier by the bed. They had been heating hemp with butter and water to make hemp cakes, thought to be the pleasantest way to take it, the way it acted most quickly and yet smoothly.

After what he had heard from Joshua just now, all this was about what he had expected to find. All the same, he was aware of feeling some sort of shock, or sudden chill. Certainly that was nothing to do with the fact that this gay scene existed at his expense. Not that at all, he said to himself. The chill had something to do with the expression on the face of the man who called himself Alpha. It was as though, during the past few days, Hop had been thinking of this young man he had rescued as a part of his life. Not just the same thing Joshua had meant when he talked about picking up phoney jewellery and kidding oneself it was sound metal. There was something of that, but something more too. It could be the way people who have sons think of their sons as separate people and yet part of themselves. Whatever his feelings had been, the man's face as Hop looked at him told him all that was nonsense. Alpha was as separate as he could be. He lay with his hands behind his head. He might have been looking at Hop from a long way off. Hop had a childish impression of having been promised something, or promised himself something, and it not being there; not available; withdrawn from circulation.

Coming across the garden he had taken it for granted this meeting with Alpha, now that Alpha had his health back, would start with some words of thanks from him. Looking at him he knew at once there was going to be nothing like that. After that first minute of chill, he was not even surprised.

Alpha said, 'So you finally got back.'

Hop, looking round the room, 'Well, you certainly haven't been lonely.'

'What was I supposed to do?' Alpha asked. 'Lie here looking at the wall? I can't run around the streets.'

Hop started to say, 'You certainly can't' and stopped there because the girls and the shady-looking young man, probably also a prostitute or as near as made no difference, were all listening. It seemed not to occur to Alpha to send them away. Hop's visit was not that important to him.

'There are a couple of things you ought to know,' Hop said, again looking round at the other three. Alpha sighed irritably and told the girls and the young man they'd better be off. 'The boss man, under the arch out there, he'll pay you off.' Sulkily, but without protest, they got themselves dressed and left, helping themselves to what was left of the hemp cakes.

'The police are after you.'

'They've been here twice.'

'Didn't it strike you as odd they didn't get tougher when you wouldn't say anything?'

'How would I know what they've got in their pig-heads?'

'You don't know. But I have a pretty clear idea. They're taking you very seriously.'

'You get this from the Civils or the Blacks or boys from the west?'

'At the moment, the Civils. They think they're on to something big and they want to keep it to themselves.'

'And so?'

'Only reason they haven't come for you already, I mean no rough stuff, no arrest, and the reason I'm still out and about, my boy, is they think I may be able to get information out of you. Stuff that'll lead them to a lot of people. Little fish to catch big ones.'

'That's standard,' said Alpha.

'They're bastards,' said Hop. 'They're mucking up my whole schedule.'

'Did you only just find out they're bastards?'

Not answering that, Hop said, 'So you can see you're certainly in a tough spot. Me too I daresay.' Trying to make a little joke to warm the cold he felt, he added, 'I'd have done better to leave you by the roadside. Maybe I didn't save you from anything. And look at the trouble you've got me into.'

Alpha let out a guttural deliberate belch. Hop stopped trying to joke and asked him was it not so? His tone told that it was important to him just then to have Alpha admit that it was on his account that Hop's schedule had been disrupted, with possibly worse to come.

Alpha stirred impatiently on the bed and belched again. Hop told Joshua later that 'just to make everything perfect' he had thought of Simon of Sachem, practically had a vision of him as if he had just walked into the room where Hop was asking his urgent question and getting belches. No one ever saw Simon laugh unless someone else fell flat on his face, and then only if Simon was pretty sure the fellow had broken his nose. Simon would certainly have been laughing then. Hop the big rescuer and saviour. Doing a lot of good. Risking death from robber bands. Walking his feet to the bone. Grave trouble with the police. Conned into paying for another man's sex life and hemp. And paid off with a belch. Simon would be laughing all right.

Hop insisted huffily to Alpha, 'Well, it's true enough you know.'

Alpha bothered himself to raise his head a little to look at him. Breathing hemp at him, he said, 'Stop it, uncle. Stuff it. You can't help being the kind of man you are. You get a kick out of good deeds. I've been around in Samaria and there's a lot of that sort of stuff in their religion. If you didn't get a kick you wouldn't act that way. So you're in trouble. The couple of men who went by on the other side of the road before you showed up are the kind of people *they* are. They're in no trouble, you can bet. People do what they want to do. Just enjoy doing different things. No difference that I can see. It's human nature.'

His voice went on and on, and it was clear that the hemp had got to him a little.

'How many more times today,' Hop said to Joshua later, 'am I going to be lectured about politics or human nature? Told the facts of life? First there was that damned police Chief and then I had to listen to this hemp-high vagabond.'

Now Alpha was going on and on about how the whole situation of the human race was going to hell anyway. There could be a revolt. Big patriotic Judaean stuff. The Romans would wipe out the lot. Or the Pharisees would start a civil war against the nationalists, God help them, and the dagger men. Cut each others' throats, and everyone else's too. 'I hear all about it, I know all about it,' Alpha said. 'That's the way it's all going to be.'

When he said he 'heard all about it' that was easy to believe. Anyone sitting around in taverns could get all that stuff off pat between the first drink and the last. People enjoyed talking that way, because if total doom was on the way anyhow why shouldn't everyone get what he could of what he wanted while the getting was still good? Some people simply invented the doom to come just to excuse the way they behaved.

Hop told him to snap out of it and start thinking what was best to be done. Alpha looked surprised for the first time. 'No trick to that,' he said. 'You go back to those pigs and hand them a lot of information from the best sources, that's me, about whatever they think it is they're interested in. Secrets of the underworld.'

Hop told him that was a notion strictly from the hemp. The police would have at least enough information to catch on immediately if they were fed a lot of inventions. They would see through everything he and Alpha could cook up in no time, and then the two of them would be in worse trouble than they were already.

Alpha said, 'But this would *be* authentic. I didn't work for Barabbas for nothing.' He looked at Hop and asked him what ailed him? Had he never heard of Barabbas?

'Strikes me you've led a pretty simple life, uncle,' he said.

Hop had felt then as though a ship had unexpectedly heaved under him and unsettled his stomach. When he got around to saying anything, he said, 'So they guessed right. The police, I mean. You really are one of that lot.'

'Was,' said Alpha. 'Off and on. Had a little trouble with them. Anyway they've got him now, up there in Jerusalem. He'll be hanging with his arms stretched out any day now. All the same, I know enough to keep the police Chief sitting quiet with his mouth open for a while, waiting for more.'

'So you aim to turn in your old friends to save your skin?'

'Yours too maybe. Don't talk a lot of hot air. That's the way it goes. A lot of them would do the same for me and be happy to. Not all of them. And I wouldn't do it to all of them unless I really had to. It hasn't come to that yet, far as I can figure. But there are some of them, some of the politicos, that I wouldn't mind seeing there on high with the nails through their hands. People like that, they move in on a bunch of professionals, men who know where the loot is and where to get it and that's all they want, and next thing you know you're supposed to be working for some phoney cause or other. The people and all that stuff. No different from the police except they're working the other side of the street. And when you get mixed up with the politicals you're really up against it. You've got every sort of police on your neck and all the other cockeyed politicos that are against your bunch.'

'All the same,' Hop said, half to himself.

'All the same what?' Alpha drawled out with a leer on his face.

Hop started to shout, then, recollecting what he was saying, lowered it to a near whisper, but whispering violently. 'I can't swallow the idea of selling anybody, anybody at all, out to that damn police Chief. He got on my nerves with his hints and jokeyness. He was trying to blackmail me. I don't stand for being blackmailed.'

'So what else?'

His question hung in the air confusingly, like the scent of the hemp. Hop got up and began to walk about.

Alpha said, 'I said, "what else"?'

Trying not to face the point, Hop began to growl at him. 'All very well for you, my boy. You've no problems. You think one thing's as good as another. Or rather you think one thing's as bad as another, one man as dirty as another. Isn't that about it?'

'You're just using words, my lily-white uncle.'

'You realize if I go back to the Chief and tell him to stuff it, you for one will be in a damn bad way.'

'Go ahead and talk, uncle,' said Alpha. 'Tell yourself if you have to do anything dirty it's all for my sake. That's what you're getting around to telling yourself.'

Hop started to swear at him and then laughed instead. 'Something like that, I suppose,' he said. 'And I daresay I'm in as much danger as you. Judging by the way that the Chief seems to have sized up in his fat mind.'

'So,' said Alpha, 'we have to play it the way I said. If I thought about things the way you do, I'd just hang on to the thought that you're only playing one lot of swine against another. Cherish that happy thought, uncle. And, like I said, what else?'

'Nothing else, I suppose,' said Hop, moving over to the curtain. He was half way out to the veranda when the drawling voice from the bed behind him said, 'You can't know which bits of what I tell them are for real and which not. Explain that to God when you finally meet up with him.'

CHAPTER FIVE

Waiting for the new cloak he had ordered to be brought from the bazaar, talking with Joshua in the shade, Hop was aware that the inn-keeper was unusually silent. Uncomfortable, he felt that this was somehow different from the silence of a man half-listening, half-dozing in the heat of the day, with the humidity as high as it was.

'What's the matter?'

'What's not the matter? Police running in and out. That guttersnipe living it up over there. And you, my dear good friend, apparently going to run to and fro between them.'

'And I ask you for the tenth time,' said Hop, 'what else is there to do? It's interfering with my business, I grant you. But if I don't do it, they'll likely put me out of business altogether, one way or another.'

'And *my* business?'

'I know, I know. It's all my fault. Hell.'

'You couldn't help it. Just our bad luck.'

Joshua repeated that remark several times while they waited till Hop could get respectfully dressed in the new, unstained cloak. The phrase began to sound meaningless and Hop had the unpleasant impression that it really had become meaningless to Joshua. The more often he said that Hop couldn't help it, that he, Joshua, didn't hold it against him at all, how could he? the more the rat-whiskers told that under these stresses and strains the inn-keeper resented the fate that had brought Hop to his door with Alpha that first day. And the rat-whisker told him there was something more than the immediate police business oppressing Joshua's forward-looking mind.

After all, Hop told himself, good old Joshua's an inn-keeper. A businessman like myself. It's natural he should be upset. He's still a good friend all the same.

Even so, when he got up from his siesta he had a new sense of loneliness. Even Joshua, he knew when he thought about it clearly, was edging just a little away from him, seeking to dig a small defensive trench between them. Hop said since he had no business to do and seemingly several days to do it in, he thought he would take a look at the sights of Jericho, famed in legend and history.

'Do that,' Joshua said. 'It's a wonderful city if you know how to take it.' He added, 'You'd better pay a man who knows it to guide you. Tell you all about it.'

'I'll be all right on my own. I don't suppose a guide like that would know anything. Tell me a pack of fairy stories.'

'You'd be surprised. These fellows have to know their stuff, within limits. Travellers from far and near pause to view the historic city of Jericho. Some of them are scholars, and if the guide gets caught out making things up, he doesn't get his little fee from the scholar.'

Reassured, Hop picked up such a guide just outside the Hippodrome. With the appearance of a jaunty class of cadaver and the manner of a professor from the big city giving popular holiday lectures to country bumpkins, this guide turned his tap on within a minute of the fee having been discussed and temporarily settled.

A truly magnificent place, this Hippodrome. Every facility for sport and entertainment. Very sporting people, the people of Jericho. Their chariot-racing generally acknowledged to be the best in the country. Don't suppose you get a chance to see anything like it up in Samaria? What? Yes, yes, you were pointed out to me as a man from that part of the country. Sharp-eyed citizens, our people here in Jericho. Not much they don't see or hear.

But always or exclusively used for sporting purposes? Certainly not. It had its serious political uses, too. You doubtless don't know, but I remember as though it were yesterday the time when it was so put to use by the late King Herod, father of our present ruler. He, you know, was for strong government; as, indeed, as nobody can deny, is also our present ruler. Therefore, subsequent to and as a result of a revolt led by two misguided school-teachers up in Jerusalem, this said revolt having been put down, the late King, well aware that there had been treachery in high places, very high places I don't mind telling you at this date so subsequent after the events, sent an order to all the notables, as one might term them, of all Judaea, to come-arunning to Jericho.

Jericho, as may not now be universally known to those coming from outlying lands such as your Samaria, was very well beloved by the late King. His city of scented gardens, he used to call it, also his green paradise, on account of the oasis our city stands in. So these notables came and without fear or favour he had them all driven into this Hippodrome. The late King was dying at the time, they said something was growing in his stomach and eating it away.

But he, good man, in agony as he was and knowing his end was near, yet was very mindful of the need for good order in the State after he was gone. And, despite his fearful pain that was doubling him up, he sent for his true and faithful sister Salome, and he made her swear that the moment he was dead she would order the soldiers into the Hippodrome and hack those unruly notables to death. They had not long to wait. None of them died of starvation or sunstroke, because the King died a couple of days later, and Salome ordered in the troops and saw them do their duty. She knew her duty and she watched until it was all done, standing right on this bit of the grandstand where you and I stand today gazing on the space before us and in our mind's eye seeing it peopled with those very very numerous notables, soaking the sand with their blood.

The event took place at night, at first under a bright moon in which everything could be seen with great clarity. But in the middle of it all there was an eclipse of the moon and, incredible as it may appear to the uninformed, some of those notables who had not yet succumbed to the sword were heard to yell out, treasonably and blasphemously, that this was a sign of God's wrath against King Herod and his sister, now standing by at her post of duty. Though it was plain to see that it was meant for a sign that heaven was darkening its face against those treacherous men.

On our right as we leave the Hippodrome, we see the former palace of the late King Herod, at present one of the summer residences of our ruler Archelaus. That's where the late Monarch died of that agonizing, truly excruciating disease just mentioned. The tale is told, and there is no reason for sceptics to asperse the truth of this interesting story, that one of his spasms came on him while he was seeking to peel an apple, a fruit in which the Jericho oasis is rich indeed. Such was the sawing, gnawing agony occasioned by that spasm that the late incumbent of the Monarchy sought to stab himself with the knife with which he was seeking to peel that apple.

He did not succeed, but the episode had an historic result and consequence for all of us living in this land of Judaea today. For before the male attendants had restrained the King and taken the knife from him, the women who had been present came shrieking and screeching out, running through the corridors of that palace we are now looking at, crying out that the King was dead. So what happened, and we can see the hand of God in it all, was that Herod's son Antipater who at one time had been his heir but had latterly been imprisoned in this palace for reasons of State, heard these cries and thought his father who had imprisoned him was dead. So with vain promises of what he would do for the man now that he was just going to be King, your man Antipater prevailed upon his jailer to unchain him and let him out of his cell, and let him rush out into the corridor. And that was where the bold Antipater found he had spoken out a bit too soon. For the King his father was not dead after all. There was life, as they say, in the old dog yet, and Herod pulled himself together, got himself up on his elbows on the bed, and mastering the delirium he'd been in, gave clear orders to the guards to find that same Antipater and torture him to death. Which was duly performed in accordance, and a couple of days later Herod died and was out of pain for ever. And it was thus that Archelaus, who was by birth the fifth son of Herod, succeeded, becoming with the full approval of the great Roman Emperor Augustus ruler, under the Emperor's protection, of the whole Judaean part of Herod's kingdom. There was the hand of God in it all.

Proceeding in a westerly direction we are afforded entrancing glimpses along the vistas of the many handsome avenues with the beauty of the site itself to endow this city with its unique blend of old and new. No doubt it was this very special character, together with the superabundant wealth of its gardens and orchards, producing as they do rich crops of bananas, pomegranates, apples, almonds, oranges and dates according to the season of the year, which so caught the eye of the late Roman triumvir Antony, that, at the height of his passionate love for the late Queen of Egypt Cleopatra, he made a present of it to her, for her use as a summer retreat. The heart of even the most unromantic of visitors to our city must surely warm and kindle at the thought of the noble lovers, the cares and travails of government and of the tented field alike forgot, enjoying in enraptured dalliance the pleasures so liberally afforded by Jericho, jewel city of Judaea.

Now retracing our steps towards the bustling city centre, a thriving mart of commerce much appreciated alike by those who come to sell and those who know Jericho as above all a good city to buy in, we cross Citizens' Square, so named by Herod in recognition of the sturdy loyalty displayed by the common people of Jericho on a famous occasion barely thirty years ago. It had been a testing time for the King and all who stood for loyalty and stable government. Misled by evil counsellors, two of the King's sons, born of his second wife Marianne, whom he had trusted implicitly, were found to be plotting against him. Marianne herself had intrigued against him, and it was due only to the vigilance of his sister Salome that her plot was uncovered and Marianne, after confessing under torture, which became necessary on account of her stubborn attitude, was executed by due process in accordance with the requirements of the given situation.

Undeterred by what should have been a salutary warning, Marianne's two sons, Alexander and Aristoboulos, entered into new intrigues against King Herod. Their elder half-brother Antipater, who had not at that time developed the treasonable tendencies which afterwards brought about his imprisonment and death, loyally denounced them to his father. They were apprehended and strangled in the fortress at Sebaste.

Men lacking faith in our people, had whispered to Herod that what they had the effrontery to term 'the people' were opposed to his rule, favoured his sons' attempted revolt. With that decisiveness which marked all his actions, Herod immediately put the matter to the test. He was holding under close arrest three hundred persons strongly suspected of complicity in the plot. They were in jail here in Jericho. By public proclamation, particularly directed to the poor quarters of our city—for even here there are poorer quarters—it was made known that the three hundred would, on a certain evening, be marched under guard to this square. The Guard would then withdraw and those citizens who wished to give proof of their unswerving loyalty to the king and their confidence that his policies, if pursued undisturbed, must lead to great benefits if not actual riches for all, would have untramelled opportunity to express their true feelings towards the conspirators. Orators were sent to the poorer districts to make the point clear.

The people responded eagerly. In many of the poorest districts, crowds assembled so early that the Royal authorities had to provide large quantities of free food and wine while the people awaited the moment appointed for them to gather at the square where the traitors were to be released to them.

When that moment came, the citizens of Jericho, many of them armed with nothing but clubs and knives, showed their mettle. Within an hour the three hundred conspirators had been literally torn to pieces. Their limbs were tossed from hand to hand by some, while others showed their indignation by tearing out the living entrails with their bare hands.

The next day was one of rejoicing among those who had taken part. Not only did they have the supreme honour of having the square renamed in memory of the event, but Royal alms were lavishly distributed among those who had best acquitted themselves. Those who had stayed at home had good reason to realize their mistake and the suspicion into which their laziness, pusillanimity or worse had brought them. Several thousand of them fled from the city.

At the close of the tour which lasted more than an hour—'and had traversed but a fraction of the city's extent'—the guide accompanied Hop to the entrance of the inn.

'There now,' he said, with his air of the big expert having done a favour to the man in the street, 'I hope this has given you something to think about. The lessons of history have their value even for those of us whose historical studies must necessarily be superficial.'

Hop reflected that this must be a phrase picked up from one of those scholars mentioned by Joshua as having, at an earlier date, lectured the Jericho guides on their lack of historical accuracy. He said the tour had been very interesting.

'*Interesting?*' said the guide, losing something of his jaunty mien and manner, and uttering the word in a kind of snarl.

'You call it merely interesting? Is that all you have to say? Let me tell you what you have just had is the equal and total equivalent of a course of historical studies such as some of the bigger scholarly mucker-mucks up there in Jerusalem would charge you the flaming earth for. They'd skin you for it.'

Hop silently handed him the previously agreed price.

The man glared at the coins in his palm. 'What's this?' he cried, beginning to jig from foot to foot. Where was culture coming to, he wanted to know. What was the end of it all going to be if people from all over could suck the brains and knowledge of men of historical knowledge and culture and think they had bought it all with a miserable payment like that?

'It's what you agreed to,' said Hop, knowing he would soon pay a little more, but wanting to hear what the man would say next. He heard it immediately. What the guide said next was:

'I just wonder,' and here he pushed his corpse-face forward so that he seemed to be examining his client like a man examining a possibly noxious insect on the wall, 'I just start to wonder whether you, being a Samaritan, possibly didn't quite appreciate all I had to say about the loyalty of our people to the Government and institutions of Judea. Could that be it, I wonder? We get a lot of queer people coming into our city these days. I dare say the police would be glad to have a little report on some of them.'

He straightened himself and stepped back half a pace, untwisting the menacing look from his face and waiting with a neutral expression. Hop said, 'We could go on bargaining and backing and forthing here for hours. I'm a businessman, and I like to strike a bargain with another businessman. But as for you, this is the only extra you'll get.'

He handed over a further sum of money, and turned to go into the inn. The guide moved quickly after him and said, 'No offence, I hope? Sometimes I get people I have to speak rough to before I get what I ought to get. I just want to tell you, when you're home in Samaria and you hear of anyone coming down to Jericho, anyone wants to see the city, tell them to go to the Hippodrome, the corner where you met me, and I'll be glad to oblige them. Only too glad. Tell them it'll be an educational experience.'

'I'll do that,' Hop said.

'And if there are some of them that aren't so interested in history and culture and all that, why I know my way around Jericho, see what I mean? Pretty well anything in what I call the sex line. Girls of course. And on from there to anything. Man must have his fun.'

'I'll tell them.'

'So goodbye for now, and may you be happy in the fine city of Jericho.'

He went jigging off in the direction of the Hippodrome. Hop went in through the arch and said to Joshua, 'Like you said, it's a great city if you know how to take it. Has anything happened meantime?'

'What should happen? The police walk by once or twice. Also one or two other people that I don't know who they are but all the same I wish I didn't see them.'

'What type of people?'

'Least said, soonest mended,' Joshua said, cutting him off.

'And the young man?'

'Your young man's gone out on the town. You seem to have given him confidence. Figures if he's working in with you and the police he can go where he pleases.'

Hop went up on the roof of the building to take the air. Looking out over what he could see of the city, he thought of Alpha running loose there through the taverns, the music-halls, the whorehouses. Somewhere close behind him a faceless detective would be following. Perhaps that would not even be necessary. All the places that Alpha, out on the town, was likely to visit would have their own police informer on the premises. It was essential for them to do that if they were going to stay in business. So that everyone Alpha was seen talking to for more than a couple of minutes would be reported on as a potential political bandit. The membership of the Barabbas gang, as recorded in the police files, would increase and multiply overnight. For the people he talked to, contact with Alpha could be as dangerous as contact with a plague carrier.

In the morning he remarked on this fact to Alpha, who, so far from looking the worse for his night out, looked the better for it. He said, 'So what? More fools they. People that are careless about talking to strangers get what's coming to them.

They ought to know better. You don't get by with being careless. That's life. That's the way I look at it.'

Hop sucked at a mint-flavoured drink. Alpha's view on life made him tired. And whenever Alpha talked of 'the way I look at things' it was always the introduction to some more or less tediously mean and vile idea. When he talked that way, Hop could hear echoes of all the mean vile people he had ever met.

'Besides that,' Alpha was saying, 'a lot of those people, men, girls, it doesn't matter, are working for the police themselves. Does them a bit of good to report on me. Does me a bit of good to report on them. Nobody worse off, and the cops up in a heap trying to figure out who's fooling who. You want to look at life the way it is.'

He made himself more comfortable on the bed and said with complacency that he had been thinking up quite a bit of a story for the Chief of Police. 'It was a smart idea you see for me to get out and about last night. Now this Mr Jericho—that's what they call him—won't know whether the info I slip to him via you is stuff I had already, or stuff this bright lad picked up from his contacts with the teeming, ever threatening underworld of Jericho, its sinister aims only foiled by the eternal vigilance of our underpaid police force. And so on and so on and so on.'

He half closed his eyes and started to talk as though he were reading out of a book, or reciting something.

'First thing, you want to tell them you've got a line on the fellow that was killed down at that farm you were at. He worked for Barabbas all right. Known to the gang only by nickname, Cock. Worked more on the protection side of the business. Job was to scout out likely ones for a shakedown and throw one hell of a scare into them. Pay up, or something not nice is going to happen to you. Your crops could burn. The bark of your fruit trees could get hacked and they'd die on you. You might die too. Seems he went down to your man Zeb's place, with two others. Seems he was over-confident. Thought Zeb was going to be a pushover. Wanted to do things nice and quietly, always avoiding trouble and rough stuff when and where possible, as per orders from the boss man. So after he's had a few words with old Zeb at the gate there on the track, he tells the other two to stay behind while he goes along up to the house with Zeb to transact business in peaceful and orderly fashion.

'And that's the last those other two see of him. They hang around a long while. And the next thing they see way up on the track to the farmhouse, is old Man Zeb and a couple of his hands coming down the track, but no Cock. So they know what that means, and they get out of there like bats out of hell. Needed to get through that village before the news spread.

'So what have you and your bright boy got to say about where those two fellows might be now? You don't know, as yet. But bright boy is performing invaluable services in seeking through his many contacts to get a line on their whereabouts.

'And then Mr Jericho is going to say: with reference to this same bright boy, that you picked up by accident and didn't have any previous contact or connection with or knowledge of etcetera, have you got any more of a line on him? And you say, on account they won't believe you if you tell different, that he admits to having had at one time contacts of an unpolitical character—don't forget that, of an unpolitical character—with members of the Barabbas gang and to have apparently gained their confidence. Can you figure anyone gaining the confidence of that bunch? What a laugh. But it sounds good. It'll sound good to Mr J.'

Hop said, 'No use asking if any of this is a bit true? I mean about the man that was killed at the farm?'

'Uncle,' said Alpha, 'what you don't know can't hurt you.' He recited, like a piece of a creed, 'What I know, I know. What two people know, three people know. What three people know, everybody knows.'

Hop wondered how he was supposed to make his report to the Chief. Just to walk in there to Headquarters and say, 'I'm an undercover agent of the Chief, I'm a recently recruited informer' seemed crude, barely decent. That, surely, would not be in accord with proper police procedure. Nor was it. Joshua came to him before the siesta and said, 'The police have been here again. Not the detectives, the ordinary cops. They made quite a hullabaloo right out there in front of my place. They claimed your papers aren't in order, and this evening you have to go around to the HQ and regularize the matter. They made such a fuss they had half a dozen loafers listening by the time they'd finished.'

Hop wondered whether anyone was likely to be fooled by that sort of crude device. It occurred to him that the police, given the position they were in, really did not have to worry whether anyone was fooled or not.

At police Headquarters he had to go through a phoney rigmarole supporting the notion that he had been summoned in connection with some irregularity in his papers, and at the end of this wearisome run-around was alone with the Chief.

He noted a small ebb in the cordiality the Chief had shown him the first time. And he thought to himself, 'Naturally. They think they've got me now. They don't have to bother with the old oil any more.'

The Chief listened to the story about the supposed member of the Barabbas gang at Zeb's place with interest, but without more than just the amount of interest a person might show on hearing a story.

'So you see,' said Hop, feeling an absurd need to demonstrate to this man the interest, possibly vital interest, of this piece of information. Then his need and the urge it gave him collapsed under him as he recalled that, for all he knew or could know, the whole story might be a pack of lies put together by Alpha for obvious, or maybe less obvious purposes of his own.

The Chief said, and the words were all right but the manner was perfunctory, as though he took all that as a matter of course—the information itself and the fact that Hop had brought it to him—'Exceedingly interesting. Not entirely unexpected. Not unexpected by me. Possibly not unexpected on your side either? Oh my dear sir,' he said, as Hop made an awkwardly angry gesture, 'I do beg you not to put thoughts into my head, let alone,' he sniggered slightly, 'words into my mouth.'

Hop said rudely, 'Anything you've got to say, spit it out. Let's have this thing in the open.'

The Chief made a solemn face and said that he was glad to hear Hop say that thing. In the open, that must be the motto. Though, he said, as though in an aside, how hard it was for an official of the police to be sure that at any time he could both act in accordance with his official obligations and at the same time keep things 'in the open', as, for example, a respectable businessman could do.

'You comprehend,' he said elaborately to Hop, 'my dilemma.'

Hop said, 'Listen, you and your comprehensions and dilemmas are damn all to a man like me. I've told you something that I suppose you need to know.'

The Chief said, 'If I may interrupt you for a moment. It isn't a question of our *needing* to know. It's just that we *want* to know. We aren't—and you mustn't run away with the idea that we are—in any sort of *need*.'

'So you know it all.'

'You are trying to tease me. And as an official I am not authorized to answer back in kind.'

'You understand that every day I stay here I'm losing business.'

'On the other hand, looked at in a longer perspective, one could say that you are doing good business—for the future, that is. I mean that if these prophets and bandits were really to take over the country, you'd have no business at all.'

'That's bogey talk.'

The Chief made a gesture of stamping his foot lightly on the floor. 'You think,' he said, 'that the situation is as solid as the ground under us? Extraordinary that a man born in these times should have such assurance.'

Hop, offended, said, 'One has to take some things for granted. Otherwise a man couldn't do business. And anyway nothing you've said, or that I've heard up and down the country about this Barabbas or the Essene or whoever, convinces me in the least that they're as dangerous as you people make out.'

'The Essene. Yes. I'm glad you mentioned him. Because in my view he may be the clue to the whole business.'

The Chief proceeded to develop an idea. Suppose that the Essene and Barabbas were in fact two prongs, as he put it, of the same fork? The Essene does the talking, the agitating, the spinning of fine stories that get people excited; Barabbas does the organizing, runs the strong arm gangs, the payment of protection money and so on. Each of course can if necessary repudiate all connection with the other. It would not be surprising to see them actually denounce one another in public.

It all fitted pretty well. For instance, there was a recent report of some of the stuff the Essene has just been getting off in Jerusalem. Heady stuff.

Here the Chief read aloud from a report. 'Nation shall rise against nation and kingdom against kingdom.... Great earthquakes and famines and pestilences ... and so on and so on ... let them which are in Judaea flee to the mountains ... days of vengeance ... they shall fall by the edge of the sword.'

One could see, said the Chief, the man's line of country. Give people the general impression that society is cracking up, general collapse just around the corner. The real strength of the established order, the Government, the businessmen an so on, is not in the final analysis, said the Chief, the police or the Army; it consists simply in the belief of the mass of people that the established order really is established. That it is part of the natural order of things like trees growing. Therefore to revolt against it is as idiotic as revolting against sunrise and sunset. The strength of our society depends on people's belief that there is nothing effective to be done because there is no alternative, this has to go on because it is all there is or can be. But once give people the notion that the whole fabric, the outfit, the entire box of tricks is going to blow apart at some not too distant date, then the strength it draws from the belief that it is here to stay just drains away. And that loss of strength is Barabbas's opportunity.

'Thanks for the lecture,' said Hop.

The Chief said, 'I have a certain gift for analysing the situation philosophically. I don't take any special credit for that. I start with certain advantages of birth. I mean, not being a Jew I can look at affairs here with more detachment than the Jews, whatever sect they belong to.'

'You're not a Jew?' Hop said, surprised.

'Certainly not,' said the Chief. 'Do I even look like one? I'm an Idumean from down south there. In other words a mongrel, but more of an Arab than anything. So was the late King Herod. That, apart of course from our remarkable native abilities, is one of the reasons why quite a number of us, sons of Idumeans who worked with Herod, hold important official positions today. Herod was a man who knew how to govern a country.'

'So I undestand,' said Hop, recalling his conducted tour of the city the day before.

'I,' said the Chief, 'also try to understand government as, shall I say, an art. You'll believe me when I say that I have no prejudices at all against the Jews or the Romans, or anyone else. But naturally I can see that the surest way to preserve order and stability—in which you, of course, are just as much interested as I am—is to preserve a certain balance between the Romans who sit on top of the Jews without understanding them, and the Jews who cannot unite against the Romans—even if rich and poor Jews could ever unite—because half of them live in an imaginary past, and the other half in an illusory future.'

The more the Chief talked in this manner, the more nervously the rat's whiskers twitched. No doubt these quite uncalled-for disclosures of the Chief's personal attitudes could be accounted for partly by the man's childish vanity. On the other hand, these apparent confidences could be, could perhaps be intended as, proof that Hop was safely in the Chief's power, might remain in his power for God knew how long, and was certainly in no position to do him any harm by telling stories.

'You read Greek?' the Chief exasperatingly continued. 'No? I often think when I am thinking how best to deal with these supposedly holy agitators such as this Essene, of the passage where the philosopher Plato comments on the death of Socrates. It was necessary for the authorities to destroy his good name; if others believed him just he would have honour and profit thereby. People must be left wondering whether he had played at goodness for an ulterior motive. He must be shown to have been thoroughly wicked. And the surest way to convince the vulgar masses that he was no good was to strip him of everything, have him whipped, tortured, imprisoned, nailed to a cross, or torn to pieces. As things turned out, the authorities did not have the courage of their convictions. By allowing Socrates to drink hemlock in a quiet dignified manner while philosophizing with his friends in his cell, they ensured that he would continue to be revered. That at any rate is the way I read the story.'

'Very, very interesting,' said Hop. 'I must go back to school and learn Greek.'

'My apologies if I've been boring you,' said the Chief. 'I get carried away on the stream of my own ideas. Still, I feel my little *exposé* may be of some practical use to you.'

'Practical use? Is that a joke? What sort of practical use?'

Seeming to pay no attention to this, the Chief proceeded to say that the thing to do was to 'concentrate on the Essene'; gain all possible information about him. 'Also,' he said with unpleasant emphasis, 'try to see whether there's anything you may know about him already—possibly some previous contact which you, quite naturally, have forgotten.'

'I thought it was the Barabbas gang you were interested in. Seems to me I've already told you more about what happened at that farm, and why, than all your damned detectives would be likely to find out in a month. Seems to me I've done quite enough. I want to get out of here and get on with my business. And there's my wife,' he added suddenly, thinking suddenly of Sarah, and saying this without asking what possible difference this could make to the Chief.

The Chief said, 'I wouldn't be doing my official duty if I let so valuable a man as yourself fade away to Samaria just at this juncture. I must seriously ask you to continue with your investigations, with the help, naturally, of the young man Alpha.'

'But *when* can I leave?'

'It depends on how the case develops. Concentrate on the Essene.'

CHAPTER SIX

The big dog jumped out of the darkness, hurled its bony, muscular weight against him, knocked the breath out of him as it landed on his chest, sent him crashing backwards like a felled tree, stood over him, puffing stinking breath into his face from a couple of inches distant. Two men came silently from, as it seemed, nowhere, one from the left, one from the right. Gripping him violently under each arm they hoisted him, half stunned to his feet. One of them wound a scarf or cloth of thick material round his head, eyes and mouth. Earlier, before the dog jumped, he had seen, dimly, numerous people strolling under the palms that lined the avenue. Now, as the cloth blinded him, he thought dazedly that some of them must have seen what was happening and would come to the rescue. Instead he heard a few scared cries, and the noise of feet running fast from that place. Soon as he was half lifted, half dragged along, there was nothing to be heard but the padding of the two men's feet, and the shuffle of his own in the dust of the roadway. Time stopped for him. He was conscious of movement but not of distance. The padding and shuffling were all that was left of the world.

Somewhere, some time the surface of the road became rougher. He began to be aware that the way they were going was twisty; also that it was narrow, twice he heard first one man, then the other, bump against a wall. Then the air changed. They were inside a building. There was a smell of fish frying somewhere, and then the air that he could just breathe through the gap in the cloth where his nose stuck out became dense and foetid, and he could smell an oil lamp burning. They dropped him to the floor like a heavy, half-filled sack, propping the upper part of his body against a wall.

They pulled the cloth off his head.

There was the lamp he had been smelling, burning dimly on a low bench. In that faint light there was no way of telling the size of the room. The first living things he saw were three big scrawny dogs, two of them padding back and forth, the third crouched at his feet, staring at him with its tongue lolling. They were like dogs in a nightmare. Slowly, as though any quick movement could get him stabbed, he turned his head a little way first right, then left. Each of the two men was taller and broader than he was. Looked at from where he was on the floor they seemed inhumanly big. Not only their size gave that inhuman look. In the uncertain light their faces seemed the faces of some unknown species of animal, dark, twisted and heavily scarred. They were of a piece with the nightmare dogs.

Hop's hand moved automatically to his belt. Naturally, his knife, last used to cut the throat of that mule, was gone. One of the men saw the futile gesture. He let go with a violent, sickening guffaw. The pacing dogs stopped pacing at the sound, and the one at Hop's feet raised his head. All three looked at the man as though trying to interpret a signal or an order.

In an accent so thick and strange that he seemed to be even speaking in some not quite human language, only just intelligible, the man started to swear at him. When he had finished swearing he could just be understood to say, 'Now you're going to see what we do to informers. You're going to be sorry you were born before we're done with you.'

Then the two of them came over to him. One of them heaved him upright. The other started to beat him savagely with punches like the kick of a mule to the mouth and nose, then to the stomach and then a fierce kick in the genitals.

Hop fainted with pain and fell sprawling to the floor. When he came to the man who had first spoken said, 'That's just the beginning, you nark. Now you'll see what the dogs can teach you. Our dogs don't like informers any better than we do.'

The other man said something in a low sharp tone. The pacing dogs moved close to Hop at either side. The one at his feet stood up and moved forward between his sprawled legs. They waited in terrifying docility. The man uttered another low sound. At the signal the three dogs lunged and, snarling in their throats, attacked. They spent a quarter of a minute ripping through clothing, tossing the rags aside. Then they went for the flesh. Hop could feel his left arm being gashed, the soft part of his right side below the ribs, and the inside of his thigh. He fainted for the second time.

When he opened his eyes, the dogs were standing a little away from him. He heard his own voice saying, 'Kill me. For God's sake kill me.'

The man who had laughed before laughed again.

'You'd like that, wouldn't you? So would we. But that's not the order of the day. Your friends might think you'd just met with an accident. That wouldn't be any use to us. We're going to turn you loose just like you are so that you can go back to them and show them what we do to informers. After that you can die of what the dogs have done to you. And your friends can die of fright.'

They let him lie there for how long he had no idea. Then one of them came over with a flask of liquor and held it for him to drink. They pulled him to his feet, and at first held him, coldly studying and evidently calculating whether he could stand alone, whether he could walk. They let him stand alone for a minute, then started to walk him about the room, holding him under the arms. Again he heard his voice saying, 'I can't walk. I can't.' And one of them said, 'You better had walk. If you can't make it, the way we want you to, we'll put the dogs on to finish you off. We'll let them take the balls off you this time.' Hop's voice said, 'No. I'll try to walk. I can walk.'

They both laughed.

They wound the bandage round his head and face again, gripped him under the arms as before, and held him between them, his feet trailing. As they seemed to be leaving the room, all three dogs set up sustained, vibrant ululation. Hop could hear them padding, furiously it seemed, up and down. A heavy door closed behind him. They were in the alley or lane or whatever it was with the houses close on either hand, and then again on the twisty part of the way, and then he could just feel the even soil of the avenue under his feet.

They unwound the cloth from his head, and stood back from him, watching him stand, teetering. 'So walk,' one of them said. He walked, seeing almost nothing and thinking of nothing except that he had to keep walking or somehow the dogs would be at him again. He was not conscious of simply following the route from police Headquarters to Joshua's inn, which he had been following when the dog first set on him. And then suddenly the entrance to the inn was there in front of him.

A nightwatchman or porter opened the door. At the sight of Hop he gave a low cry and put his hand to his throat in dismay.

Hop said, 'Let me in quietly. Get me to my room.'

In the nightmare he was living, he was suddenly and violently obsessed with a single demented idea. For Joshua to see him like this would be the last straw for Joshua. Joshua, erstwhile friend, could have him thrown back into the street and there those dogs would nose him out and go for him. Lying on his bed he directed the porter to strip him of the rags the dogs had made of his clothes and then used what strength he could to explain to the man where to find the medicaments and bandages still unused after he had treated Alpha by the roadside. Sure that if he lapsed unconscious at that moment he would die of his wounds, he ground his teeth with the effort to retain consciousness and explain to the porter how to clean the wounds, apply the proper ointments and salves, and bandage them. Before he finally became unconscious, his last words to the porter were, 'Just tell Joshua I came in late. Say nothing of this before I see him myself in the morning.' His last conscious sensation was one of great pain at the thought that he was entirely alone: that even Joshua was no longer his friend.

Hours later, at around noon of the following day, he came to, with Joshua and a doctor standing by his bedside. He looked dumbly at Joshua, who mumbled some monotoned formal words of sympathy and concern. Controlling a groan, Hop managed to say, 'Warn Alpha. It could happen to him.' Joshua nodded briefly, and Hop, foggy as everything was to him, could yet see that this, the way it struck Joshua, had been an exasperating thing to say. Then the doctor talked. Said the wounds were not infected. Lot of blood lost. Head badly bruised, shaken up—no doubt by fall. Lie quiet. The doctor made no comment on the fact that the flesh wounds had been caused by dogs.

Out of his fog, Hop asked, 'Is that standard here in Jericho?'

'Is what standard?'

'Getting bitten half to death by dogs.'

'Certainly not,' said the doctor. 'I know nothing of such things.'

It seemed that before Hop had been sufficiently conscious to know that the doctor was in the room, the doctor had given him some drugged drink. Now he felt himself dropping into a deep sea of sleep. He woke once when it was dark and the second time when he could see by the shortness of the shadow in the garden that it was somewhere near noon. A servant brought him soup, and while he was still eating it Alpha came in from the veranda.

Alpha said, 'So can you talk straight now? I've been in and out of here every few hours. But you weren't making much sense.'

Hop said, 'Did Joshua warn you? I remember I told him to warn you.'

'Warn me what about?'

'About how what happened to me could happen to you. I suppose you've stayed under cover.'

'Nobody did any warning to me. And I wouldn't have stayed under cover anyway. Just for now I'm all right in this town. Seems I've got friends both sides of the street.'

'You're an informer, just like me,' said Hop bitterly. 'That's why this thing happened to me.'

'Tell,' said Alpha.

His head was clear now, Hop told him of what had happened to him after he left the Chief's office. Alpha sat slightly slumped, his face apparently vacant, except for a sulky sag of his mouth. But when Hop had finished he began to ask questions showing that he had listened to and memorized every word of the story.

Hop said, 'So you see they're on to us. The same thing could happen to you.'

'It won't,' Alpha said. 'They're the ones are going to get it in the neck.'

'You been at the hemp?' Hop asked.

'Get through your head, uncle, this is a game you don't begin to understand one little bit of.'

'And I suppose you do. All right. Go ahead and tell me.'

Alpha went into the monotone, like a person reciting something from memory, which he used when he had to speak more than a couple of sentences at a time. He said that getting around and about in Jericho the way he did, he had picked up a lot of bits and pieces of information, enough of them to be put together and make a picture. Naturally, he had met some of the people he had known when he worked —'off and on'—with the Barabbas outfit. There had been fallings out, but they didn't hold that against him. It seemed that ever since Barabbas got arrested in Jerusalem, the organization had looked like splitting apart at the seams. Too many people were trying to take over. And some of them figured that the first thing to do on the way to moving in on Barabbas's empty seat was to show they were tougher than anyone else: tougher, maybe, even than Barabbas, with his political notions that could get in the way of business.

Hop interrupted to say that he had understood that was the way Alpha himself felt—against the politicos.

'Hell,' said Alpha, 'that's the way I may have felt. Seemed to me at one time those politicos were messing things about. I thought they were on their way out. Now it seems they've made a come-back in the organization. I'm for whoever's on top. Looks to me now like some of the elements I thought were out are in, and running things. So I know them, and they know me, and we're all bugs in a rug.'

The monotone continued. What Alpha called the Old Guard, the people who had been closest to Barabbas before he was jailed, were pretty much in control, but not quite. There were still these members of the organization who wanted to show themselves tough, and fit to be the new leaders. They'd got, it hadn't been difficult, the news that Alpha, through Hop, was passing information to the police. The Old Guard people knew that too, of course. But they calculated that working through Alpha they could feed the police a lot of false leads: and they could use the situation to put the police on the necks of people within the organization they would be glad to see eliminated.

The tough fellows decided to play the game the other way. Possibly they thought, and possibly rightly, that the Old Guard was feeding the police information against them. Whatever might be about that, they certainly saw in this situation a chance to show one and all just how tough they were. So they bring off a big spectacular display of beating up and savaging nearly to death that Samaritan informer and undercover agent of police. That would be something to boast about. And it could maybe throw a big scare into the members of the Old Guard.

'And they've got away with it,' said Hop. 'Look at me.'

Disregarding him, Alpha said, 'Only trouble is, we don't know quite just exactly who these fellows are. Might be these and those or those and these. And we don't know just where they're holed up.'

'Seems they're sitting pretty,' said Hop.

For the first time Alpha's face came out of vacancy. The whole of it seemed concentrated in a rasping snarl.

'You poor dumb ox,' he said. 'They're not going to be *allowed* to sit pretty. Don't you get what it could do to the organization if they get away with this? *We're* going to get *them*.'

'You are?'

'You too,' said Alpha. 'You're going to help get them.' He went on talking. Hop listened, at first, as though he were listening to a story about someone with whom he was not concerned at all. The points of the story were simple enough. One, two. One: there was a chance that, starting from where the dog first jumped him, Hop might be able to remember the route taken after that.

'Not a chance,' he said. 'I was all muffled up and half stunned. How would I remember?'

'Your feet might tell you,' said Alpha. 'Anyway you might get us to the section of the city those fellows are working from. That'd be a big help to start with. We could likely get a line on them around wherever it is.'

Point Two: If they got a line on one or two of the people that might have been responsible, Hop could tell them whether they had the right men or not. 'It wouldn't do,' said Alpha, 'for us to go for some fellows that might not have done it. Not at the present time. That could be dangerous—make more bad feelings.'

Hop was going to say, automatically, that he wanted no part of such doings. For a moment he saw himself still as the respectable travelling man, grotesquely asked to go roaming through the slums of Jericho, helping one lot of gangsters find another lot of gangsters. The prize for his charitable deed. Then that picture slipped. He saw and heard the men who had beaten him. On top of all he saw those nightmare dogs.

He said to Alpha, 'Give me a hand up. Let's see can I walk.'

He could walk feebly. Alpha watched him, and said as though he were buying some object in a bazaar, 'That's OK. You'll be OK for the evening. You can find your way back to where the dog got you?'

'Yes.'

'So we'll meet there,' said Alpha. 'Near police HQ.'

Hop had a moment of panic. 'Listen,' he said. 'I'm there on my own and suppose they do it again? Suppose that dog, those dogs, suppose they get me again?'

'You won't be on your own,' Alpha said.

'What time then?'

'Same time as when they got you. Same time of the evening. Maybe it'll help you remember.'

Walking shakily through the darkening streets from near police HQ, Hop felt panic again, a horror of getting nearer and nearer to that exact place where the dog had come at him from nowhere. Alpha had given him a new knife. But what use had his knife been before? As before, there were numerous people walking or just strolling on the avenue. He could just distinguish, even count them, when they were close to him. If he had thought, that first time, that anyone was going to attack him, he would have got confidence from the presence of all these citizens. Now he could hear again the noise of their feet running away when they had seen him attacked and muffled up in that cloth and dragged along by those two men. Thinking of it now, his feet slowed, his heart pumped, he could hardly walk.

Then he heard Alpha's voice just behind his shoulder. 'Don't look round at me? Was it about here?'

Hop nodded.

Alpha said, 'So keep walking. Our boys are around.'

Hop walked on, uncertain, and stopping every few yards to find lost bearings.

Alpha spoke again. 'I'll come alongside and catch your

elbow. Then you shut your eyes. Maybe your feet'll think for you.'

Hop felt the hand holding his elbow, closed his eyes, and after a little stumbling really did find his feet vaguely remembering, counting off the steps of that first journey along this avenue.

Presently he said, 'I think it was about here we left the avenue.'

'Well you'd better open your eyes and we'll nose around.'

They went a little forward and a little back. Then Alpha said, 'Look. This could be your twisty lane.'

The entrance to the lane was not much wider than a hole in the wall. They went through that hole, and the lane did begin to twist, with a rough surface under foot. Once when he paused Hop could just hear the soft sound of feet somewhere behind them. The boys. Repeatedly from one side or the other came the yelping and yapping of wandering dogs. He stretched his arms wide and his fingertips touched walls on both sides.

He said, 'This was the way it was.'

Alpha said, 'Sure. Unless it was some other goddamn stinking rat-run.'

Hop went on and then stopped as suddenly as if he had run into a wall.

'What is it, uncle?'

'Listen.'

'Dogs. But there's a million dogs around here.'

'Not that sort of dogs. Listen again.'

What Hop could hear was the sound he had listened to as the door closed behind him on the room where those three brutally trained dogs had savaged him.

Alpha listened and said, 'More dogs. Anything special?'

Hop told him what was special and added, 'Those dogs are trained dogs. Like in a circus show. They even howl together. Not like these strays all around.'

'It adds up,' Alpha said, and turning went a few paces back the way they had come. Hop could hear first a little murmur of voices, then the sound of Alpha coming back and of other feet moving up close behind him.

He said, 'There was an archway, I think it was an archway. Somewhere along here on the left.' They edged forward with small steps, watching the wall on the left. Then there was an archway. From some courtyard beyond it came the smell of fish frying. The dogs had stopped howling.

In the darkness under the arch, Hop spoke low into Alpha's ear. 'Those are trained dogs. They don't move without they get the word from the man. We'll need to rush them before they get the word.'

There was a door in each side wall of the arch. 'Which door?' Alpha asked.

Hop stood tense, shaking with the effort to remember. 'I don't know.'

The doors were solid. No sound came from behind either. Hop could hear nothing but the breathing of the men behind him. Then from somewhere beyond the door on the right came a small, nearly musical whimper. Another dog's voice joined in, and a third, until the whimpering was a low, clear chorus.

'Now!' said Alpha, and took a running leap for the door.

Hop was thrown aside and nearly over by the thrust and spring of the men from behind going for the door. Their huge impact smashed it open. He heard a man behind the door scream as it hit him. Moving up fast behind the others he saw in the light of the oil lamp Alpha stab twice at the throat of the man he remembered as the dog-master, the one who had given the signals. He saw the dogs poised, alert and waiting just behind that dog-master. The man twisted his head away from Alpha towards the dogs. Blood choked him before he could get out the signal. The dogs quivered, seeming to strain at an invisible leash which a word would slip, but there was no word.

Two of Alpha's boys were holding another man, while a third of the boys was stabbing him to death so fast he had no time to cry out. Hop was aware of three figures, figures in a flimsy dream, flitting past him with little cries. He understood that they were women, running for the opening where the smashed door had been. While he looked dazedly after them one broken leaf of the collapsed door heaved, and Hop saw, crouched and coming for him, the man who had been with the dog-master on that other night when he had been in that room. Panting and snarling like a dog himself, Hop lunged with the long knife, hit the man somewhere near the jugular, felt his knees giving in weakness and his whole body sprawling forward. The other man's knife struck his back, but ran askew and got caught in his cloak. By the time Hop got to his feet it was the other who was on his knees, blood jetting from his throat before his eyes rolled up and he toppled over sideways.

Hop saw a group near the light: the boys: five of them with Alpha in the middle. He heard Alpha say, 'That's about it. Let's go.' His voice reminded Hop of his own when, way back when he was a boy, he had led a little gang to strip an orchard and got them away again quick. As they went quickly away from there, each first looking carefully to make sure he had no blood on him anywhere, it seemed as though they had done no more than rob an orchard. As they left, the dogs, still quivering, still waiting for the secret signal to attack, stood where they were but set up a low howl which could have been one dog howling instead of three all together.

By the time the end of the lane was reached and they were on the avenue Hop found himself alone with Alpha. He had not noticed just when and where the boys had faded into the shadows. He said, 'Those women. They rushed out. I saw them.'

'So what?' said Alpha. 'They'd have got killed if they'd stayed any longer. Bad night's business for a whore.'

'But they could tell what they saw.'

'Be your age. Who'd they tell? The cops? They'd be crazy. Be inside for weeks with no money coming in and getting screwed for free by every cop on duty. They didn't see a thing.'

Hop said surprisedly, 'It's hardly any darker than when we started out.'

'Why would it be?' Alpha said. 'We didn't take very long. It was a quick job. You've time for a nice evening chat with friend Joshua.'

'And you?'

'I'll be meeting up with a couple of the boys in that wine shop none of us left all evening. We'll be putting together a real good story for you to take to that Chief. He'll be well and truly glad to hear that three dangerous political elements of the sinister Barabbas organization just met with sudden accidental death at the hands of a bunch of old-fashioned criminals trying to take over control. Hell, that's what he'd like to hear. So let's have him hear it. He won't turn much heat on those handy criminals.'

'You think he'll believe that?'

'Why not? Just because it didn't happen that way, it doesn't mean it couldn't have. Could have easily. And like I say if he thinks it's the politicos that got rubbed the less trouble he's going to make. Well look at it through a cop's eye. Cop reckons he knows all the answers when it's criminals he's got to deal with. Politicos give him ulcers.'

'And I'm supposed to take this story to that Chief tomorrow evening? When I go to have another row about my papers?'

'When else? It's a good story. He certainly ought to show gratitude.'

'They'll have found those bodies by then.'

'Too right they will. So the man who can tell the big Chief just what it was all about is going to help that same Chief get quite a bit more reputation for knowing all that occurs in Jericho's fair city. Mr Jericho knows all.'

But in the afternoon, half-way through siesta time, Alpha came to the part of the veranda where Hop was resting in the shade. He said, 'Wake up, uncle. Something a little greasy, something not just as nice as you'd wish just happened.'

CHAPTER SEVEN

It seemed a man had just got into town from Jerusalem who had been at a little meeting the Essene had been talking at.

'Damn that Essene,' said Hop. 'He's been hung on my neck all these days.'

'Just wait till you get the rest of it.'

So this Essene had been talking, privately, to a gathering of disciples, friends and well-wishers. A man from the Barabbas organization—'one of the political boys who has the job to follow the Essene around'—was among those present. And this man, busy with a lot of urgent business, had come on down into Jericho and, in the course of conversation had happened to mention a couple of things the Essene had said, not himself attaching much importance to the same.

'So what *did* he say?' Hop demanded.

The affair had been, as usual, a kind of philosophical gab-fest. Somewhere along the line the Essene put out as an axiom or whatever that a man should love his neighbour like himself. Listening keenly, and seeing a chance to show off the fine legal brain he had, some legal eagle who had been brought along to the meeting, asked the smart question, 'Who is my neighbour?'

It was just then that the Essene said the thing that was going to cause a hell of a lot of trouble.

He had got hold somewhere, somehow, probably from some long-eared lout in Jericho, the story of how Hop had picked up Alpha that day on the road.

'So what?'

So what had the Essene done but take this story and carpenter it around into a shape where it fitted just sweetly into the line he was putting across. There was this Samaritan, was there not? A heretic. A man whose beliefs were low-life blasphemies to respectable Judaeans. A real outsider. What happens, says the Essene. There's this certain man lying half dead in the ditch and first a Judaean priest goes by, and then one of those upright and respectable persons known as Levites. They each in turn take a look at the man in the ditch and being the both of them respectable citizens and they feel that if a man keeps the kind of company where a thing like that is apt to happen to him it's his affair, and decent people should not be asked to mix themselves up in that kind of business. One after another the two of them keep to their own side of the road and proceed in due order to Jericho.

And then comes our bold Samaritan, and what does he do? He stops and looks and then, save us all, he gets off his mule, goes to work on the man's wounds, hefts him on to the mule, gives him a free ride into Jericho, and not only puts him up at an inn, paying in advance, but promises the inn-keeper he'll pay for anything extra the man has while this Samaritan is out on his rounds in the countryside.

It doesn't need much understanding to see that this story is loaded against the priests and the Levites. But he could have told a story or so against them without dragging in the Samaritan as an example to one and all. Those are fighting words. They could be taken to mean that the Essene in his general subversive campaign is lined up with or trying to line up with the Samaritans. And if he were to be successful in that, he would just about double the strength of whatever following he has. And a lot of that new support wouldn't be riff-raff like some of the Judaeans that cheer for him. There'd be some pretty solid Samaritan citizens joining in because this was a way of moving against the hierarchy there in Jerusalem.

'It won't be more than just a day or two before the news of the Essene's new line, this bid for the Samaritans, gets reported to the High Priests. And you can see,' said Alpha, 'where that puts us.'

Hop saw very well. First of all the High Priests and the Sanhedrin police would want to know all about this Samaritan on the Jericho road. They would be asking about his connections with the Essene on the one hand, and with this suspect member of the Barabbas organization on the other. Secondly, when the news reached, as it quickly must, the Police Chief of Jericho, what was his reaction going to be? The story would entirely confirm the suspicion he had cherished all along that this Samaritan, giving out to be an innocently respectable businessman was in fact associated with the Essene outfit. And this connection with Alpha would go to show how right the Chief's instinct had been when it told him that Barabbas and the Essene were two prongs of the same fork. There could be two answers to the question what would the Chief do then. And both answers meant danger for Hop.

He might decide that in the light of this new development the smart thing to do was, after all, to turn the Samaritan and Alpha over to the Sanhedrin police, receiving their congratulations on his efficiency and co-operation, and staking a claim to equal favours from them at some future date. Or, playing it another way, he could use the new situation to tighten further his hold on Hop, maybe keep him in Jericho indefinitely, harassing him mercilessly, exploiting him to the limit as a helpless tool of the police. And when the tool wore out its usefulness it could be broken up: Hop could be jailed, or worse, on some faked charge.

He spoke these thoughts aloud, stringing them out for himself and Alpha to look at.

Alpha looked at them sulkily and then said, 'If the two of us could get out of here and up there into Samaria, what's the betting we'd be left alone there?'

Hop considered. 'So far as the law's concerned there's no difference that I know of. The Romans put in Archelus as ethnarch over Samaria as well as Judaea. The Civil Police Corps could pick us up there just as easy as here or in Jerusalem if they wanted to.'

'Hell!' said Alpha.

'Just a minute. That's only one way to look at it. The plain fact of the way things really are, or anyhow the way I've been told they are, is that the Romans are none too keen to look as though they were taking sides between us Samaritans and those Judaeans. Why should they, the bloody pagans? They don't believe in what we know about the true faith any more than they believe what the Judaeans pretend to know. What they don't want is trouble. Especially religious trouble. Keeping them out of that sort of trouble is one of the things their procurator up there in Jerusalem, old man Pontius Pilate, is paid for. I can think of a couple of cases up in

Sachem when the Romans have definitely given the Civil Corps the word to lay off our people. And of course that would go double for the Men in Black.'

'Sounds like a soft option. Do I have to bone up on your religion?'

'You damn well have to be civil about it. Not just up there in Samaria. Here, too. To me.'

'OK, OK, OK. What are we waiting for?'

'A miracle, I should think. To whisk us out of here into Samaria before the police get us.'

'No miracle. But it'll cost a little money.'

'How much?'

Alpha talked figures. Probably, thought Hop, doubling what was really needed and about to pocket the difference. And what, he thought, can I do about that?

There would be the payment for a guide, one of the boys. He would know how to get out of Jericho after dark without being challenged by the police. There was a network of abandoned irrigation ditches on the north side of the city which the boys used for coming and going. Then there would be the mules. And a man to mind them, have them ready at a place outside the city limits. Three mules, because the guide would have to clear out of Jericho for the sake of his skin. He had his reasons. That was why he would do the job cheaply.

'And then we'll be on the road to Sachem,' said Hop. 'God speed the hour.'

Alpha snorted. 'Are you soft in the head or something? We have to reckon on word getting to the Chief here some time late tonight. Let's just hope not before it's dark enough for us to go. But what happens next? The police rush round here, find we've gone, and they think that for sure we've taken off for that Sachem of yours. On the Sachem road the patrols would be up with us before we were half-way to Samaria.

Angrily he drew a word map. Here they were, north-east of Jerusalem. And in a straight line, going north and then north-west, they would be heading straight for Samaria and Sachem. What he proposed was that they leave Jericho on the north side, but then—unexpectedly to the police—cut across country, turning first southwards and then, when far enough from Jericho, westwards again towards Jerusalem.

That way, they would come out on the Jericho–Jerusalem road from the east side, and very close to Jerusalem.

'Now *you're* crazy. In Jerusalem the Men in Black have us just where they want us.'

Alpha spat viciously on the ground. 'Don't go calling me crazy. I don't like it. You understand? It just happens to be one of those little things I don't happen to like.'

'All right. So what's the idea?'

'We don't go into Jerusalem at all. We go to an inn the boys know. The first inn on the route before you get to the city. The boys know it and, better than that, the man that has the inn knows the boys. We hole up there till we get word of how the heat's going off and on.'

'This inn,' said Hop. 'You mean the last inn on the route out of Jerusalem?'

'That's what I said. The first you come to going from here. Kept by the man they call Simon the Knower.'

'That fellow?' said Hop. 'A bloody rogue in my book. I've been there. He's either just a bag of gas or a crook or both. Both, I'd say.'

'So maybe you'd rather go some place where they have a certificate of good conduct from the police?'

'How do we know that fellow isn't a police spy? Just listening and looking at him I wouldn't be at all surprised.'

'Answer to that, Mr Pick-and-Choose, is we don't know it. We do know that if the cops are paying him he isn't earning their money. If he had been, a lot of the boys would have been picked up that haven't been. Besides, he's half crazy.'

'That's damn nice to hear. Makes a man feel safe.'

'Not all round crazy. Just crazy against the police and the Government and God Almighty. It's some sort of religion as they call it.'

'How can it be a religion if he's against God Almighty?'

'Search me. It's got a name, though. They call them The Knowers. That's why this guy's called the way he is.'

'Well yes. That's so. I've heard talk of them. They think they know about a God that's beyond God or some such.'

'Well,' said Alpha, 'damn all that. He's our man.'

Just as Alpha was going off to see, as he said, the boys, Hop said, 'What'll I tell Joshua is what I'm wondering.'

Alpha stopped sharply and said, 'You tell him nothing. We

just go for a look at the night life and don't come back.'

Hop brooded. He said, 'Can't be done. I've got him in plenty of trouble already. We have to warn him about what's going on. He has to have time to get a story ready before the police get to him. They'll suspect him anyway. But at least he has to be ready with a story. Otherwise they'll put him right out of business. Into jail too, maybe.'

'So let them put him out of his business. We have to get away, and nobody has to know we're going.'

'Joshua has to know,' said Hop.

'What's this in bloody aid of?'

'He's my friend. And what would have happened to you if he hadn't taken you in on my say so?'

'Bet he charged you plenty for it. Anyway he did that because that's the way he's made. Some people get a kick out of being friendly to other people.'

'You said that before. To me.'

'It's the way I look at it. And you can't tell that Joshua anything.'

'I'm going to tell him. He's my friend. Also...' he stopped.

'Also what, damn you?'

'Something you wouldn't follow. Something we're taught in our religion.'

'Your religion? Haven't you any common sense? You'll get us both jailed or stoned or crucified. Have you thought of that? What about me?'

'I suppose you could get away alone.'

'No you don't. Because I know that if I split up with you now you can go crawling off to that Chief of Police and tell him a tale. Tell him all about how we boys get in and out of town. All about those irrigation ditches. Have me watched right along. You could save your skin that way.'

Astonishment turned Hop's stomach puking sour. He had to swallow several times instead of shouting a protest against that insinuation. In the moment for thought thus gained he saw that it was useless to protest, and positively useful to pretend to accept the possibility.

He said, 'I suppose I could do that.'

Alpha said, 'It's what anyone in your position would do. Stands to reason. That's where you've got me. I can't stop you talking to Joshua. I just hope your God's got enough know-how to take care of us. Well, if that's the way you want it. Give me the money.'

Hop counted out the amount they had calculated for the guide and the three mules and the man who was to have them ready outside the city, and Alpha, his face blank with sullen anger, went off, saying only, 'Don't go out and about. Just in case you've got any new religious ideas, I can tell you the boys are out and about too. You'd never get to police Headquarters if you tried.'

Hop stretched himself on the couch, sniffed at the scented air from the garden and felt weak from all the blood he had lost a few days before, and the fears and strains and fighting of the night. He was aware of being light-headed. He could hear himself beginning to mutter to himself. To keep his brain from spinning he seemed to need to mouth words. Just why, he murmured to himself, did I have to talk about our religion to that young ruffian? I'm not a man that talks about such things to strangers. Why give him of all the scallywags on earth a chance to laugh at it?

In an angry flutter of the brain there flickered in front of him precepts from the scriptures mouthed at him by Samaritan preachers when he was a child. They had taught that 'thieves are not to be shunned, so as to be left to their own evil devices, but are to be treated as friends and shewn other ways'. The thought of Alpha danced mockingly through that bit of memory. The preachers had also said, 'A Samaritan must not deceive a man who is not a Samaritan because, when that other man finds he has been deceived he will never accept the truth of the Samaritan religion.'

Now it was Joshua whose bothered face pushed itself forward. 'He must not be deceived,' said Hop, quite loudly, before his thinking apparatus collapsed into a quicksand of weakness and a sleep shot through with furiously bright dreams.

Clear-headed after the siesta he went in the late afternoon to see Joshua and told him the whole story.

Joshua: 'I knew all this.'

Hop: 'How come? I only just told you.'

Joshua: 'Had a bad feeling about it from the minute you came with that man. When the police came round it got worse. And when you told me what you told me about you and the Chief of Police it was really bad. And then there were those men I saw on the street. About then I made up my mind.'

Hop: 'To do what?'

Joshua: 'Up stakes. Sell out. Get out. I've talked to a man. He'll take over the whole business. He's paid a good price for it. All things considered.'

Hop: 'Paid?'

Joshua: 'Sure. I could see what was going to happen and I sold and he bought. It's the way it goes.'

Hop: 'You say it's not just the police. Something to do with those men you saw on the street. You said you wished you didn't see them.'

Joshua: 'I know Barabbas's people when I see them.'

Hop: 'And what's the trouble with them? They haven't anything against you. Just the contrary I'd have thought.'

Joshua: 'You're simple-minded. A person can't ever tell what's going to happen. One day, like it might be the police could happen. But think ahead a bit and it could be the Barabbas people could take control. Burning and destroying. Either way I'm out of business.'

Hop: 'You've got jitters. You're seeing things. No need to yell before you're hurt.'

Joshua: 'I'm not yelling. Not at all. I'm quitting.'

Hop: 'How? How'll you get out of town?'

Joshua: 'How're *you* getting out of town?'

Hop: 'I just told you.'

Joshua: 'So that's the way I'm going too. What's the matter? You going to faint or something? It's not much I'm asking. The spot I'm in, you've put me in it.'

Hop: 'And O God! that's the truth.'

Joshua: 'So what's so hard about it?'

Hop: 'They'll have to get another mule.'

Joshua: 'I'll pay for another mule.'

Hop: 'They won't like it. They'll say it's raising the risk.'

Joshua: 'So you brought the risk on us all in the first place?'

Hop: 'Let's hope they see it that way, Alpha and the guide and whoever's really making the arrangements.'

Joshua: 'I can see that in just a minute you're going to start suggesting that I'm deserting my wife and family.'

Hop: 'Never even thought about it.'

Joshua: 'Got them out of town, days ago. To a quiet place where it's peaceful.'

Hop: 'Days ago? So that was the something else you did just after I showed up. Like getting ready to sell the place. You mean you saw something coming? Like a dream?'

Joshua: 'I don't just remember. It was a feeling I had.'

Hop: 'Suppose it was a dream, and part of it's come true already. So you won't tell me the rest. Maybe better so.'

Feeling discouragement and some fear regarding what Joshua might have seen coming in some dream, if he really had had that kind of dream, Hop stood up and began to narrow his thoughts down to the question of how he would explain to Alpha that the sort of stupid, dangerous thing Alpha had been sure would happen had happened. Hop had insisted on telling Joshua that they were going, and how. And as a result they were going to enlarge the party, get another mule and take Joshua along with them. Thinking, he got a little way across the courtyard and was aware of a small hubbub in the entry-arch behind him, and then, with a sensation as unpleasant as though someone had spat on his neck, of the sound of his own name being uttered in a tone that was harsh and plaintive at the same time.

He stood stock still, looking up at the evening sky. He told himself that he had to believe his ears. He had to believe that Simon of Sachem had come from afar; had put in an appearance; was here in Jericho; now. He felt as though that snuffling nose were already almost at his back. And that was no figment. It was actually so. For as he turned, making an effort to do so against numbing exasperation, there was Simon coming out from under the arch, squealing something at Joshua out of the corner of his mouth, and now half squealing, half snuffling at Hop. Behind him under the arch stood a mule with saddlebags bulging.

At such a moment, this Simon induced a sense of hopelessness in Hop. Cocooned as Simon was in his own fuss and hubbub, how could he be reached, have matters explained to him, be told the facts of life as they were that dangerous evening in that hotel yard in Jericho? No way at all, it seemed to Hop, who looked over Simon's twitching shoulder at Joshua. Joshua stood looking from Simon to Simon's mule with the air of a man who has gone into a trance. Hop had time to wonder whether Joshua had foreseen this, too, in his dream.

It was barely possible, and was unnecessary, to distinguish just what Simon was saying, to make it coherent. It was like a silly chant by a child who is somehow at the same time senile.

'You. You. You. Here. Here. How? What? No news. Money.'

All that Hop had imagined Simon gibbering to himself in the office in Sachem was being gibbered here in Jericho. Hop had left on his trip with a big sum of the firm's money, hadn't he? He had promised to report immediately, hadn't he? He had not reported, had he? Day after day he had not reported. And, if he didn't know, everyone else in Sachem certainly did that he had an irregular, unsound type of streak in him. A man could never be entirely sure, as a man ought to be able to be, what Hop might get into his head next.

Might have taken off on some crazy trip to parts unscheduled and unknown. Might have gambled the money away and then killed himself. And Simon waiting there day after day after day with no news. Couldn't stand it a day longer. Had to follow. And now finds Hop lurking like a runaway dog in this inn where the inn-keeper looks like a man that believes he's going to be flogged to death and for good reason and refuses information requested. So what's the explanation? If any, if any.

'If any,' thought Hop. He said, 'Simon, the situation's got just a bit confused.'

Simon wriggled and twitched like a pricked insect.

'Confused? I'll say it's confused. You've gone and got it confused, quite personally yourself. I want your quite personal explanation. If any. And I have to get back there and see to my bags. Don't trust that inn-keeper. Looks an all-round sneak-thief. Or worse.'

Spinning round, as dizzy as a dust eddy, he held Hop by the cloak and started back to the arch. So why not. Best, Hop thought, to go into Joshua's room and talk there. Joshua knew the entire situation anyway; even knew about Simon of Sachem from satirical, contemptuous things Hop had said when Simon was just a bad joke, safe out of the way, up there in Sachem.

They got the bags off the mule and then the three of them

were sitting—Simon more twitching than sitting—on the couches in Joshua's place.

'Well then, what's the explanation?'

O great moon above and myriad stars, Hop thought, what *is* the explanation? There are two explanations: the explanation of what and why these things have really happened to me, and some other explanation that might make some kind of sense Simon Snuffler. And the trouble is, I don't know either one. Just one thing's certain: there is no hope at all, none at all, of proceeding as though Simon had not poked himself like a stick between a runner's legs into our plans for tonight. He's going to stay as close as a hound. No chance whatsoever of giving him the slip.

His business instincts are aroused. Which in his case means principally that he believes he is being swindled or is about to be swindled. And that makes this wretched snuffler keener and more determined than a trained, paid policeman. And, just completing that thought, if he were to get a whiff of something he thought a little suspicious, a little unusual, he would waste no time at all before he was round at police Headquarters with his story.

Thinking thus, and at the same time talking off the top of his head, Hop got as far as 'explaining' to Simon of Sachem that a lot of matters had arisen which he could not go into now, but that the upshot and sum total of these events was that Hop had to get out of Jericho that night.

'Have to? Out? Get out?'

Simon quivered all over. The words about having to get out tonight, meant to him only one thing: that his partner Hop was a wanted criminal. Hop noted, wearily, the quiver and the suddenly fixed glare in his eyes. It was easily seen that this was just precisely the kind of thing Simon had all along thought more than probable. But it could be seen too that the fact that he had suspected such things did nothing at all to lessen his furious resentment at the confirmation of lurking suspicions.

Indeed, the news that his suspicions had been correct caused him to resent the situation worse than would have been the case had he never had any such suspicions at all. This state of mind expressed in a thin jet of bitter words. They were to the effect that almost since the first months of their partnership he had sensed something unsound, not quite regular about Hop.

Had Hop on any occasion admitted to Simon that he was basically unsound, irregular in his manner of thinking and behaviour? Oh no. Quite the contrary. He had gone on for months and months hypocritically deceitfully playing the part of the reliable man. His accounts were always in order. His business deals on behalf of the firm which were continuously profitable, were also reported on fully and accurately. In a word, although given to woolly talk, he never, by a single act of commission or omission, gave the least grounds for distrust.

As a result of this impeccable behaviour, Simon had been lured, against his better judgment into trusting him. And look now at the results. Simon's partner on the run. The firm disgraced throughout Jericho. Throughout Judaea. Liable now to be boycotted by potential customers in all that territory. Crippling financial losses.

He jumped himself up off the couch.

'I'm going to get to the bottom of this. I shall go now, at once, to the police.'

'You're not in Sachem now,' Hop said. 'You'll get yourself arrested.'

'Or killed in the street,' said Joshua, speaking for the first time and evidently thinking of Barabbas's people.

Simon's knees gave way, his buttocks bumped back on to the couch. He was still quivering and glaring. He seemed to make an effort to control himself and take command of the situation in the name of sanity, justice and business.

'Let us,' he said, in a judicial manner, 'get this quite clear. You are now, if I have understood you aright, threatening me with arrest or—if I heard you correctly—murder. Or have I misinterpreted your meaning?'

Joshua looked mournfully at Hop. 'Maybe,' he said, 'we'd best tell him the whole story.'

Hop looked briefly across the big room dim in the fading light. There was a curtain, and beyond that a door which normally stood open.

'The door's shut and bolted,' Joshua said.

'Of course,' said Hop. 'But I think there's someone out there.'

Simon was on his feet again. 'Someone after my mule.'

Hop pushed past him, went across the room through the curtain and while he was unbolting the door someone was knocking. Alpha was there. He looked Hop quickly up and down. Then his sulky, sultry eyes looked beyond Hop into the room.

His low, rough voice said, 'May I join the party?' and he walked in, studying Simon as he came. Simon stared at him with an expression of disgust and possibly fear. His stare at Alpha's face, clothes and general appearance said as plainly as though he had spoken 'I know your type. Seen it before. Layabout. Hooligan. Or worse.'

'A little conference?' said Alpha. 'Who's this?' He jerked his head insolently towards Simon.

'My partner from Sachem,' Hop said. 'He's come to see what's been happening to me.' After a small hesitation, he added, 'I've had to explain to him that I'm leaving town tonight.'

Expecting a snarl from Alpha, he got instead a long, thoughtful look and a nod. It occurred to him that Alpha had the kind of experience which would enable him to understand instantly just why it could be more dangerous to try to give Simon the slip than to tell him that much of the facts.

Simon said, 'You're associated with this young man?' and sat down, looking like a prosecutor who has made his point and now rests his case.

Alpha scowled, and let himself down on to the couch beside Joshua, his legs sprawled, his eyes looking malevolently round the room.

He said to Hop, 'You've got us in a mess of manure.'

Hop said, 'I got you out of one once.'

Alpha spat on the floor.

Simon started to say something, but before anyone could hear what it was Alpha gave a low, brutal growl. The growl developed into violent words.

'Listen, you,' he said to Simon. 'Don't talk. Just listen. You don't know what goes on. Just get in your head that if you start to bother me I'll get you killed. Just killed.'

CHAPTER EIGHT

Not killed, but trembling all over and losing control of his bowels, Simon crouched in the old irrigation ditch with those four others—Hop, Joshua, Alpha and the guide.

Back there hours ago in Joshua's room, Alpha, talking as though it were a question of what to do about a troublesome dog, had thought aloud that to have Simon killed could complicate and possibly disrupt the arrangements for escape from Jericho. He certainly could not be left behind, alive. So he must be taken with them.

'You'd better bring your partner to understand the situation,' Alpha had said to Hop. After Alpha's cold talk, the situation was so evidently simple that there had been no difficulty in bringing Simon to understand it.

'You see how it is?' Hop had said to him. 'You have to come with us and do just exactly what you're told to do. You can see for yourself what'll happen otherwise.'

For the first time since his arrival in Jericho Simon said something unexpected. He said, 'I see I have no alternative. But let me tell you that, as of now, I consider our business partnership dissolved.'

At this Alpha let out a snarling cackle of laughter. Joshua and Hop looked at Simon with nearly admiring astonishment.

That had been hours ago. Their escape through the out-buildings at the back of the inn to the alley where the guide waited for them was delayed on account of the extra work Alpha had to do. He had to arrange to provide the mule for Joshua. He had to try, but in this failed, to get yet another mule for Simon. Simon had seemed to understand why it would be impossible to use his own mule in the flight from the city. It must be left behind. But as they went stealthily on foot through the out-buildings, Hop heard him say, apparently to himself, 'I knew all along they were going to steal my mule.'

His plump saddlebags had to be left behind too. He had been able to carry nothing but his money.

It seemed to Hop that by now a whole section of his life had been spent moving in danger and terror through the twisting lanes and alleys of what that other guide had described as 'Jericho, jewel city of Judaea'. He thought, in order not to think of anything much else, how things had come to the point where these same dangerous alleys meant, now, for him, the only safety. No police would venture here in the dark, probably not even in daylight. And against thieves and murderers the presence of Alpha and the probably criminal guide, were a protection. It would be known among such people that it could be dangerous to obstruct the friends of Alpha. So now, thought Hop, this shameless thug is my protector; and this is not just a notion. This is real.

It was real all the way through the lanes and alleys to the edge of Jericho. There were people moving, or just standing. They were sometimes a little ahead or a little behind, or they could be faintly seen at doorways or under arches. With one half of your mind, Hop thought, you could suppose them to be dangerous criminals, only daunted by sight of Alpha and the guide. Or, if you looked at the matter sanely, normally and without fear, they could be quite simply very poor people, living here in those stinking alleys, talking bitterly but harmlessly about how much it costs to live.

The old irrigation ditch, where the insect and animal sounds of the night took over, was noisier than the alleys of the city. The going was mostly smooth, where the masonry was intact. But every couple of hundred paces or so the man-made bed of the ditch had collapsed. They had to go gingerly across patches of earth sprouting thorny scrub and tilted slabs of stone. The guide was a little ahead with Alpha. Joshua and Simon came next, Simon puffing and sometimes even groaning as they clambered across the rough patches. Hop, moving easily on his strong legs, was behind them. Alpha had said this was the best order. As though, Hop thought, those other two might make a break for it, try to escape. Why? And, at this stage of the game, where to?

They had been going for maybe an hour, sometimes fast, sometimes slowly, when the challenge came. This was a shallow part of the ditch. Two men in the uniform of the Civil

Police stood in it, with their weapons at the ready. Two, perhaps three other men of the patrol were on the bank of the ditch, just ahead of the point reached by Alpha and the guide. Someone in command, up on the bank, called harshly to 'you two', meaning Alpha and the guide, to come forward slowly with their arms stretched out.

It seemed they had not sighted the other three, who were still behind a clump of furze. But Hop could hear the voice of the corporal in command throwing violent questions at Alpha. Just a couple of questions, then the corporal and two others jumped down into the ditch and Alpha and the guide were ordered to come forward. Although he was closer now, the corporal continued to shout. 'You two,' he was saying, 'are under arrest. Don't make a move or we'll chop you up.'

The rat-whiskers, much used to detecting states of mind from tones of voice, told Hop that this fellow was more than a little scared. The corporal could be heard ordering his men to search and disarm Alpha and the guide. These same two policemen were to march the prisoners back to Jericho. He gave his orders as though he were memorizing instructions given in training. To Hop, a man of tough deals and hard bargaining, this corporal's whole manner suggested that this must be the first time that the patrol had actually had to do what it was posted to do; namely to apprehend criminal elements trying to cross the outer edge of the city's limits.

Even so, if Alpha and the guide were marched off, and the corporal with two others remained on guard, there was no way forward for the rest of the party. Joshua and Simon would be useless in a fight, however scared and astonished the police might be. Hop, talking to himself in a low voice, as he did when he had to make up his mind and was unsure whether he was making it up right, said, 'I am a businessman. This has to be a matter of business.'

At the moment of the challenge, he, Joshua and Simon had all crouched low. Hop now stood up, stepped forward between the other two, and with his arms stretched out advanced towards the police. They were puny-looking men. From the way they jumped and put themselves on guard you could have thought that they were being attacked by a superior force. The corporal barked at him to stop where he stood. He jabbered out questions. Who are you? Where going? How many? In his nervousness the official questions became confused. Instead of being a corporal of police he might have been no more than the leader of one band of travellers suddenly confronted with another band.

Hop said sharply, 'We have to leave town.'

The corporal said, 'It's forbidden.'

'Of course it's forbidden,' Hop said. 'Otherwise you wouldn't be out here on the edge of things.'

At that, he saw the corporal and two of his men look automatically towards the city, measuring just how far out on the edge of things they were. Then the corporal could be seen trying to peer past Hop towards the bushes, trying to see how many more men might be there.

Hop roughed his voice. He said, 'If you whistle or make any kind of signal you'll be sorry for it.'

The little corporal shifted on his feet, made an evident effort to pull himself together, to assert himself in front of his men.

'*We'll* be sorry for it? It's *you'll* be sorry for it if you try to interfere with police officers in the discharge of their duties.'

Hop saw the man next to the corporal give a quick tug at the corporal's tunic and step back a pace. The corporal stepped back too and leaned his head sideways to listen to whatever the man was saying. Hop watched them in this small, agitated conference. Then he said loudly, 'So maybe we'll all be sorry. All of us get hurt. And all for nothing. Is that reasonable?'

He took a couple of steps forward, and nobody ordered him to halt. He was close enough now to look at the policemen in the manner of a businessman looking round a group of other businessmen with whom he is going to do a deal. He said aloud, 'I am a businessman.'

Experience of deals in many market places told him that from the moment the corporal had failed to challenge those few steps forward there was going to be neither an arrest nor a fight: there was going to be a deal.

In the bargaining that followed, he was hampered by one fact. He knew how little money he had left after the trip. He had no exact notion how much money Simon had with him. That meant that while he could decide on the low figure of his first offer, he had no way of knowing how far he could safely go towards meeting what would be the high figure of the corporal's first demand. He decided that the only way to make his bargaining convincing was simply to guess at the amount Simon might have and then behave as he would if he knew it for a fact. Though the corporal naturally was the spokesman for the other side, the members of the patrol repeatedly broke in with greedily excited interjections which prolonged the business. Alpha, on the other hand, still standing between two of the policemen, remained watchfully silent, except to say at one point that of course the knives taken from him and the guide must be returned as part of the bargain. And later still as the bargaining reached crisis point, Alpha, to Hop's admiration, turned sharply upon Hop and said, 'Why can't you be reasonable? Can't you see the corporal here has a problem. Whyn't you come a little bit further to meet him?'

The trick, the pretence that a member of the opposition had changed sides, was as old as the hills, and very familiar to Hop. It was not so to the corporal. His nerves were, his voice and manner showed, nastily strained by the dealing.

There were his men, greedy and ready to turn on him if he failed to get a good enough price for letting these birds fly free. There was the possibility that, before all the dealing was ended, some Inspector of Patrols would come riding out from Jericho, and then there would be no money at all and not much credit either. And there was that other possibility that the fellow he was bargaining with might have enough men hidden somewhere in those bushes to put up a fight in which, as he had said, everyone would get hurt and from which nobody would profit.

The suggestion that one of those others, this first prisoner, had unmistakably come over to his side came to him as a profound relief. He had no way of knowing that this was precisely the object of the trick. With relief he listened to Alpha explaining to Hop that Hop was not to be unreasonable, that he ought to increase his offer. The suggested increase, naturally, was a long way below the increase which the corporal had not only demanded, but had declared with violent oaths to be the absolute minimum he would accept. But the long tussle with this tireless Hop had tired him exceedingly. Hop's method of bargaining gave the impression that the thing could go on for ever. To anyone but a professional dealer the prospect must have been so wearisome as to be terrifying. Thus the corporal now turned to Alpha in gratitude, as to a friend in need. Hop, with a look of simulated reproach at Alpha, as though the fellow had betrayed him, finally shrugged and agreed in a surly manner to the sum suggested that he pay, a lot less than that which he had expected he would have to hand over.

Throughout the tussle Hop had been aware, out of the back of his head, of Simon of Sachem from time to time coughing and grunting behind him. Since Simon was several yards away behind the furze bushes these coughs and grunts must have been loud indeed, either deliberately uttered, or jerked out of the man by the excitement of his interest. Now Hop said Alpha, 'Get the needful from you know who.'

Stepping for the first time from between the two patrolmen, Alpha went back along the ditch. Hop could hear his voice speaking harshly, contemptuously to Simon, and Simon's voice putting up some kind of plaintive argument. Simon's resistance, as though any kind of resistance were at this point possible, was all to the good. It would help to convince the corporal and his men that they had skinned these refugees, squeezed them till it hurt.

Alpha returned with the money in a small skin bag and handed it to Hop, who counted it. Then he tossed the bag on to the ground about midway between himself and the corporal, who came forward, squatted, and counted it, while his men watched, counting with him.

'Correct?' said Hop.

'Uh-uh,' said the corporal.

'Well then,' said Hop, 'jog.'

In accordance with the terms of the agreement, their knives having been returned to Alpha and the guide, the corporal gave an order to the patrol. As he did so his voice changed. He had stopped being a dealer bargaining with another dealer and became once again a corporal of the Civil Police of the City of Jericho. Under his renewed command, the patrol moved off along the bank of the irrigation ditch in the direction of the city.

The guide watched them until they were far enough away so that neither their voices nor footsteps could be heard. Then he made a signal to Alpha. Hop in a low voice told

Simon and Joshua to come on. Joshua started walking as though this dreadful walk had never been interrupted and might have no end either.

For a moment Hop looked at Simon expecting some kind of protest, outcry, expostulation. None came. His eyes were about on a level with Hop's neck, and he looked at it with hatred, contempt and despair. He turned his head slightly and gave the same sort of look at Alpha: the two of them accomplices from the underworld, experts in crime, getting a man like Simon far on to the wrong side of the law.

The ditch ended, and they crossed a wide stretch of bush. A whistle told them where the man with the mules was waiting in a shallow saucer of ground. There were, as Alpha had said, just the three mules. The biggest of them, a huge animal, was to carry two. The guide mounted one of the smaller ones immediately. Simon, either as a reaction from the alarms just experienced or in sheer disgust at the entire situation, squatted down.

Alpha said to Hop, 'I'm a lot lighter than you. He'll get up behind me on the big fellow.'

At this, Simon, who had been getting to his feet, squatted again, his bowels convulsed and spattering the ground. The stench seemed to be his comment on the pass things had come to. Alpha said, 'How much more've you got in that belly? You aim to crap all night?'

Simon, still squatting, said, 'I had a good mule of my own.'

Alpha said, 'Get that crap out of you and come on.'

Simon got to his feet and took the few steps to the big mules like a deathwalk. Alpha mounted. Hop hoisted Simon up behind him and then mounted the remaining mule.

'Jog,' said Hop. They jogged, and about the time they could smell dawn coming the guide said, 'Nearly there. That's the back side of the inn.'

The rest of them could see nothing until the mules, stumbling and slithering on stony ground, were almost on top of a low boundary wall. Beyond it, a man, alerted by the noise, was coming cautiously towards the wall. The guide called out to him, uttering a string of words unintelligible to Hop; some password.

The man beyond the wall said, 'The gate's this way.'

He led them to it, opened it, and stood watching them file

through. He called out to the guide to ask did he know the way to the stables. The guide walked his mule down a steep slope of rough ground and then the bulk of low buildings could be seen. The man came from the gate and stood waiting while they dismounted, and unsaddled. He said they should go on to the back door of the inn and he would attend to the beasts.

In the dawn twilight they stumbled along behind the guide. In a building ahead of them a door stood open. The guide told them to wait where they were while he went ahead. They could hear him talking with someone at the door. Hop recognized the voice of the Babylonian. The guide called to them to come ahead.

The inn-keeper had turned from the door, and moving with bearish gait, lumbering and neat at the same time, had gone in front of them down a broad passage, pushed aside a curtain, and now awaited them in a courtyard, where the tops of a few trees rustled in the slight wind of dawn. It was not the courtyard Hop remembered from his first visit to the inn. The place must be bigger than he had imagined.

The inn-keeper turned to face them, extending his arms in a wide gesture of welcome. He rolled words around his tongue. He said, 'I myself, personally, will conduct you to the available quarters. When available food and drink is in readiness, I will summon you.' Then, looking at Hop he said, 'I told you the road was dangerous, and it was dangerous. You didn't believe me. I told you other things, and you didn't believe them either.'

Hop shrugged.

The inn-keeper said, 'You've experienced some frightening experiences? You've had the living daylights scared out of you?'

'You're right there.'

'Anyone,' said the inn-keeper, 'who isn't frightened is a fool.'

'OK, OK,' Alpha said.

'Maybe there are worse things to be scared of than anything you know.'

He put his head back and looked up at the sky where a few pale stars were still shining.

He pointed upwards. 'Speaking personally, myself, that's what I'm frightened of,' he said.

Joshua spoke suddenly and irritably. 'Let's not bother about the stars. Let's get some food. You don't think the stars bother about what happens to us, do you? Some people do.'

The inn-keeper, still gazing upwards at space said, 'No, I don't think the stars bother at all.'

'Well then,' said Joshua testily.

'That's why they frighten me,' said the inn-keeper.

CHAPTER NINE

'News? News? Any news?' On the evening of the second day at the inn of Simon the Knower, Simon of Sachem was asking, for the hundredth time, what was happening outside, how long were they to stay in that place, when could they get back to Sachem and attend to business?

The Knower, the Babylonian, said, 'The dogs barked on the road. It was a party of businessmen going down from Jerusalem to Jericho. Later, the dogs barked again. It was the postal courier on the way to Jerusalem. Perhaps the third time they bark it will be the police.'

He smiled round at the company gathered for supper. There was a silence while everyone listened for the barking of the dogs. There was no barking. Simon of Sachem broke the silence with a snuffle and said, 'But how is there no news? I had assumed,' he said pompously, looking at Alpha, 'that your people would have been on the alert and thus kept us reasonably informed as to the state of affairs.'

'What people, loose-guts?' Alpha asked.

The Snuffler said, 'I was always under the impression that certain types of what I may call underground organization, maintaining a network and so on in the country, up and down the country as it were, are in a position to furnish their members with information on matters arising. An underground network.'

'Is that so?' said Alpha.

'It was my understanding,' said the Snuffler.

Evidently speaking hurriedly and more or less at random to prevent trouble, Joshua said to the Babylonian, 'Wanted to ask you about a thing you said yesterday. Just after we got here, remember? you were talking about the stars. You said you were frightened of them because they didn't bother about us. Well what I mean to say is, if you follow me, is if they don't bother about us why should we be frightened of them? See what I mean to say?'

There was a coughing noise outside, one of the dogs was coughing and maybe starting to bark at something and then perhaps the other dogs would bark too. Everyone listened but the coughing stopped and there was no barking.

After listening, the Babylonian puffed himself out a little, a little of the frog-puff Hop remembered from their first meeting. He said to Joshua, 'Listen to me, I have to use words when I'm talking to you. Words mean one thing and another thing to you and to me. So I'll use words and maybe you'll understand them and maybe you won't understand them. It comes to the same thing in the end.'

'If that's how you feel about words,' Joshua said sharply, 'what's the use of using them, if you see what I mean to say.'

The Babylonian continued without attention to this remark.

'With promises and guile astrologers persuade people to believe that those black stars, bright to your eyes but really black, black as endless hell, care about this man's fate and that man's and yours and mine. Not so. They care no more for you and me than you and I care about this, that and the other ant on an ant-heap.'

'Well then,' Joshua began.

'But,' said the Babylonian, swelling a little more, 'but without caring about any one of us they are among the dark rulers of all of us. All the ants in the ant-heap. There are many rulers, the stars among them. They are among the black evil rulers of all men. We are the prisoners, they are the gaolers. Do you imagine,' said the Babylonian, raising his voice, 'that by prayer or incantations or spells you can ever reach the ears of those eternal gaolers? If they were to hear you scream your little screams they would laugh. But they are beyond hearing. They follow their black purpose deaf, deaf, deaf to the yells of men.'

'Purpose?' said Joshua.

'Their purpose,' said the Babylonian, 'is congruent to that of the Archons. It is to numb and suffocate the inner spirit of man, to put out man's small spark of light, his tiny breath of life. The breath,' said the Babylonian, making himself and his voice swell until he seemed to be preaching to a big congregation, 'which is his part of the Unknown God, the Alien God, the God beyond the rulers and the gaolers, beyond the Archons of Space and the Aeons of Time.'

'Interesting,' Hop said, taking a swig of wine.

'Big deal,' said Alpha.

'I'm sure I don't know,' said Joshua, 'what authority you have for all that. Forgive my saying so, sounds lot of claptrap to me, more or less.'

'Because you are without knowledge or cognition,' said the Babylonian. 'You are numb, drunk, obfuscated by the air of your prison. Which is the world. I tell you the Fate of man, and you call it claptrap. Your thought is directed by the manipulation of your gaolers.'

'What I want to know,' said Simon Snuffler, 'as I said quite some time ago before my question was evaded, is just how long we are likely to have to stay here. I want to know is there any *news*? And if not, why not?'

The Babylonian started to say something, then abruptly raised a finger and was seen to be listening in a manner which caused all the others to listen too. During a long stretch of silence they were unable to hear whatever it was the Babylonian had heard. Then they heard the noise of hooves coming from the direction of the enclosure at the back of the inn.

Simon Snuffler started up from his place. 'Look here,' he said in a furious hiss, 'this may be the police or whatever. You said the dogs would bark. Warn us.'

'If the dogs didn't bark,' said the Babylonian, 'it's because whoever's coming is a friend. Someone they know. This may be the answer to your need for news.' He got up and began to leave the room in his quick, lumbering, bearlike manner. Alpha stood up and said, 'I'll come along with you.'

'No,' said the Babylonian, stopping to turn round and look Alpha in the eye.

'May be one of the boys,' said Alpha. 'May be someone I know.'

'And may be someone you don't know,' said the Babylonian, turning his back on Alpha and moving fast out of the room. Alpha sat down, pouting, but got to his feet again when the Babylonian returned, bringing with him a man who, evidently, was after all a person known to Alpha, 'one of the boys'. A messenger from Jericho.

'And so?' Alpha said.

So there was hell, it seemed, to pay in Jericho on account of many matters arising, here, there and the other place.

'Such as, for instance?'

For instance the escape of Hop, Joshua and Alpha from the city had naturally caused a major scandal in the Police Department. It had not taken the detectives long to learn, from one or more informers in those black alleys, that a group which included Alpha, had been seen moving by night through that section of the city. This news led to discovery of the secret entrance to the irrigation ditch. And that piece of information led straight to the arrest and violent interrogation of the corporal and the members of his patrol. Under torture they had confessed, and been executed—secretly, in order to try to stop news of the scandal becoming public knowledge.

'Silly bugger didn't have much time to spend the money,' said Alpha. 'So what else is going on down there?'

Given the state of the country, and the particular preoccupations and obsessions of the Chief of Police, Mr Jericho, the simple fact of the trio's escape had been only a beginning. According to information from inside Police HQ, the Chief had chosen to take this skilfully conducted escape as support for his theory that the Samaritan was a valued agent of the Essene and Barabbas. He further chose to speculate that the unknown man (in fact Simon of Sachem) who had ridden into Jericho that night, was an emissary from rebel headquarters in Jerusalem, bringing them urgent orders to get away, presumably to Samaria, without delay. And this in turn suggested that the rebel plot was coming to a head.

Further, the personal prestige of the Chief was evidently involved. Even without special information from the inside of Police HQ everyone who knew anything could see how the Romans, and, especially, the Men in Black would suspect, or pretend to suspect, that the Idumean was playing some dangerous game. The man from Jericho who was one of the boys, had a face anyone could easily forget, which stayed blank except when a corner of his mouth twitched. He looked at the floor and said:

'Everybody's wondering. There's the story that the Chief doesn't move yet because he's waiting for you to lead him to others in the conspiracy. Maybe for them to come to you. The only sure thing about that story is that the Chief's certainly spreading it himself.'

'Then how does it make sense?' said the Babylonian. 'He spreads that story. He knows that it will reach this inn. It has just reached it. So all of us are forewarned of his intention. No. If he makes no move to apprehend you—though not to apprehend you gives the Romans and the rest ammunition against him—he has a deeper reason than that.'

He took his beard in his hand, closed his eyes, and assumed the posture of a man meditating. The others sat watching him in silence.

Then, speaking as though out of a trance, he said:

'First, we know that he says he believes you,' he gestured at Hop, 'are an agent of the Essene. Secondly, we know that his enemies on high allege that they suspect him, the Police Chief of Jericho, of in fact being in secret league, complot and conspiracy with the Essene, the Barabbas people and other dissident elements. Then suppose,' he slowly straightened his back so that without getting up he was looking down a little at Hop, 'suppose the thing he says he believes and the thing they suspect are both true?'

The remark sent out ripples like a stone dropped into water.

Hop started to say something. The Babylonian spoke before he could utter.

'What can you say my travelling friend? You deny it. You say you are a simple businessman. Your story is that you gave aid and comfort to a wounded traveller by the roadside, an act of simple goodheartedness. It has involved you in discomforts, dangers and delays. All you want now is to be back in the arms of your wife in your little home in Sachem.'

Hop said, violently, 'It's true. What's strange about it?'

He thought vividly of Sarah and remembered saying just the same thing to the Police Chief. Futile then, futile now.

'Nothing strange,' said the Babylonian. 'It is what you would say if you were that simple man of business. It is also what you would say if you were an agent of these and those.'

Hop sighed resignedly. Then a useful thought came to him. He pointed at Simon of Sachem and said to the Babylonian,

'And what about him? You can't believe he's anyone's secret agent, can you?'

The Babylonian smiled. 'But suppose he is simply a particularly good actor? Acting, overacting a little perhaps, the part of the snuffling, fussing, pigheaded little moneybags?' He appraised Simon of Sachem with a cruel grin.

It seemed that Simon, in the bubble of his own ideas had not bothered to understand these exchanges. The bubbles now fizzed out in words.

'I have been thinking,' he said, 'I have reached certain conclusions. It is crystal clear to me from what this messenger whom I presume to be reasonably reliable, has reported this evening, that the difficulty and, I may say, danger of our situation results in large measure from the fact that the civil authorities in Jericho suppose us, myself and my former partner, to be agents of the so-called Essene. Am I right?'

'Well and?' Hop said.

'That,' went on Simon Snuffler, 'is the nub of the matter as I see it. Therefore what's required is that means should be found to disabuse the authorities of a misunderstanding which is manifestly absurd.'

Hop said, 'You weren't so sure about it back there in Jericho. You were all set to believe that I might be mixed up in anything and everything.'

'I concede that point,' said Simon. 'I am even prepared to admit that I still have an open mind on the point. But that point is not, and must not be regarded as, the point.'

'And what is the point?'

'The point is that at this juncture, as I may term it, the essential, regardless of this, that and the other thing, is to make it clear beyond a peradventure that we neither of us have any such connection.'

'Great idea,' said Alpha.

'It just so happens,' said Simon, 'that, mere businessman as I am, I am not entirely ignorant of what I call the political situation. The general state of affairs. For instance, it is crystal clear to me that, for reasons best known to himself, this Essene is anxious to give the impression, to suggest in other words, that we Samaritans are in sympathy with his ideals. So-called ideals, aims, etcetera. *Now,* my friends,' continued Simon, 'it must be crystal clear to your goodselves as it is to me, that conversely, if I may put it that way, conversely the various authorities must be anxious to demonstrate that the Essene's claims are false. In other words, putting it that's to say in a different way, they'd be glad to have it shown that when he claims support in this, that or the other quarter, these claims are demonstrably false: in other words can be shown to be baseless. Such a demonstration would be very much in line with their desired line. Am I right?'

'So what?'

'So it is necessary, indeed urgent, to find ways and means, all ways and means, of making clear to the relevant authorities not only that we have no connection of any sort, kind or description with the Essene, but that we are prepared to so state in the most public manner in any terms, and by any means, which said authorities may deem advisable.'

Hop in an angry voice started to say something. The Babylonian interrupted him.

'You,' he said to Hop, 'are going to say that you would rather feed your body to the worms than do anything that might give pleasure and solace to that Chief of Police in Jericho. Save your breath, friend and brother. In the circumstances of the case no such decision is called for. The answer,' he said, turning to Simon Snuffler, 'to your proposition is that it lacks at every point perspicacity and a due sense of the feasible realities of the given situation. Your brain-children gibber unproductively. Your mental activities are unavailing. One may consider your contribution to the discussion every way from which way and yet end up with one's head in a pig's bladder.'

'I resent that,' said Simon. 'I tell you in so many words I resent it. I'm not accustomed to that kind of language.'

'The reason being,' continued the Babylonian as though Simon had not spoken, 'that no operative means are available for encompassing the end you have in view. Who, let me ask you little man, is going to embroil himself in the endeavour to convey your message to the authorities? Nobody at all.'

'But, but, but,' said Simon. 'What about him?' He jerked his head in the direction of the corner where Alpha and the messenger talked inaudibly.

'If you believe he's your man for a job like that you'll believe anything,' said the Babylonian.

'Well,' said Simon, 'he's supposed to be a messenger, isn't

he? I was given to understand that he's just a messenger.'

The Babylonian now turned his eyes on Simon with an expression of loathing and contempt. The effects of the hemp he had been chewing for some time could be noted. Also, Hop vaguely recalled that in the code or lingo of the Knowers the word 'messenger' could have a special, holy significance. It evidently had such significance for the Babylonian in his present condition.

Taking his time with the words and somewhat rolling his eyes, he said:

'You are pleased to speak lightly of messengers, beasts of burden only fit to carry your stupid baggage.'

'Look, look, look,' said Simon, showing alarm at his manner. 'I said nothing of the kind. I simply meant that I thought, in the circumstances...'

The Babylonian's speech sailed on. 'The human messenger,' he said, 'who, at risk to his life, carries messages through the evilly watchful outposts, patrols, lurking spies and houseguards of the enemy, is the lowly yet noble image of that other messenger. The other messenger.'

'What other messenger?' said Simon nervously.

Turning now to Hop, the Babylonian said, 'I know, and you have at least heard, of that messenger. The messenger who with artifice and holy guile penetrates to the innermost cells of this dungeon which is the world. The messenger from the Unknown God. The messenger who eludes the seven circles of dark and deadly power that surround the world. Each Ruler of each circle seeks to entrap, seize and destroy him. Yet he slips through their defences which are the many walls of our prison. He comes to bring the message of light through darkness. To bring the light of the Unknown God to that tiny imprisoned spark of the light which is like a little gasp of breath in imprisoned man.'

'We must all listen to the word of God,' said Simon piously.

'*Your* God,' cried the Babylonian. 'Your God is no God but a devil. He is in league with the Rulers. His laws, his commands to you, which you seek to obey on your crawling knees, are nothing but tricks of the evil Rulers to keep you in your prison.'

Simon was suddenly on his feet, shaking his fist in some

silent declaration. From the Babylonian the words continued to flow.

'I tell you that *your* God is tirelessly at work to help those Rulers of the spheres to imprison those sparks which fell into the world from the great light of the Unknown God. Your God is one of the gaolers of our prison.'

Words had been struggling in Simon's throat and now he let out a half-choked screech.

'Stop it! I won't listen to such stuff! If you talk like that I shall...'

'What will you do?' said the Babylonian.

Simon stood looking at him and trembled all over. Then he said, 'I shall simply leave you to your own filth. I shall go to bed.'

He left the room, his indignation giving his gait a kind of hopping motion.

The Babylonian looked after him with a sneer. Swelling himself up a little, he said, 'A prisoner. A slave. A crawler.'

It was Hop's opinion too. But he felt at the same time that this Babylonian in his arrogant fashion was taking too much upon himself and in a general way looking down upon Sachem, and all that that implied.

He said, 'That's as may be. But all the same it could be reasonable to ask you how you *know* so much about an *Unknown* God?'

The Babylonian said, 'D'you think I'm not asked that question two thousand three hundred and thirty-three times per year? Ninety-nine out of a hundred of the people who ask it are cheapskate mockers. They think there's no answer to their witless inquiry and anyway they're not going to wait to hear it. The hundredth? Well, that might be you, friend.'

'And why does the hundredth ask the question?'

'Because,' said the Babylonian, 'he already knows the answer.'

Hop said, 'I'm slow in the head this evening. Get me some more wine.'

The Babylonian let out his puff, became a natural-sized inn-keeper. As he went off to get more wine, Alpha and the messenger got up too. Alpha came over to Hop and said, 'We're going to see that woman. Want to join the party? The word is she's a great lay.' Hop said, 'I'm tired. I want to go on drinking.'

Alpha said, 'The Knower says she's the Fallen Thought of the Unknown God. Doesn't that give you a bit of a stand?'

'Tomorrow maybe. Tonight I want to drink.'

'Anything you say, uncle.'

'That's if we ever get to tomorrow night,' said Hop.

'We'll keep trying,' said Alpha and went off with the messenger. And in the morning the messenger was gone; into Jericho, Alpha said. In the evening he visited the inn again for a short while, but was not seen by Hop. He had gone on to Jerusalem, Alpha said.

But on the fourth day he was seen again at the inn. During all these hours Simon of Sachem had not appeared; stayed in his own quarters. And when Hop would force himself to visit him and inquire how he was, Simon replied with insults. His line was that by consorting with the Knower, insulter of true religion, Hop was himself among the insulters, and therefore could not complain when Simon insulted him in turn. Past bothering much about what Simon did or did not think, Hop still let himself say that if Simon could think of some way by which it would be possible for them not to consort with such people as the Babylonian and yet not get themselves arrested and possibly executed, he would be glad to hear it. Then Simon would come out all over again with his notion about making some kind of public repudiation of the Essene. And Hop would say, 'Listen, I've talked with that Chief of Police and you haven't. Just try to get it into your head that even if you could get your damned repudiation or whatever it is, about the Essene, to that Chief, which you can't, the only effect, I'm telling you, the *only* effect would be to convince him more than ever that we are secret agents of the Essene, up to some new trick.'

'But it doesn't make sense,' said Simon.

'It would to him.'

'In that case,' said Simon, 'the man is quite unfitted to hold such a responsible position.'

'You'd better complain to someone and get him fired,' said Hop, and left Simon alone and went into the big room at the end of the back court of the inn.

This was the fourth day and the messenger had come. He

came from the direction of the stables and the field with the wall beyond it. His face was bandaged. He was not alone. There was a stranger on each side of him, each holding him lightly by an elbow. The Babylonian walked behind. The two strangers guided the wavering messenger to a couch and now Hop saw that the inn-keeper had a flask of wine in his hand. While the strangers stood aside he leaned over the messenger and put the flask in his two hands and told him to drink. The messenger took a long swig at the wine.

The Babylonian said to Hop, 'He was caught. They put his eyes out. He's blind. So they let him go. They thought they'd done for him. But they hadn't cut the muscles out of his legs or torn out his tongue. He is here, and he has news.'

'But if they blinded him? How?'

'There are hands along the way, Hop man. Helping hands the others don't know of. When a man is blinded there are other eyes to see him, and to see for him. These men,' he gestured at the strangers, 'saw him, knew who he must be, and then saw for him. He's a messenger.'

He turned back to the messenger and said, 'Take more wine. Drink. The wine's good.'

CHAPTER TEN

In the big room at the Inn of the Knower an exhibition of obscene dancing was now taking place, and was of a high standard. Chief performer was Helena, the Babylonian's woman. Other women had evidently been whistled up from the city and were doing well in supporting roles.

'Where,' Hop asked the Babylonian, 'have all these people come from?' For in the few hours after the arrival of the blinded messenger a diversity of people had filtered, slouched, sauntered or lurched into the inn by doors back, front and, it seemed, all around the place.

'When the solid earth shakes about the burrows,' said the Babylonian, 'all sorts of creatures run out.'

'The earth is shaking?' Hop said.

'The earth is shaking in Jerusalem,' said the Babylonian.

Upon a daïs at the far end of the room Helena and the other women were doing their dances. Musicians were in action too. Where had the musicians come from, Hop asked.

'What a band, eh?' said the Babylonian. 'What a tight little bunch of musical bums. Strum, strum the bum.'

On couches opposite the raised place where the dancers were dancing, lounged Alpha and a couple of other young men of criminal appearance. They could be seen to be tumescent; any one of them, it could seem to the observer, might have an orgasm on the spot. Hashish, however, prolonged the pleasurable prelude. Anything could take ten times as long as it otherwise would.

Between Hop and the dancers numerous strangers were lounging or moving about. In the corner of the room to his right sat two men whom he recognized as the 'helping hands' who had conducted the messenger to the inn.

Sitting, a little puffed up, on a stool opposite Hop, the Babylonian leaned forward and said:

'The Essene is on the run.'

'Not here?' Hop peered quickly round the hazy room.

'No, no. Nobody knows. Bethany, some say. It seems he got word a stoning had been arranged. His people are dispersed. In times like these people come to my inn.'

'But these,' said Hop still looking round the room, 'aren't the Essene's people, are they?'

'I think only those two who brought in the messenger,' said the Babylonian. 'The others? What a collection of layabouts. What low lifes, what real swine. Dregs of humanity you might well say.'

'So why are they here?'

'They are part of my reputation, the reputation of my inn.'

'Meaning?'

'Meaning that whichsoever one among them is the police spy will be able to report that the Inn of the Knower is, as always, nothing for the political police to brood, ponder or worry about; nothing but a dive, a fun-house, a place in the suburbs nice for a nice little orgy or whatever.'

'You mean you've invited them with that in mind?'

'No invitation necessary. Matter of instinct. These people smell thunder in the air. Political situation? About that, they don't know. Procurator? They don't know. High Priest? Just part of the architecture to them. The Essene? The prophets? The soothsayers? Which one, what one? They don't know one from one. But when the thunder's near enough they smell it. Probably they think, if they think, that if the world's going to end, this is the kind of place they'd like to be when it happens.'

'And the thunder?'

'You get about the country. You know and I know and the dogs in the street know the whole country can blow up any month, any week, any day or night. Meditate upon that Police Chief down in Jericho. He's no fool. He knows the pot's boiling, the ground's cracking, the earth's heaving, the lightning's ready to flash. The Judaeans could rise against the Romans. Or the Romans could go for them first, massacre the bastards. Or the dark ones—you know what I mean? the people down below who don't care whether the man on their backs is a Judaean or a Roman or the big baboon of Babylon —they might rise and make shit of the whole fucking lot.'

'And the Essene? Where's he in the whole picture?'

'I tell you; gone underground. Bethany or wherever. Want to know what's he up to? You could try asking his people here. But I wonder if they know the answer any more than you do.'

'You say he's afraid of a stoning?'

'So they say. And wouldn't that be a queer thing for a man that's cracked up to be a miracle worker? One of all these Saviours and Sons of God and whatever that go up and down the country. You know they tell of him that when he was a little lad, two bigger lads annoyed him and, big as they were, he beat them to death with a magic stick. And when their pa's and ma's came running and complaining, he twiddled his fingers and struck them all blind. Maybe,' said the Babylonian with a twisted smile, 'he's planning to blast the whole Roman army the same way.'

An obese young man who had been lolling at Hop's left, suddenly sat up and pushed his face forward. His permanently bulging eyes gave him an amazed expression. He stuttered slightly and blew a little spittle from his lips, either because he naturally stuttered and dribbled or under the influence of excitement.

'Now listen while I tell you something,' he said. 'I know it for a fact. Happened in Bethany just the other day. Actually happened. Matter of solid fact.'

'Get on with it. *What* happened?'

'There was this man Lazarus. Perfectly reputable citizen. Nothing fishy or hanky-panky about him, and there he was, dead. I mean he was definitely dead. Got sick of some illness and it killed him.'

'Very interesting,' said the Babylonian. 'Except I never heard of the man. Friend of yours?'

'No but listen while I tell you this. This man Lazarus had two sisters. And these two were friends of the Essene, d'you follow me? So when the brother gets sick that way, and the local medico can't do anything for him, just naturally they think of the Essene because it's well known he's a faith healer that's done cures up and down the country. So they get a message to him to hurry on down. But he can't hurry because he's on the run, see? Has to dodge about. And by the time he gets there the man's been dead four days. Been in the tomb four days and stinking.'

'Too bad about that,' said the Babylonian. 'Very sad story.'

'Just a minute, just a minute just a minute,' stuttered the fat young man. 'I haven't got to the point. Point is the Essene told them to take him to the tomb and roll away a big rock they'd put there to close the entrance. And then the Essene shouted out, "Lazarus, come on out of there!" And sure as I'm sitting here, out steps Lazarus, with the grave clothes still on him, hale and hearty as they come.'

'And stinking?' queried Hop.

'Never mind that,' said the young man. 'He was alive and walking. Went home with his sisters and had a big meal. So what d'you think of that? It's a fact, sure as I'm sitting here talking to you.'

'You know all this?' said Hop.

'Of course I know it. That's what I'm telling you.'

'I mean, were you there?'

'I didn't need to be there. Man who told me is a cousin of mine. Sound level-headed businessman. No flies on him at all. He was there in Bethany just after it happened, and he ran into a man who was right there on the spot, saw the whole episode. Friend of the family, too. Said it was the most amazing thing he'd ever seen. Well you have to admit it's amazing. I mean there the man was dead and there he was alive. Makes you think, doesn't it?'

Hop said, 'It makes me think I'd like to know your cousin.'

'Oh, I see,' said the fat young man. 'I see your type of approach. Well let me tell you *I* would like *you* to meet my cousin. You wouldn't get away long with calling him a liar near as makes no difference. I'd like to see you confront him and you'd find you hadn't a leg to stand on. You're the type thinks because a thing's amazing it isn't so. Well let me tell you, the opposite's the case. Or damn near it.'

He got huffily to his feet and moved away across the room. Hop shrugged. The Babylonian suddenly shifted his weight from one buttock to the other and somewhat changed the key of his voice, too. He leaned a little in the direction of the two men in the corner.

'You,' he said, 'you who are followers of the Essene, you believe he can bring a dead man to life?'

The men glowered at him.

'No, no,' said the Babylonian, 'I'm not laying traps, playing tricks. Do you suppose that I, I Simon the Knower, would do such a thing? You imagine I want to get you to make a statement before witnesses disclosing your view as to whether your Essene can bring a man four days dead to life? So if you say "No" you admit he's an impostor. And if you say "Yes" you're saying he's a sorcerer, a necromancer, supporting his claim to possess powers contrary to accepted doctrine, and the police—one lot of police or another—they could surely get you for that.'

The man nearest to him swallowed deep in his throat and said in a Galilean brogue: 'If the one you call the Essene says he raised a man from the dead, I believe he raised a man from the dead.'

'And why not?' said the Babylonian gustily. 'Can anyone prove, can you prove my much travelled friend,' he said, looking at Hop, 'that a man cannot be raised from the dead? You can't answer that, can you? You think because something didn't happen last year it can't happen this year. Nonsense, my dear travelling friend. Something utterly new can happen at any time.'

He turned again to the followers of the Essene, who continued to look at him with suspicion.

'You believe,' he said, 'that your leader, your teacher-man, your prophet or how you like, is what people tell me he claims to be? Saviour, son of God? Or maybe God himself?'

'I believe,' said the man nearest to him, 'what he tells us of himself and his mission here on earth.'

'You believe him when he calls himself the son of God?'

'I believe him.'

'Anyone can say he's the son of God. This entire country's full of such liars. They wander about the streets of our town and villages, they uplift their voices on the edge of the Roman camps, hoping to give the troops a bit of a laugh and get paid for it.'

'But only one can be the true son of God.'

The Babylonian swung round on him, tilting his head back and seeming to take a sight on him along the length of his beard.

'So to which God do you have reference?'

'Which God?' said the Galilean adherent of the Essene. In

his young weather-beaten face his eyes were light and puzzled. 'Which God?'

'I am asking you,' said the Babylonian, 'whether the God you chose to bring within the orbit and ambit of our discussion is the creator, arbiter or carpenter of this world we are in? The God, I mean, who rules this world on behalf of the imprisoning Archons? The God,' almost shouted the Babylonian, 'of Cain?'

'Cain? How are we talking about Cain?'

'Because Cain was a first victim of that God. Cain the simpleton, the greenhorn. As a sacrifice to that same very good God, Cain brought the good fresh fruits of the earth. Corn and roots and suchlike. He imagined that such healthy good things would be pleasing in the sight of the good, good God. And that was where he made his very very notable error, his eternally fatal slip-up.

'He was unaware, my dear friend, that the God of this world is a God of blood. Blood he wants and will have. He took Cain's little sacrifice as damn near an insult. But Abel, that conniving lickspittle and devious toady, whose other name, the books tell us, was Eloim, meaning "cat face", had observed and taken note of the character of that same God.

'With cunning, artifice and unholy guile, he came with his blood sacrifice; sent the blood of a beast gushing out for the slavering pleasure of the great and good Artificer. And did he find favour in the sight of the Lord? He surely did. Great was the shock and horror of Cain to have revealed to him the true nature of that God. And God used that moment of shock and horror to cause him to strike down Abel dead. And in revenge for Cain's not making him the blood sacrifice, he drove him out to wander for ever and ever on the face of the earth.

'By this act he made plain for all to see that the simple people of this world, people who take more pleasure in a green growth than in blood, are outcasts. The bloodthirsty triumph and are richly rewarded. Because in their bloodiness they obey the laws of God and the Archons.'

To this tirade, the second of the 'helping hands', and adherent of the Essene had paid scowling attention, not looking at the Babylonian but listening and playing with the big knife he had. He now said, 'There has to be blood. We have to be ready, it's no secret is it?—for the armed revolt against the enemy. There are some don't believe that.' He looked sideways at his fellow disciple of the Essene.

The other sounding timid and firm at the same time, said, 'That's for the Master to decide,' he said. 'We must wait for the word from him.'

The scowler with the knife spat on the floor.

'Yes, yes, wait. But also we know that the Romans and the Men in Black are getting ready to mop us up? They're not the ones to bother about a drop of blood. And what are we doing about it is all I want to know?'

The Babylonian looked them over, a quick look at each, and said: 'I hear tell, it is reported, it is bruited abroad that your Master has advised submission to Caesar in all earthly matters.'

'People can take that several ways,' said the Scowler, scowling more than ever.

'But,' continued the Babylonian, 'it is also rumoured, declared and stated on good authority that your Master has said that he comes to bring not peace but a sword.'

'Indeed it'll come to that,' said the Scowler. The man from Galilee looked from one to the other so perplexedly that he seemed to be squinting.

'Thus,' said the Babylonian, 'we have a mystification. It is one among many in the utterances of your eloquent Master. Are we to take these mystifications as evidence of subterfuge, artifice and guile? Or, friends and fellow travellers in the great desert, are we not to see in these contradictions proof that this individual has permitted himself to become encompassed by a misconception?'

Watching the faces of the two others, the one scowling suspiciously, the other in a visible pain of puzzlement, Hop said, 'Are you saying something, or just talking?'

The Babylonian swung his beard around towards him and sighted along it haughtily.

'I am,' he said, 'saying something. I have to use words when I'm talking to you. This Essene, I am saying, is encompassed by a misconception of the nature of this world. He believes two contrary things at two different times. Perhaps at the same time. Which is to say that sometimes he is near to having Knowledge, other times the hood of the world is over his eyes.

'With hooded eyes he believes that good and evil are to be found in this mundane world, and among the men and things of this same mundane world. In this state of obfuscated delusion, friends and brothers, he looks with bleared but loving eyes upon that Power to which, according to credible report, he alludes as his Daddy-God.'

The Galilean made a movement as though about to interrupt.

'Yes indeed,' intoned the Babylonian, his voice now vibrating in a key to cut through any muttering or murmur. 'He thinks of his Daddy-God as one who is both God of this world and above this world. He thinks that with himself, the sacred Sonny-boy, as go-between, agent, drummer or what have you, the people of this world will rally in righteousness to Pa almighty, and Pa almighty for his part will do them a bit of good, if not now, then hereafter.

'And this is where he makes his notable error. For in the inspissated darkness of his mind and soul, he cannot see that his Daddy-God is not above the wickedness and black ruin of this world, but is part and parcel of it. He is as evil as the world he pretends and purports and sets up to be ruler of. But in reality he rules it only on behalf of the Archons, helping to further their great design upon our freedom. He was created by the Archons to aid them with the eternal imprisonment of the true spirit of man. He is not even the Warden of the jail. He is, my dear friends'—the Babylonian paused and rolled his eyes—'he is a *trusty*.'

The Galilean spoke up loudly and slowly, pushing out his words like a man pushing against the current of a river.

'If he were here himself,' he said, 'he would give the lie to all that. He would tell you things to open your eyes and shut your loud mouth.'

The Babylonian bowed extravagantly. 'He will be welcome at any time. Most welcome at the Inn of the Knower.'

'Maybe not so welcome when he's given you a straight talk and knocked a little air out of you. He can hit hard, the Lord Jesus.'

'He can punch with his mouth all right,' growled the surly Scowler. To him the Galilean gave a bright, furious look out of worried eyes.

'I said,' remarked the Babylonian, 'that your Master believes in two different things at different times, or even at the same time. I have dissected one of those beliefs and laid it out before you for your ruminative edification. Now, naturally, you are all eagerness to know about the second of these beliefs entertained by the individual in question to whom we have reference.

'For he can, from time to time, move in a different sphere or orbit of spiritual operation. He can—for such are the workings of the spark within—believe that all upon which in these last minutes I have been partially expatiating is true. He sees, in a blink and flash of light, that his Daddy God, what the Tiber men call The Pater, is what I, the Knower know him to be, and that the only true God is the Unknown God, the Alien God, as alien from the earthbound body and soul of man as man's little spirit spark is from this world and all that's in it.

'It is the spark, sir, that counts. The spark alien to body and soul alike, and related only to the Unknown and Alien God of which it is—how shall I say?—a chip, my friends, like as it might be a small sliver of silver brought to this land from some mountain of purest silver far down there beyond Egypt, beyond the lands beyond Egypt, beyond, beyond.'

He made the last two words ring like the dying notes of a trumpet blown at sunset.

'There are times, if my reports of him are correct, when there shines upon your Master a glimmer of the truth: when he knows something of what the Knowers know.'

Through the thin haze of hashish in his head, Hop had been looking across the room at the dancers, or rather at Helena, the principal dancer. 'What a lay,' he said to himself, 'what a lay.'

It seemed to him that it would be simple and good to go over to the place where she was dancing, buffet Alpha and his lewd friends right and left, knock them flying, pick Helena up with his big hands under her armpits, throw her on to some couch somewhere or on to the outside grass, and have her again and again. That being so, it seemed at the same time needless to move. It also appeared to him that there was plenty of time for free and full discussion with the Babylonian and the others. He was inclined to say something essentially succinct: summing things up in a manner both comprehensive and precise.

'So,' he said, 'it's clear that if the world, including the God of Moses and Abraham, is all evil, a desert of evil in which we are going, if you follow me from nowhere to nowhere, and the only true God is this Alien one you've been on about, there's nothing a man can usefully do, can do effectively about anyone or anything. That's your position, old friend, and you think it may be the position of this same Essene.'

'I said "at certain times".'

'Certainly. At certain times. Such times to be ascertained by one means or another.'

The Scowler jumped in, by his vehemence giving the impression that he had made an actual physical jump with his powerful legs.

'That's it,' he said, 'action. Where's action? Lie down and let the bastards shit on you. Is that the word that's going round? The hell with that. And the hell with anyone that takes that line. Anyone, I say, Master or no Master.' He glowered defiantly at the Galilean. 'Turn the other cheek, is it?' He spat violently. 'If the Men in Black or the Tiber boys came after him he'd soon change his tune. So would a lot of others that still don't know which day from what day. We'd see some action if that happened.'

A light draught blew across the room. The Babylonian became quite still, seeming to sniff it. He clapped his hands loudly and one of the men who were usually about the stables came over to him. The Babylonian said:

'The wind's changing. See to the dogs.'

The man nodded and went off. The Babylonian said, 'The wind's starting to blow towards Jericho. We're up wind now. The dogs will have less warning of anyone coming. They have to be positioned further out.'

'But suppose,' said Hop, 'the police come from the other side. From Jerusalem.'

'They will not,' said the Babylonian confidently. 'You and your friends are Jericho's meat: they will retain you within their sphere of operation. That police chief wants to keep you all to himself. He as good as told you so. I would hardly think he'd even reported the whole of your affair to Jerusalem: not in detail. I wouldn't think he's told them where he thinks you are. Question of prestige, question of jealousy.

'My partner,' said Hop drowsily, 'still thinks we should ge out of here now and get into the city.'

'And as I've told you five times,' said the Babylonian, 'in m opinion, just for the moment, you're safer here. Unless yo ditch your young friend.' He looked across the room at Alpha 'You and partner could maybe pass for respectable citizens i Jerusalem. With him tagging along, chances are pretty goo someone—cop-man, informer, what they call a crimina element—recognizes him: probably has a record as long a your arm. Then they pull you all in and you'll have plent of explaining to do.'

'Just so, just so, just so,' murmured Hop, watchin Helena.

'And if the lads come up from Jericho, you know how t get away from this place. Just a hop skip and jump to th city. And you take your chances there.'

'Just so, just so.'

'For us,' said the Galilean, 'Jerusalem is not so safe.'

The Scowler glared and played with his knife. 'It could b made safe,' he said.

'You speak,' said the Babylonian, not looking at him, 'o armed revolt. Of battle in the streets. But for that you nee a leader.'

'We have a leader,' said the Galilean. 'It's for him t decide.'

'But,' said the Babylonian, 'first of all he's on the run And secondly there are these many reports and speculation we just spoke of suggestive of the possibility that he is o principle and according to his lights opposed to armed re sistance. With a man like that, who knows but he may decid to let himself be arrested: a sacrifice to some one or othe of those same principles.'

The Scowler broke out violently. 'If he were arrested, thou sands would rally to him. They would fight to fre him. The people are ready for a fight like that. It woul be ...' he looked at his hands, as though looking for word there.

'You were going to say,' said the Babylonian, in a cooin tone, 'that it would be the best thing that could happen. A word in the right quarter, an arrest, and then your rallying o the pee-pul, your armed resistance, your blood-letting and revolt.'

The Scowler made no movement. But the Babylonian chose to admonish him as though he had. 'No, no,' he said to the Scowler, 'don't jump and start back aghast; don't tighten your hand on that knife as though to cut off the flow of my ruminative speculations.'

Hop and the man from Galilee were now looking at the Scowler as though he really had jumped, started back, and tightened hand on knife.

'Such thoughts,' went on the Babylonian, 'can pass through some heads. Not all,' he glanced sideways at the Galilean, 'but mine, for instance, or others. It is necessary only to be capable of appreciating the destination of the situation. Any given situation, on any road it travels may come to a point where the road forks three ways. As in the matter we have currently under advisement. Along which of those three ways will the situation move? Looking back from the future people will know which it really did move.'

The man from the stables came across the room again and whispered urgently to the Babylonian. When he had gone, the Babylonian told them that the only news was that a dog at a farm four miles down the Jericho road had been poisoned. The boy from the farm had mentioned it as he went by on the way to the city. It could mean nothing. But there had been a piece of meat near the dog which did not come from the farm. So that could mean that police scouts, knowing of the guard dogs at the inn, had mistaken this farm dog for one of them and poisoned it with specially doctored meat. And that in turn would mean that the police were moving towards the inn, but also that they were moving with the utmost caution, were still very much afraid of making a false move.

'And that leaves us where?' said Hop.

'I'd say it still leaves you right here,' said the Knower. 'You could make a bolt for the city. But, point one to which I have already drawn attention, the city is not under all circumstances safer than this place. Here you know where the danger is. There it can jump on you from anywhere. Also, this thing about the dog could mean that perhaps the Jericho people have scouts in the waste land between here and the gates. Whatever their orders, a couple of them might recognize you, get excited, hack you down. Safer here. There'll be plenty of warning before they really move on this inn, if they ever do.'

The Galilean had seemed not so much to listen to this information as to wait for it to end. He kept on looking at the Scowler as though he were doing sums, trying to add up figures written on the Scowler's face. He now said to the Babylonian, 'You were talking about the future.'

'I am truly gratified by your attention,' said the Babylonian, with a bow that was a little insulting. 'So the situation can go bowling, bowling, bowling along a road where soon the eyes of the people are opened, where the Jews and the Romans and this man and that man and the next man are subjected to a great enlightenment seeing all through the eyes of your man, the Essene; and recognizing that Sonny-boy is verily, verily the son of Daddy-God, they bow down and call him blessed, bringing blissful peace to this tumultuous world of ours...'

'What a chance!' said Hop.

The Galilean nodded gravely.

'Or,' said the Babylonian, 'the big mules of Fate drag the situation along a road where despite all the preaching of the Essene nobody is enlightened, nobody in that great city of Jerusalem gives more than a small bloody damn what he says or what it's all about. They persist in apathetic miasma and bemused inaction. The well-informed agents of Law, the inexorable forces of Order, reach out with just one hand and they nip that helpless Essene between their finger and thumb, and they say, "Enough of you, little noisy fellow," and they first give him a beating, and then they give him a hanging, with rope and nails as is correct procedure in certain cases of malfeasance duly certified by the relevant authorities.'

The Galilean dusted his forehead with his hand.

'Or,' said the Babylonian, 'the situation gets jolted on to another track. A rutty one. The miasma is seen as susceptible of sudden dispersal, of vulnerability to the whistle of a keen wind. It is considered, it is shrewdly calculated, that if such an event as the ruthless arrest of the Essene were in fact to occur, broad masses of the citizenry would envisage so dramatic and overt a gesture by the authorities as presaging some kind of general attack upon themselves, as a prelude to further acts of wide repression, damaging, restrictive and dangerous to citizens seeking only to earn enough to eat, the wherewithal of continued existence. But the authorities are aware of the consequences of such an act. They are slow to move. Procrastination is their chosen strategy. What then is required? It is required that from some source or quarter deemed credible by them, information be transmitted indicating that the Essene is no negligible little fellow but rather is one with his hands upon the ropes and pulleys of a vast and truly dangerous conspiracy, destined to, and capable of overthrowing the edifice of Government, of putting down the mighty from their seats and exalting those of low degree. Information would also be made available as to the movements and lurking places of the Essene so that the forces of Order may move swiftly to his apprehension. On this information they are constrained to act. On the news the Essene is seen now by all men of low degree as their man, their threatened leader, they rush together for defence and to mount the counter-attack. Revolt spreads through that seething city of Jerusalem. The forces of Order, ill-prepared for so sudden a happening, are overcome. The Government is overthrown and all that that implies. The Essene and his men are swept to the power, the kingdom and the glory.'

The Scowler kept looking at his hands and his knife. After a bit of silence he said, 'Words.'

'Just words,' said the Babylonian. 'Adumbrations of the hypothetical.'

The trio began to float gently out of Hop's area of interest. He turned away from them to watch the dancers again, got up, and took a step in the direction of the dancing-platform. Pausing, and hefting his balance back and forth between one leg and the other, he said half over his shoulder, 'I'd like to meet that Essene of yours.'

'So would a lot of other people, from all we hear,' said the Babylonian.

The Scowler paid no attention. The Galilean had the mixture of wariness and welcome which could come natural to a man often approached by people who wanted to meet the Master.

'You want to know why?' said Hop with a bit of cloudy haze in his voice.

'It's very natural,' said the Galilean. 'People that have heard of the Master's teachings, his doings...'

'Let me tell you,' said Hop. 'It isn't natural for me. A businessman. Not at all one for the soothsayers and so on.'

'A lot of people feel that to begin with,' said the Galilean.

Hop spoke with a thick truculence. 'I'm not a lot of people,' he said. 'I'm me. And the reason I want to see your man the Essene is on account of that thing he told about me.'

'You mean his telling of that action of yours there on the Jericho road a little while back?'

'You're right that's what I mean,' said Hop. 'I was told how he told that story. Shall I tell you something? There was this nephew of mine, just a little kid and one day I heard him telling one of our neighbour's kids about his uncle. That was me, you understand? Well, listen to me now. Make you laugh to hear the things that kid had to tell about his uncle Hop. Seems Uncle Hop rides the roads, goes up and down and back and forth on the broad earth, and he brings rich goods to the peoples of the earth, uplifting benefits to one and all. And when all the people see Uncle Hop approaching, riding high upon his beast, their hearts swell up with joy and thankfulness and with one voice they cry out, "Blessed be Uncle Hop, bringer of good things." And in happiness and gratitude for all the good things, they bring out their bags of silver and gold and open them and pour out the silver and gold at the feet of Uncle Hop, and he gathers it up into his saddlebags, and rides home to us here in Sachem singing a song of triumph. And now, my nephew says to this neighbour's kid, you know all about my uncle Hop.

'Well, I thought to myself, that certainly is one way of looking at uncle Hop. And when they told me the way your Essene had told about me and that thing that happened on the Jericho road, I had the same kind of a feeling. What a man! I thought. Mind you, that story got me into a hell of a lot of trouble down there in Jericho. All the same, it was a damn fine story.'

CHAPTER ELEVEN

Uplifted by his own words and recollections, Hop stood up and looked down on the Galilean with benignity, as one who had done the fellow a favour, conferring the privilege of making acquaintance with such a one as Hop, the Samaritan, a man of character and understanding.

Returning his attention to Helena, who was briefly lolling on the daïs with the other dancers, Hop made as though to carry out his design to hurl aside all others and drag her off to a more private place. Instead she immediately uncurled herself, came towards him as if she had long been awaiting his signal, and then slid close past him, and went a little ahead, leading him out of the big room on to the broad veranda, round an angle of the house and into a curtained and carpeted room, well appointed for its purpose with couches and mirrors, and lighted by lamps beside the central couch, but not brightly enough to show whether it was large or small.

He recalled that at very first sight of her, all those days and days ago, he had been angry that he was just at that time in no condition to enjoy her. He had said to himself then that she would be a fine woman to have, and now he was feeling in very fine condition, and she was even finer than he had imagined.

However much it was later, and he had certainly had her two or three times one way and another and was relaxing briefly and most cheerfully, almost dozing, when he was just a little astonished, though nothing seemed very astonishing, to hear a mutter of voices from a short distance away, and from some place above his head.

He became aware that the murmur, and the sound of one voice in particular, which was the voice of the Babylonian, had been sounding for some long or short time previously, during which they had been to him like voices in a dream.

Now, coming more alertly awake, he understood that there

was a low gallery, barely visible, in the obscurity of one end of the room. Listening now to the intelligible voice of the Babylonian, he grasped that the keeper of the inn had invited a small circle of friends to witness and appreciate the scene.

'You observe, you must be aware,' the Babylonian was now explaining, 'that you, my fellow-Knowers, are not mere spectators of this episode in the earthly experience of the woman, but are participating in it. Your presence is to her as a whip, as a stiff stroking of her in her entirety with a branch of rough yet tender leaves.

'She is of the highest and the lowest,' said the Babylonian. 'The Fallen Thought of the Alien God; fallen, fallen, hiding from the Archons in the lower depths, brought by me from the lowest brothel in the notably corrupt and licentious city of Tyre. She personifies all resistance to the evil will of the Archons and the laws and precepts of the God of this world. By cherishing the hidden light of the Alien God, she flouts them. And thus may all Knowers among men do. By covering their moral precepts with the filth of the brothels, she flouts them again. Thus, too, may all Knowers do. Withdrawing from the fleshly world they make mockery of that world of the Archons; they are subjects who have defected and become flee. Or, by wallowing in what the Archons and their trusty-God call sin, they mock them otherwise. Watch. Watch.'

Hop, turning again to Helena, forgot them. A half-hour later, hazed with hashish and sexual happiness, he found himself going back along the veranda, finding at last the big room.

The Babylonian and his most intimate guests now formed a small group a little apart. Although many of the inn's clientele were sleeping, or in somnolent reverie, others were talking and calling to one another so noisily that the roar and vibration of voices was much greater than before, and the musicians had ceased trying to make their music heard. Hop rested himself beside the Babylonian on a heap of cushions. For a while he floated into sleep, and then was awake again without knowing how long he had slept. Now Helena, in a voluminous robe of dark material, was half sitting, half lounging in the circle made by the Knowers, and the Babylonian was conducting, or beating time with his hand as he put her through a number of chants, songs, verses to be recited. It seemed this singing and chanting had been going on for some time. Helena began to say that her voice was tired. They begged her to continue, asking her to chant or recite songs traditional among believers in their creed, many of them Hop thought, religious in character, and dolorous, but moving.

Now she was chanting, huskily:

> 'When I loved life, real life,
> 'When I loved Truth, true Truth,
> 'From that day, from that day
> 'I trust no more, trust no more
> 'Nothing, nothing in the world.
> 'Not father not mother, nothing.
> 'Not brother, not sister, nothing.
> 'Not what's made, not what's created,
> 'Nothing in the world.
> 'I looked for the light in me
> 'Felt the light in me
> 'Bigger than the world.
> 'I found light. I found Truth.
> 'Truth I found her,
> 'There where she stood
> 'On the rim, the far rim, of the world.'

And all of them together chanted the last words after her, 'On the rim, the far rim of the world.'

One moment there was this low chanting, and the uproar going on all around, and then two men, the man from the stables and another, came marching fast across the room to the Babylonian who, before they reached him, was already on his feet, his head and beard pushing forward towards them in his eagerness to get the message.

What had been expected to happen was happening. The trained dogs, on the northern approach, out in the scrub were barking, signalling 'danger' to one another and to the watchers from the inn behind. The police scouts were moving up. By sounds which one of the men from the inn had heard, it could be judged that one of the dogs had worried the throat out of a police scout.

Hop had got to his feet almost as soon as the Babylonian,

who at once made a shushing motion with his hand. 'Not time for you yet,' he said. 'The word will go whipping round this place and this whole mob will panic. Just see how they'll run. Why? They'll just run because when they hear police they run.' His face twisted sardonically. 'To escape danger here they'll go running, running, running back to the city which they left to get out of danger—back and forth and back and forth and who cares? If a couple of the Jericho scouts really are out there between us and the city this crowd will draw plenty of attention. And looking the way they are, scum of the earth like I told you, dregs of humanity, they'll probably be held up for a little examination when they start trying to get into the city. You and your friends and associates should wait, go a little round about: in a half-hour—and you probably have that long—it will be a lot darker. Get ready to go, but wait.'

He made a signal to Helena and his guests. They filed out of the room, Helena in the rear, bundled up in her dark robe, looking like a bale of stuff with feet under it.

It was correct that the news spread at once, and there was panic. As the word rippled through the room Hop watched them gaping and chattering, heard the previous uproar sink to a large-scale whisper. Some made straight for the door. Others seemed to be arguing in those alarmed whispers. Others again were trying to shake awake their sleeping friends to tell them the news and whispering frantically to startle others out of their meditative reveries. Observing them, Hop asked himself the question the Babylonian had asked: What in God's name were people like them running from? If they were in my shoes, he thought, then they really would have something to worry about and fear. But that lot? What have they ever done that's serious enough to get them in danger, real danger, at a time like this? So they beat and starve their wives. They pimp boys and girls. They run crooked gambling saloons and brothels where the customers get rooked and maybe some of them are organizers of small-time pickpockets. Maybe they've even arranged for a murder here and there. What do the police care about all that at a time like this? The way things are going in this country, pretty soon one murder, two murders, three murders, a couple of little gang battles, are not even going to be something people will talk about when they meet for drinks next day. Like the Babylonian said, there in Jerusalem the earth is shaking. These people don't know why it's shaking but they're running all the same.

He watched till most of the pushers and thrusters were through the door and then made off in the direction of the room where Simon of Sachem spent most of the time with his deep sulk. But before he got there, Simon himself was coming along the veranda at a waddling trot. From yards away he began to call out in his scolding voice. Had Hop heard the news, heard the news? Very bad situation, no time to be lost. No time this to be lounging about with women. Time to be going. Hop told him what the Babylonian had said. They ought to wait a little.

'Not me,' said Simon of Sachem. 'Not me. I don't trust that man. Never have from the beginning. Suppose he aims to delay us here and then hand us over to the police? Eh? How do you know that isn't his game? Eh?'

'If it was,' said Hop, 'he'd have had plenty of time to play it all these hours and hours we've been here.'

'I don't trust him. There's been a lot too much of this delaying and trusting. I insist, as the senior partner in our business, that we take appropriate and immediate steps to leave this place, to proceed to the city, there to procure respectable means of transportation, and thus make our way decently home to Sachem. High time. More than high time. For all we know the business may have gone to smash. I fairly tremble to think what situation we shall find when we get there.'

Hop said, 'You might tremble to think too what could happen to you if you got caught at the entrance to the city with that mob. Find yourself detained as a pimp, like as not.'

Simon puffed and snuffled as indignantly as though he had really been called a pimp. He wanted to know why such a thing should happen? to a respectable businessman from Sachem?

'Lot of pretty strange things happening. Better wait a bit. Besides I have to collect the others.'

At this Simon's mouth first puckered in puzzlement, then burst out in rage.

'Others? What others?' he wanted to know. Was Hop so much as daring to suggest that they should once again attach to themselves, get mixed up with, that stupid old fellow from Jericho of whom they knew nothing except that he had joined them in their flight from the city, and that young delinquent and criminal thug they called Alpha? At a pinch they might take the Judaean if he was ready and not going to delay their getaway from the inn. But as for Alpha, no, absolutely no. Simon stamped his foot. 'We've had enough trouble,' he said, 'with that fellow already. Just being with him gets us a bad name. He isn't the kind of individual a couple of respectable businessmen are expected to be seen in association with.'

'He got us out of Jericho,' said Hop irritably. 'If it hadn't been for him we'd have been in gaol down there still.'

'If it hadn't been for him,' said Simon, 'you wouldn't have been in any trouble in Jericho in the first place. It was him having you rescue him off that roadside that started the whole trouble. You certainly made a proper fool of yourself there. I've said so all along.'

'So you have.'

'Said all along if you'd exercised due caution, made a few inquiries, called the police as you should have before you made a move and got mixed up with him, you'd have kept out of trouble. You wouldn't have got me and the whole business into all this trouble. You never stopped to think how it was going to affect the business.'

'Well, he's with us now. You stay here while I go and find him and tell him we're all going to be off in a half-hour or less.'

'You're crazy,' shouted Simon, beside himself. 'I tell you, I insist that not only are we not going to take him with us but that in my opinion the very best thing that could happen to that young man is that he should stay here and be taken into custody by the authorities. Whoever he is and whatever he's up to he's up to no good. You know that as well as I do. Let the police have him.'

Hop brushed past him furiously and hurried on. Looking back from the angle of veranda he saw Simon give himself an angry shake and then start waddling off the way he had been going when Hop ran into him.

Stepping out into a small courtyard at the end of the veranda Hop saw Joshua sitting on a bench in what looked like a mood of melancholy meditation. Hurrying across to him he said, 'Listen, Joshua, if you want to get into Jerusalem in the company of a respectable businessman, now's your time. My snuffling partner is on his way there. I've told him there's a chance of his being taken up for a pimp or something of the kind if he goes now but if you're with him and stay a little behind the rest of the mob I'd say the two of you together would be pretty impressive as models of blameless citizenry. You may have a pretty big belly on you, Joshua, but you still walk faster than Simon. You'll catch him up before he's even out of the back door of the inn.'

'And you?'

'I suppose,' said Hop, 'I have to look for Alpha. Of course Simon thinks I'm crazy. Thinks that lad means nothing but trouble. Won't have him along at any price. And if you come to think of it,' he said broodingly, 'Simon may be right at that for once.'

Joshua smiled gloomily and said, 'Naturally, he's right, my friend. And if he hadn't said that I dare say you wouldn't feel the way you do about bringing Alpha along.'

'You mean,' said Hop, 'I'm just doing it to spite the old snuffler? It could be. Whenever he tells me what I ought to do I feel I ought to do the opposite. The same in business. When he wants me to act as though prices were going up I can't help trying to act as though they were going down. All the same ...'

'All the same what?'

'Well, I took such trouble with that fellow Alpha at the beginning and he got me into such a lot of trouble already I'd feel kind of a fool dropping him here now.'

Joshua shrugged in a more philosophic manner than ever. 'It's a reason like another,' he said.

'Well, and so? What about yourself?'

Before Joshua could answer there came from a long way off the sound of a dog barking and then of another. Hop listened, cocking his head on one side as though that made it easier to hear. 'With them down wind,' he said, 'they must be a good deal nearer than two miles.'

'The wind's dropped a lot,' said Joshua. 'While you were inside I've been sitting out here listening to it. It's a pretty still night. One could hear a bark like that a very long way off. A trained dog can throw the sound of his bark a long way.'

Hop made an impatient gesture. 'Two miles, a mile and a half, it doesn't make much difference. We'll have to be out of here pretty damn soon. You've still time to catch up with Simon.'

Joshua looked up at the sky, now turning the colour of night, and spoke as though he were reading something off it. In melancholy tones he said: 'I shall stay with you. God knows, I see nothing good coming of it. Nothing good has come to me since the Lord God saw fit to send you to my inn in Jericho, you and that damned Alpha. He brought the trouble on you and then you brought it on to me. It's too late to change it all now. I'll stay along with you and see if anything turns out for the better instead of worse.'

'I'm sorry about it all. You know that. But what difference does that make, me being sorry?'

'None at all,' said Joshua. 'Perhaps you will take comfort in the thought that all this is part of all the evil that is happening in the world, that it is just a little tiny drop in the ocean of horrible things to come. Some people can comfort themselves with such thoughts.'

'Wait for me here,' said Hop, and started across the courtyard. Then he stopped and swung round on Joshua. He spoke suddenly in a strange fierce voice. It was like the shaking of a fist. 'Just listen to me, Joshua,' he said, 'and the same goes for Simon too. I brought trouble on you. So I did. And then you say Alpha brought trouble on me. And that's where you make your error. He didn't bring the trouble on me. If there was trouble I made it. Nobody pushed me into it. It was a thing I did. Me. It was me did what I did and brought about all that was to come. I personally myself. Get that into your head and keep it there.'

He swung around again and went on towards a room where there was a lot of light coming from behind the curtain in the doorway and the sound of music. Inside there was an exhilarating smell of sex and hashish and wine, and the loud hoarse voice of Alpha greeting him. 'Come on, uncle,' he was calling, 'come and join the party.'

'The party's over,' Hop said.

In that bright room, seemingly crowded with three, four, five or more young men and girls, he felt sad that the party was over. Everything that had to be done seemed to him wearisome, dreary and a harsh pull on the nerves. Now Alpha's companions were shouting at him, saying that the party was not over, he must stay and join them. He went across to the couch where Alpha was, took him by the hand and started to pull him to his feet. Protests broke out. At least two of the voices were getting angry. Alpha, standing up now, looked angry too but also puzzled.

'What is it, uncle?' he said. 'What goes on? Meet my friends. We're all friends here. All happy.'

'I know. You may be the belle of the ball. Lots of fun. Would like to join you.'

'So why not?' the voices rose around him again.

Hop looked at Alpha, who looked back at him with that half angry, half confused and stupid look. Against that look and with no time to lose Hop spoke urgently, not caring, with no time to care, whether it was safe to say what he had to say or dangerous. Probably it was safe, these people wouldn't understand what was really going on if you spelled it out for them. He said to Alpha: 'The dogs are barking. You know what that means. You stay here and have a party and at the end of that party you'll be hanged, h-a-n-g-e-d, up on a cross till you die, unless some of those policemen forget themselves and beat you to death first just for the fun of it.'

Somebody let out a falsetto cry: 'Oh, oh, listen to the bogey-man.' A girl snarled at him, abusing him in a general manner as being a horrible dirty old man, the type that goes around breaking up parties with a lot of talk about hanging and police and such like. 'You'll soon see whether it's just talk,' said Hop, looking at Alpha. 'On the level?' Alpha said.

'Never more so,' said Hop.

'Well,' Alpha said, 'if that's the way it is.' He walked a little shakily ahead of Hop out of the room and into the courtyard where they saw Joshua still sitting like a man in deep meditation. But as they drew near him he got up and silently joined them. Hop said: 'We have to find this Knower. He has to give us the signal when to go and send the man to show us out of the side gate.'

'He may be anywhere in this rat warren,' said Joshua gloomily. 'We may go wandering through the place looking for him until it's too late.'

But this did not come to pass. In the big room where the

dancers and the music had been they found the Babylonian seated on a pile of cushions. After the way it had looked earlier the room seemed gauntly empty. But the Babylonian was not alone. Seated with his back to him was the Scowler seemingly looking at nothing. Although these two were silent there still seemed to be a noise in the room. Looking over to the side Hop saw Helena still wrapped in her dark robe, and standing over her with his hand raised in what seemed to be a warning or threatening gesture, the Galilean. It was he who was making the noise. He seemed to be intoning something. The Babylonian looked at Hop and his companions and said, 'Not yet. Something strange is happening.'

'Such as?'

'Such as for five minutes there has been no noise from the dogs.'

'Meaning?'

'Well,' said the Babylonian, 'they can't have killed them all, that's for sure. And if there was one of those dogs left alive he'd be barking. So it means the dogs have had an order from my men; an order to be quiet.' The Scowler turned half round and said: 'They could have double-crossed you, your men? Gone over to the police?'

'Perhaps you think too much of such things,' said the Babylonian. 'In any case, if so, then so, and there is nothing we can do about it.'

Alpha was looking almost goggle-eyed across at the Galilean, who continued to intone and gesture. The Babylonian looked at Alpha and then at the Galilean and the Scowler. 'These two,' he said, 'thought it wiser to take the same advice I gave to you. They did not rush out with the mob. They are waiting to see what happens next.'

'But what is he at?' asked Alpha, still absorbed in the behaviour of the Galilean.

'He is reciting,' said the Babylonian, 'some verses from the great prophet Isaiah. This man is what they call an evangelist, a maker of converts. He sees in this chance meeting with Helena an opportunity I suppose to convert her to something or other. He believes that the observations, animadversions and strictures of the well known prophet will be of value in attaining his objective. It is his mode of operation.'

The Galilean was now raising his voice and they heard that he was indeed reciting verses.

'Come down,' he intoned, 'and sit in the dust, O virgin daughter of Babylon, sit on the ground: there is no throne, O daughter of the Chaldeans; for thou shalt no more be called tender and delicate.

'Take the millstones, and grind meal; uncover thy locks, make bare the leg, uncover the thigh, pass over the rivers.

'Thy nakedness shall be uncovered, yes, thy shame shall be seen, I will take vengeance. And I will not meet thee as a man.'

'Well, screw me,' said Alpha. The Galilean half turned to him and gave him an angry look. He raised his voice as though determined that the whole company should hear his prophetic maledictions.

'Sit thou silent,' he chanted, 'and get thee into darkness, O daughter of the Chaldeans, for thou shalt no more be called the lady of kingdoms.

'Thou saidest I shall be a lady for ever so that thou didst not lay these things to thy heart, neither didst remember the later end of it.

'Therefor hear now this, thou that art given to pleasures, that dwellest carelessly, that sayest in thine heart I am and none else beside me.

'Thou hast trusted in thy wickedness: thou hast said, none seeth me. Thy wisdom and thy knowledge it hath perverted thee; and thou hast said in thine heart I am and none else beside me.

'Therefor shall evil come upon thee; thou shalt not know from whence it cometh and mischief shall fall upon thee, thou shalt not be able to put it off and desolation shall come upon thee suddenly which thou shalt not know.'

As though trying to break a spell, Alpha shouted out: 'Watch your step, sister!'

Speaking louder still to drown the interruption, the Galilean shouted: 'Stand now with thine enchantments and with the multitude of thy sorceries wherein thou hast laboured from thy youth; if thou so be thou shalt be able to profit, if thou so be thou mayest prevail.

'Thou art wearied in the multitude of thy counsels. Let now the astrologers, the stargazers, the monthly prognosticators, stand up and save thee from these things which are come upon thee.

'Behold, they shall be as stubble; the fire shall burn them; they shall not deliver themselves from the power of the flame; there shall not be a coal to warm at nor fire to sit before it:

'Thus shall they be unto thee with whom thou hast laboured, even thy merchants from thy youth, they shall wander every one in his quarter, none shall save thee.'

'It appears,' said the Babylonian, 'that with those last lines he is seeking to insult me.' He called across to the Galilean. 'Tell me, young man,' he said, 'are you not only trying to frighten and insult the woman but threatening me too? Am I to be burned like stubble, and wander on the earth?'

'It is not I but the prophet Isaiah who is speaking,' said the Galilean stubbornly.

'Then let me tell you,' said the Babylonian, 'that personally I care nothing at all for your prophet or anything he says. Nor does Helena. I know and she knows, she who has sat at the rim of the world and seen truth standing there, that you and your prophet and your God are agents of the evil Archons. You threaten us because you hope to put out the light that is in us. But let me tell you that the Alien God, the Unknown God, will endure when your God and his Archons have perished in darkness.'

In a matter of-fact tone Hop said, 'With all this talk going on, what happens if the dogs start barking and we don't hear them?'

'My ears are good,' said the Babylonian.

'All the same,' Hop began, and Joshua interrupted him. 'All the same,' he said, 'what's the use of this waiting about anyhow? We're not gaining anything I can see and we may be losing a lot.'

The Babylonian said, 'I've told you it's better to wait. There's some change in the situation. Until we know what it is, better to wait.'

'And supposing it's a double-cross?' repeated the Scowler. He continued to fiddle with his great knife. The Babylonian shrugged and turned to Hop as though explaining the behaviour of an unfamiliar animal.

'You understand,' he said, 'that he is one of that group or

element of the population known as the Zealots. The aim of these Zealots as I understand it is to take vengeance for the massacre of the people who revolted in Galilee some years back. They decided that what was wrong with those people was that they did not have enough weapons. Nor, maybe, a powerful enough urge to use them. Openly or secretly the Zealots go armed. That is why a man of their persuasion is called a Knife Man, or as the Romans say, Sicarius. Our friend here is a Sicarius. Those fellows stop at nothing: murder, blackmail, treachery of every type: these are their chosen modes of operation. They really revel in it.' He smiled benignly at the Sicarius. 'I find,' he said, 'a warm place in my heart for them. They spit on all the laws of God and the Archons. To say the least they are out to make trouble and often enough they make it.'

'Using what for money?'

'Sometimes they steal it,' said the Babylonian, 'sometimes they get paid by one of their enemies to eliminate, inactivate and lay to rest beyond possibility of doing further harm, another enemy they think more dangerous at a given moment. It is not, as you know, at all difficult to get a man killed in this city. It is even quite cheap in most cases. But the people like this Sicarius and his friends get bigger money because they are prepared to encompass bigger enterprises. In the interests of course of their political objective, whatever that may be. Me, I am not interested in their objectives. But I like their style, their attitude to life in this world. They say always "No". And such an attitude is most disconcerting to the Archons. People without understanding of the real nature of this world think it simple to go about saying No to everything, but really it is not so at all. These fellows play the most complicated games. Their mode of operation requires finesse and much holy guile.'

As the Babylonian finished his sentence his ears, Hop thought, seemed actually to prick up. He sat up straighter on his cushions and raised his hand. For quite a while as they all sat there in attentive silence Hop could hear nothing. Then quite a long way off on some distant veranda he could distinguish the flap flap of feet. And not just one man's feet but several pairs.

With a look as though this had confirmed his suspicions of

treachery, the Sicarius got to his feet with his knife at the ready. Then the well known voice of one of the men about the inn hailed them, giving some kind of password. To this the Babylonian replied and waited rigid on his cushions until the curtains at the entrance to the room parted. Four men came in.

Three of them were familiar figures about the stables and the inn premises. All were armed with clubs. One of them carried in addition a light spear which he held clumsily as though unused to such a weapon. The sight of the fourth man explained this. He had on his tunic the insignia of the Civil Police. But he was unarmed and it was obviously his spear that the man from the inn was carrying. The man from the stables who had brought messages to the Babylonian earlier in the afternoon stepped forward. 'This policeman,' he explained, 'was apparently one of the scouts or had been sent up from the main force behind to join the scouts.' He had hallooed and shouted and when the dogs had been ordered to stop barking he explained that he wished to deliver an important message to the people at the inn. He said if they would keep the dogs off him he would come forward alone holding his spear above his head. After some suspicious consultation among themselves the men from the inn had agreed. He had refused to tell them anything more and demanded to be taken to the inn.

'He has a message for you,' said the stable man.

'To which of us?' asked the Babylonian.

'To you I suppose,' said the stable man. But at this the policeman also took a couple of paces forward.

'No,' he said, 'to this one.' And laid his hand on Hop's sleeve.

'Me? How do you know it's me?'

'You were described to me. Besides, I saw you once at Headquarters in Jericho. You're the man, no question about it.'

'Well, then,' said the Babylonian, 'the message.'

'The individual in question,' said the policeman, obviously reciting from memory, 'is requested to follow me together with not more than two of the servants of the inn to guarantee his safety, to the spot where I shall conduct him where he will learn something to his advantage.'

The Sicarius gave a sneering snarl.

All present gazed at Hop who in his turn gazed at the policeman as though he were the emissary of some business rival who, under stern looks and after a few sharp questions, might be prepared to disclose the intentions of his principal. The face of the policeman, however, remained so blank that Hop, experienced in reading faces under conditions of that kind, came to the conclusion that the man knew absolutely nothing, was a messenger and nothing more. Rather than cross-question the man he said simply, 'How far away is this spot you speak of?'

'Not far,' said the policeman. 'It's inside the walls of your land.' The Sicarius burst out angrily: 'It's some trick,' he said, 'either it's some plan for this fellow,' he nodded towards Hop, 'to get clear of us and go over to the other side, or perhaps the people on the other side for some reason want him as a hostage.'

Hop seemed not to hear the suggestion of treachery, treating it with an indifference which was like an insult. Instead he looked questioningly at the stable man. The man said, 'I don't see how they can do you any harm. None of them could have got through as far as the wall or anywhere near it without the dogs letting us know all about it.'

Hop considered for a moment and then said: 'All right, let's go.'

With darkness and the rough ground the walk from the inn buildings towards the wall of the wide field that surrounded it seemed very long. The policeman, who had evidently been given careful directions by someone who had familiarized himself with the inn and its outbuildings, walked ahead. Hop went between the two stable men, one of them still holding the policeman's spear and both plodding doggedly along. One of them had a trick of shaking his head every few steps as though to emphasize the puzzling and even nonsensical nature of the proceedings. Hop was affected by this gesture to the point of asking him once: 'What's your idea about all this then? Do you see any point in it?' To this the man made no reply, not even with a repeated shake of the head.

Then they saw the wall and the low bulk of what might have been a small barn or large hut. The policeman stopped. He said to Hop: 'This is where I was to bring you. You are to go in alone. We,' he looked at the stable men, 'are to stay outside, at this distance.' They were thirty or forty paces from the hut. Hop stood quite still, not hesitating but simply wondering.

'It's as silly as a dream,' he said. He walked forward away from the others and found the solid door of the building, which was now seen to be more like a small barn than a hut, hanging a little open. He went in quickly, stooping in case there were low beams and keeping his hand on his knife. Inside he straightened himself cautiously and stood quite still, letting his eyes get used to the deeper darkness inside.

'Good,' said the voice of the Police Chief of Jericho, the Idumaean. 'You will forgive me if I doubted whether you would come. My message was necessarily obscure. You are not I hope unduly surprised to see me or rather I suppose I should say hear me?'

And in fact the moment the man had spoken Hop felt that he really was not surprised. Feeling that, he could not help coming out with another question, which, the moment he had asked it, seemed to him trivial and irrelevant. 'How did you get here?' he asked. 'They said nobody but that policeman could have got past the dogs.'

He was astonished to hear out of the darkness a low exclamation, half a laugh, of pure pleasure. The voice said, 'I told you, I'm an Arab or Berber, anyway a mongrel from the desert like our ruler Herod. In such situations blood will tell. I was never more than twenty paces behind that policeman of mine. When they let him through the dogs they let me through too without knowing it. Those obedient dogs,' he laughed again, 'thought they had orders not to touch me either. I lay there on my belly in the scrub and while the others went off to take my message to you I made my way here.'

Hop was annoyed with himself for his question which had given the opportunity for this outburst of boyish triumph and self-congratulation. The voice said: 'My eyes have got quite accustomed to the darkness here. There is some kind of a bench just to your left there. I suggest you sit down.' Hop fumbled his way to the nearly invisible bench but found that already he could just distinguish the outlines of a muffled figure seated a few feet away. There was a small silence and

Hop said gruffly, 'You said in your message I should learn something to my advantage.'

In the dark he tried to picture the Chief of Police in the flesh, or rather as he had looked in his office back in Jericho. It was hard to understand that this was the same person. Police Chief, Idumaean, Mr Jericho. The voice, coming now from a vaguely seen body, said, 'to your advantage. Yes. I think so. If I had not thought it perhaps indiscreet, even very dangerous, I might have added "to our *mutual* advantage".'

CHAPTER TWELVE

The darkness, abolishing distances, swallowed up time too. Hop lost count of how long it was that he had been listening to the light, high-class voice of Mr Jericho, talking, it occurred to him, like a book, its passages elaborate and controlled, and so phrased that a plain man's first thought must be that the whole thing was a tissue of lies. But how could it be so? Nobody would bring himself so near to a hanging with lies like that. Underneath all that there was desperation. Only a desperate man would commit himself so far. There was also a savage purpose designed to convert the desperation into triumph.

The voice was painting maps in the darkness. Maps of a country, maps of a city. But not flat maps that stayed still after you had drawn them. These maps were like maps of the sea: heaving and straining with changing tides and currents and winds. But these now were tides and currents of people; groupings of people, hopes and fears, needs, ambitions, allegiances, traditions, powers physical and spiritual. It was a picture of a storm, but of a storm that yet might be controlled or directed in its violence to one objective or another. In the violence of the storm everything shook or became fluid. Positions of power which a man busy minding his business took to be as solid as the mountains; forces of power, and administration and organization; these changed shape, collapsed out of sight, moved across the map in clouds, or wobbled like a line being drawn with three people trying to hold and guide the same pen.

Disconcertingly, while Hop was still deep in contemplation of these peculiar maps, Mr Jericho changed tone and said sharply: 'So you see my position. You understand what has to be done.'

Hop said gloomily that it was not entirely clear.

'No?' said the voice. 'But it had better be. Certainly it had better be. In fact, I think it is probably clear enough to you already. You are an intelligent man. But it is easily to be understood that in a matter of this magnitude you would wish the main points to be repeated. It is like the natural demand for confirmation in writing of a vital agreement. In this case of course confirmation in writing is hardly...' He laughed.

'That much is clear at least.'

'So I will encapsulate,' said Mr Jericho, 'encapsulate in brief my situation and my proposition.' Already almost invisible, he seemed abruptly to become more distant: like, Hop felt, a person in a drama, or in a history book. He even spoke of himself, the Police Chief of Jericho, as though speaking of someone not himself.

At the juncture now reached, he said, the Police Chief of Jericho, nicknamed Mr Jericho, faced a crucial decision. The following were in his view, the essential factors in the situation:

First, the profound unrest, stirring towards an explosive climax, now seen to exist in the city of Jerusalem.

Second, the fact that the Roman authorities, while convinced that the Essene, in secret alliance with Barabbas, was the focal point of the agitation, at the same time admitted that they had so far not dared to arrest him in the city for fear of provoking just the explosion they feared.

Third, in this supremely critical condition of affairs, the Police Chief of Jericho occupied a key position. He had massive popular support among the ordinary citizens of Jericho. More important, he had at his command the best, militarily-trained Civil Police Corps in the country—a small highly efficient army. He was neither Judaean nor Roman, but Idumaean, like Herod himself, 'with all the freedom of manoeuvre which that could be made to secure.'

In the imminent event of an armed popular uprising in Jerusalem—a direct confrontation between the authorities there and the mob—his intervention could be, one might almost say must be, decisive.

Fourth, the Roman and Jewish authorities in Jerusalem were as alert to these factors as was the Police Chief of Jericho. All of them suspected, some of them were convinced, that he was already in secret communication with the Essene. Whether they fully believed it or not, they could not afford to disregard the possibility. Sooner or later, and probably sooner, they must act against him: perhaps by assassination.

'So you see, the Police Chief of Jericho, this powerful Idumaean, is forced to an instant and fateful decision. He might, certainly, retreat. Short of resignation, or a trip abroad, he could reach some administrative compromise with the Roman authorities, involving a reassuring diminution of his power. Or'—his voice became lower and more intense at the same time—'he can advance—with all that that implies.'

'For that advance to succeed, one element is indispensable: there must be a link, a line of communication between the Police Chief and the Essene. The Police Chief must be in a position to co-ordinate his action swiftly with the action of the Essene. Were either the Essene or the Police Chief to act too quickly, each without pre-arrangement with the other, the result could be defeat.

'It is essential, it is indispensable, that at the very moment of the popular uprising, the military police forces of Jericho must be at hand to support them against the military force of the enemy.'

The voice broke off. And then, sharply:

'You understand this?'

'I understand what you say.'

'Then you understand your role.' The voice now had an edge of military command.

Hop said violently, 'No. That's what I do not understand. My role as you call it. What role? What are you trying to tell me?'

'Simply that you are that essential link and line of communication between myself and the Essene.'

'I?'

'You, you alone. You are the line of communication. Given time I could perhaps have found a better one. But who gives me time? Who gives the Essene time? Hurry's the word.'

Perhaps, Hop thought, if there had been daylight, or so much as a lamp, he would somehow have found words to put things back, so to speak, into shape: to bring real life alive again. He could have told this Idumaean to get on with his dreams, play his games of power and battle in his own world and leave Hop in the world where he lived. Instead, the darkness, the strange voice, the paralysing danger, caused him to feel as though that world where he lived had already folded up or dissolved.

He said, not to the other but to himself, 'How has this come about?'

But the other took it as a question to be answered. He said:

'I might answer that you are the obvious link simply because, as I know, you are already in touch, there at the Knower's Inn, with two intimates of the Essene. They can take you to him.

'But that's not all of it. This has come about because you came to Jericho when you did, and because there was a flaw in your story about your arrival there.'

'A flaw?'

'Or, if you like, an explanation of the circumstances so flimsy that it at once drew my suspicious attention.'

'I told you the truth.'

'We've been through all this before, in Jericho. First my subordinate, then I myself—twice—asked you just how you happened to pick up that young man—a known member of Barabbas's gang—on the Jerusalem road. You insisted, quite stubbornly and rudely, I may say, insisted that you acted simply on some kind of impulse. A fellow man in distress, feeling of sympathy, vague desire to lend a helping hand. And so on and so forth.

'*But,*' the voice was coldly emphatic, 'you know and I know, my dear Samaritan, that in this day and age, conditions being what they are, level-headed men of the type you profess yourself to be simply do not act, involving themselves in danger and expense, on that sort of impulse. It's not human nature to do so.'

Hop made a noise in his throat, seemed to begin to say something, and finally said nothing.

'That being so, there could have been many reasons for you to tell such a story. The most likely explanation for you offering me this unlikely tale was that you actually wanted me to see through it. By your manner of arrival with the young man you had ensured that my attention was drawn to you. As an agent of the Essene, anxious to establish communication with the Police Chief of Jericho, that was a way of making that contact without exposing yourself more than absolutely necessary. Under cover of my story, which you knew I was most unlikely to believe, you could sound me out, take your bearings, without either of us being prematurely compromised. As for the change of plan which caused your sudden flight from Jericho, I can only guess at what it may have been. On reflection, I concluded that for some reason you wanted to continue our contact on—for you—somewhat safer ground. And here,' said the Police Chief, with a sudden lightening of his tone, 'we are.'

When Hop sat silent, the Police Chief said impatiently, 'Well now. I've opened my mind and hands to you. Now it's for *you* to act. I've already told you what must be done. My proposition. You understand it now? And your role? To a man of your intelligence I don't need to repeat that?'

'No,' Hop said. He reviewed the 'proposition' and the 'role' which the Chief of Police had outlined at the beginning of this conversation in the barn. He was to make immediate contact with the Essene. He was to convey to him the Police Chief's proposals for joint 'popular and military action'. He was to establish a line of swift communication between the Essene and the agents of the Police Chief in Jerusalem. Along this line the imminent actions of each could be co-ordinated.

Still groping confusedly for some way of putting things back, as he saw it, into shape, but now without much hope of being seriously listened to, he said:

'But that business on the Jerusalem road. If I still tell you that was the way it happened, and that's all there was to it?'

'You would be asking me to believe that you are that sort of man.'

'The sort of man I am?' Hop had a recollection of Alpha saying something like that when, lying on his bed in Jericho, he had refused to give any thanks for his rescue. The Essene had said the same sort of thing in his reported version of the episode on the road.

Again the Police Chief spoke impatiently.

'Very well. If that be so, then that is the answer to your question. How has all this come about? You are the sort of man you are. In any case, it makes no difference—even if your improbable story were true after all.'

'No difference? How can you say that? No difference?'

'For whatever reason, your situation is what it is and not otherwise.'

Hop's thoughts meandered, and came abruptly to the thought of Sarah.

'And suppose,' he said, 'I simply tell you that all I want to do is to go home?' As he said it, he was aware that even this simple statement had become, in some terrible fashion, absurd.

'Home?'

'That's what I said.'

'And where is your home going to be?'

'Sachem, of course. I've told you over and over again.'

'It used to be your home.'

'Still is.'

'Not, if you come to think of it, so. And now that you are on the blacklists of all the various powers that be in Jerusalem you are not likely to be at home for long anywhere. If you were to go to Sachem you would find out too late the truth of what I tell you—namely that appearances have imposed themselves upon reality and have in fact become the reality, the reality for you.'

'There are,' said Hop, 'a dozen men in Sachem who can testify that all these blacklists and so on are lies. Sound businessmen who know I'm a sound businessman. They've known me for years.'

'In conditions,' said Mr Jericho in his most elaborate manner, 'such as those existing now and likely to exist in the immediate future, you will find that your dozen of sound men is liable to shrink with alarming suddenness. Three of them will be out of town when the critical moment comes, four when the authorities come to question them will explain that they know nothing whatever of political matters, which will be taken of course to mean that they repudiate you. Three will visit you with tears in their eyes to explain that although all the suspicions and accusations of the authorities are nonsense, and although they are perfectly aware that you have never had a seditious thought in your life, you must please remember that they have wives and children who are dependent upon them and who may be brought into poverty and ruin if their menfolk allow themselves to get into bad odour with the powers that be. They will most humbly beg for your forgiveness for the fact that they are about to rat on you.

'Two will stand firmly by you. One of them will be arrested on a trumped-up charge, the other will be made the victim of an organized whispering campaign of calumny and vilification sufficient to ruin his trustworthiness as a character witness for yourself. And then there was one. The thirteenth man. You.'

Both men remained for a while perfectly motionless in the dark. Then Hop spoke, in a quiet tone as though of a minor business deal.

'Your plan,' he said, 'like you said of my story, is full of holes.'

'You are wondering,' said Mr Jericho, 'why I have overlooked the possibility that you and your friends might simply disappear into Jerusalem, making no effort to contact the Essene. I don't deny that would be a great blow to my plans. But I shall be no worse off than I am now. You would.

'For of course as soon as I was sure that that had happened I should take steps to provide the Romans with absolutely cast iron evidence against you and naturally your wife—Sarah is it not?—and associates in Sachem. It would do me no particular good but would be a revenge and I am a vengeful man. It is one of the characteristics of my people, the Idumaeans.'

'I am not a fool,' said Hop. 'I can see that that would happen. So I wouldn't act that way. But I can't control Alpha or these two followers of the Essene, men I scarcely know. Suppose they blab the story? Suppose,' he sarcastically imitated the Chief's voice and manner, 'they commit an indiscretion?'

'But if you come to think of it, what good would it do them? Who would believe them? Or putting it another way, assuming that people did believe them it's obvious that they would themselves be regarded as in some way accessory to these iniquitous and seditious proceedings and at the very best be arrested and held for questioning of a most savage kind. They would simply be running themselves into danger even more serious than they are already in.'

Hop pondered and nodded in the dark. He said: 'It's your affair, not mine, but suppose you're wrong about the Essene. I mean supposing after all he doesn't what you call "agree in principle". I know and you must know that there have been times when he's said things which make you think he would maybe not want to get involved in the kind of bloody affair you have in mind.'

'He is reported as having said, "I come to bring not peace but a sword." '

'I could think up some other things he's reported to have said that seem to mean the opposite,' said Hop.

There was a small abrupt noise and movement across the barn. Mr Jericho was getting to his feet. 'In that case,' his voice said from a point above Hop's head and a few feet off, 'the Essene will bear a very grievous responsibility. He will have betrayed the faith and hope of the masses.'

For the first time Hop laughed. 'A shocking thought to a man like you,' he said. 'Very very shocking to betray the masses.'

'I am not the Essene,' said Mr Jericho coldly.

'That's noticeable,' said Hop, also getting to his feet.

'But I repeat,' said the other, 'that for him it would be a shocking responsibility. He has a chance to help change the history of the world.'

Hop was about to say something when he realized he was alone in the barn. He had not felt Mr Jericho glide past him. The words 'history of the world' floated back at him from nowhere through the open door. One other word followed them. 'Hurry!'

CHAPTER THIRTEEN

The Babylonian stood just inside the main door of the inn. Hop asked, 'How late is it? How long to first light?' and when the Babylonian told him, said sharply: 'Then the mules must be ready by that time. For me, Alpha, Joshua and the two men of the Essene.'

The inn-keeper tilted his beard at him and said, 'So something has moved.'

Hop said, 'I'm a businessman. When a thing has to be done, I like to get it done.'

'And you are starting *after* first light?'

'It's slow travelling in the dark.'

'Slower still in the light if the police scouts are in the way.'

'They'll not be in the way.'

'Oho,' said the Babylonian, and moved off.

The Sicarius and the Galilean awaited Hop, their faces almost distorted with their unspoken questions.

Hop said, 'There is not a lot of time. I'll explain the thing to you quickly. Listen.'

He had to explain more than he had first intended. He had had in mind to say no more than that circumstances had arisen, or something of that kind, which made it necessary that they bring him together with their Master. But it could immediately be seen that the Sicarius, who had already made clear that he was a man who thought constantly of plots, treacheries and violence, had got by instinct to the heart of the matter.

'Is it an offer of help, then?' he said. 'From the Jericho police quarter?'

'Think what you like,' Hop said. 'I'll tell you two things: first, it's absolutely necessary that I see the Essene; secondly, I guarantee that to the best of my knowledge and belief, I'll bring him no harm and may bring him good.'

The Sicarius's eyes glowed. 'You've no need to tell me any

more. I'm not a fool. The police scout with the message. Your meeting out there—whoever it was. What you've just said. It's an offer of help from Jericho. An alliance.'

His voice was low, but the tone was like a shout. As he drank in the news, it affected him like wine. 'This is the hand of God,' he said. 'This is God's finger showing us and our Master the way to go.'

The Galilean watched him with an expression both bewildered and furious. His Galilean brogue thickened with his emotion.

What sort of alliance? he wanted to know. Were they to disclose the Master's hiding-place to a stranger? For what? To serve the interests of some gang of uniformed butchers in Jericho? His words flowed on and on.

Aware of time passing, and exasperated by this obstacle, Hop could see that the quick way to remove it was to reinforce the Sicarius. He told him more of what the Police Chief proposed. The dispute between the two followers of the Essene flared and guttered and flared again. Once Hop said, 'It's simply a question of putting the thing to him. It'll be for him to decide.'

'I'd be ashamed to put the thing to him at all,' said the Galilean, huskily.

The Sicarius looked at him and sneered. 'I suppose,' he said, 'it wouldn't be that you're afraid the Master will accept the plan? That's what it is. You're afraid he'll understand that this Police Chief, butcher if you like, is a chosen instrument of God to help us and our Master to victory. You're afraid when he sees the way God's pointing he'll be apt to forget some of the things you seem to remember best. The soft things. He'll forget them all right, the Master. You know it and you're scared.'

Then the Galilean suddenly made an unexpected remark. 'Aside from all that,' he said, 'what's all this about the rising of the masses gathered in Jerusalem for the Passover? I suppose you've forgotten that there's a regulation forbidding people even to carry knives during the Passover celebrations. The crowd won't just be badly armed, it won't have any arms at all.'

'Do you think,' said the Sicarius, 'that at a time like this people are going to worry about a bloody little regulation like that? I expect there's a regulation against burning down the Procurator's palace. That's not going to stop people doing it.'

'We must talk this out between ourselves,' said the Galilean.

As they withdrew to the far corner of the room, by the dais where the dancing had been, Hop called out to them, 'Hurry!'

And a little before the Babylonian came to tell Hop the mules were ready, it seemed that the Galilean had gloomily and reluctantly agreed. Just at first light they were mounted, together with Joshua and Alpha, at the gate of the wall enclosing the field of the inn.

'Which way now?'

The Sicarius pointed north-east—more north than east.

At that Alpha looked sharply at Hop as though expecting an objection. It was certainly not the way to the city, a half-hour's ride to the south-west. North-east—a long way north of the Jericho road—would take them into high rough country of valleys and ridges. So far as Hop could remember there was no town or even village there of any size, between them and the big village of Ephraim, which might be a half-day's ride away, more or less, according to the going.

It could be some dangerous trap of the Sicarius.

Still in that matter of danger it was a fact that the farther they were from the city, the less risk there was of stumbling across some patrol of the Roman Garrison, it would be assumed that such patrols would be particularly active at this time when people were pouring into Jerusalem for Passover. Also it was common knowledge that these foothills of the mountains to the north-east, north of the road running down to Jericho, were full of caves, large and small; and that these caves were often occupied by groups or communities of people travelling from one part of the country to another, or even from other countries across Judaea; going, for instance, to Egypt. People on the run used this country. Perhaps in one of these caves was sitting at this very moment the Essene. Perhaps the Sicarius and the Galilean had days ago arranged a meeting there with him and his other close followers. Hop sat motionless in his saddle while all these thoughts paraded across his mind. Finally he nodded to the Sicarius. 'What ever you say, let's jog.'

The going was rough but the mules were less tired than their riders, and they could be said to be making fair progress if only it were known just what they were progressing to. Time and again, Hop discerned from black against grey in the half-light what he made sure was the entrance to a cave and for a moment or two made equally sure this was the cave they must be going to. But the Sicarius in the lead made so far as could be seen no sign of interest in any cave, if caves they were. Once Alpha called out to him impatiently, Where were they going? After a long while irked by weariness that was an active pain and becoming slowly exasperated by this blind and perhaps meaningless journeying, Hop reined in his mule. 'We need a rest,' he said.

Alpha seemed simply to roll out of his saddle and get himself stretched full length on the ground like a person long accustomed to snatching any rest he could get before it was snatched away from him. His voice came up from the ground. 'You're right, uncle,' he said.

At the idea of a rest, the Galilean looked doubtful. 'It's a long way to Ephraim,' he blurted out.

'So that's where we are going? that's where the Essene is at?'

The Galilean shut his mouth and looked as though he wished he had not opened it. The Sicarius shrugged. 'It doesn't matter now,' he said, 'we are taking them to him, aren't we? And who could they tell about it even if they wanted to?'

The Galilean tried to insist it was a long ride and they should be pushing off. Alpha from the ground laid obscene curses on him. The Sicarius shrugged again and dismounted. Joshua sitting on his mule at the tail of the little party gave the impression of a man asleep in the saddle. And he could have been a sleep walker as he got to the ground made a few jerky steps and pulling his cloak round him sank down to sleep. It might seem that the whole journey appeared to him so strange a dream that it made no difference whether he was awake or asleep. Alpha too was already asleep. In his sleep he smiled.

The smile suggested an indifference to the dangers of lying asleep unguarded and without any precautions taken in that place at that time; or else it could have been, Hop thought, that he was simply the sort of man who imagined that any wearisome precautions that had to be taken would be taken by someone else. And the other end of the sleep if you woke up too late, Hop thought, could be a long ride between policemen with your arms tied, a beating with iron chains until you were half flayed and your bones broken and maybe hanging on a cross to finish up with.

'We ought,' he said sleepily to the Sicarius, 'to set a watch.'

For the first time the Sicarius looked as though something was amusing him. He jerked his head in the direction of the Galilean. 'The question doesn't arise.' Indeed the Galilean, although dismounted, remained standing beside his mule in a posture of alertness. His expression when he looked at the others was scornful. He said, 'Sleep if you like, I shall keep watch.' The Sicarius said, 'We can sleep an hour.'

They had been sleeping for an hour or more when, crouching, the Galilean came to where Hop and the Sicarius were sleeping and kicked each of them in turn. In the light after sunrise they could see a long way over the country. Over and between the tops of scrubby trees they could see the ground falling away steeply from the ridge where they were, to a broad valley of which the other side was a long gentle slope stretching up to another, lower ridge opposite. The valley ran from north-east to south-west and in the centre of it very clearly visible was a track much broader and more level than the path they had been following.

The Galilean pointed away to the north-east where this track came into view and dipped down with the valley.

At that place there was a confused, fast-passing movement. Then the movement, with dust rising above and behind it, could be seen as the movement of a band of horsemen moving fast. Now they could hear the clop of the hoofs. As the horsemen came on, and were almost opposite the watchers on the ridge, they were still too far away for their faces to be seen.

But it could be seen that there were three of them, riding hard, leaning forward in the saddle. Three were bunched together. One was a little ahead. In the fury of his gallop, his body clung to his horse, but his head twisted quickly in a backward look, like the look of the leader in a race, judging the length of his lead. His head turned forward again, they could see his arm flailing his horse with a stick, and now he was near enough for them to see that his mouth was wide open, shouting.

Out of the tail of his eye Hop saw the tense faces of the Sicarius and the Galilean.

'Is that the Essene?' he said.

The Sicarius, without taking his eyes from the track, nodded.

And now the eyes of the watchers could espy what it was that was pressing the riders so hard. Over the top of the opposite ridge came two, and then another two, and then two more horsemen. Even at that distance there could be no mistake about who they were. The uniforms and accoutrements of the Roman police were striking and familiar enough. The ground they had to cover was rough going but they came on down quickly. The two bands must have sighted one another higher up on the track before it dipped into the valley. Evidently the Romans had cut across the high ground beyond the further ridge, and now they were moving down slant wise at an angle that would bring them, if there in time, across the track at the point where the valley dipped out of sight again towards the south-west. Despite the rough ground on the slope and the better surface of the track it was going to be a close-run thing.

Alpha jumped out of sleep to his knees staring bleary-eyed across the valley.

'My God,' he said hoarsely, 'it's the bloody Mounties.'

'Not us they're after,' said Hop, pointing.

Alpha looked down and saw the men on the track.

Now that the hunted horsemen were just below them, they could see the strain on the leader's body, coiled on the horse. Through his open mouth he might have been shouting or gasping for breath.

Alpha, on his knees, looked from the hunted to the pursuing police with the look of a man used to watching races. 'Poor buggers,' he said, 'they'll never stand that pace.' He broke off watching intently. 'The police'll get them.'

The Galilean was crouched with his hands on the rock in front of him, and his fingers trying to dig into the rock. His tense muscles distorted his mouth. His eyes flashed furiously for a second from the scene in the valley to Alpha beside him. 'Never, never!' he said. The word came out like a rattle in the throat.

'They can't make it,' Alpha repeated. And as the fleeing horsemen went away towards the left, the mounted police were finding the going easier, and the three horses on the track were under pressure. The gap between the two groups was closing. Alpha watching with that same look of an expert suddenly said, 'My God! They may make it yet!'

And then the others could see too that the leader of the three horsemen had somehow pulled an extra turn of speed from his horse, and in a moment the three of them were past the point on the road where the mounted police were due to hit it with the police still fifty yards or more away. There was still a steep rise in the ground between them and the level of the track itself. The Galilean let out a low cry either of relief or exaltation. Alpha looked at him. 'What's the use?' he said. 'Those police horses are a lot fresher than the others. They'll catch them for sure on the level.'

Then a strange-seeming thing happened. The six mounted policemen clambered up on to the track and then just stood there, they and the horses quietly getting their breath. They looked down the track towards the dip where the three horsemen had disappeared but seemed to have no further interest in the matter as though it was no longer their business. As the watchers watched in astonishment they lumbered down off the track again, and started at walking pace up the slope down which they had come. The Galilean stared after them, his eyes looking half mad with excitement. His eyes fixed on them he said in his rattling voice, 'It's the hand of God, God has put his magic and his spell on them! He stopped them and sent them away!'

His customary puzzled look had gone. He had a smile as a perfect understanding. The puzzlement was all on the faces of Hop and the Sicarius who watched the policemen moving away up the hill as though at any minute they might give a clue to their mysterious proceedings. Alpha suddenly brought his hands together in a soft clap.

'What is it?'

Alpha tapped his head. 'This boy, this city boy knows a thing or two. Any of you others know what is just beyond there?' He nodded his head towards the place where the track went out of sight.

'Well what?'

'You go a little way along that track and there is a stone there, kind of little pillar. And what's on the stone? Markings. A sign. And what's that sign mean? it means that'—he mimicked the reading of an official document—'that this marks the outer limits of the civil boundaries and jurisdiction of the city of Jerusalem and its authorities and government duly appointed by the powers to safeguard the lives and the interests of all good citizens and true.'

'What's that to do with it? If you're so clever, tell us. And hurry!'

Alpha looked sulky.

'How should I know,' he said, 'what it's got to do with this business? All I know is you will find stones marked like that on the tracks all round the city. They can be pretty damned important to a man who's been in a little trouble with the law. If you'd been on the run from the law as often as I have you'd know things like that. What they call indispensable pieces of general knowledge. Now that I've had a chance to look it over properly I remember this track, but I was running the other way than those fellows were running. Little matter of a break-in. Stolen goods. Property not recovered. Thieves believed to have made good their escape beyond the jurisdiction of the city police. Oh, what a night, shall I ever forget it?'

'What good did that do you? Getting beyond the mark? It doesn't seem to stop the police roaming around.'

Alpha sneered. 'Good citizen doesn't have to know things like that. Poor city boy came from a bad home, never had a chance, he learns about those things. School of adversity. Those Romans are from the Garrison, Military Police.'

'But,' Hop said, 'they're allowed to operate inside the city limits. You can see them any day in the city. I don't get it.'

The Sicarius laughed abruptly. Coming from him a laugh of any kind was an astounding sound. He kept nodding his head in the triumphant manner of a person who had at last seen a sum tot up to a satisfactory conclusion.

'It means that those fellows,' he gestured in the direction of the retreating police, 'are under orders not to try to arrest the Master inside the city limits. Instructions to obviate so far as is possible, the commotion liable to prejudice public peace, etcetera, etcetera. It means the Big Men from the Presidium are very scared. Means everything I told you, everything your Police Chief told you about that situation, has proved what we said it was. Confirmation. They know and I know and your Police Chief knows that anyone who tries to lay hands on our man is liable to touch off a public revolt. Rising of the masses. Just like I said and your Police Chief said. If anyone does it they want it to be the Men in Black or the civil police. Shift the onus. And you can certainly guess they'll have told the Civils and the Blacks to watch their step, play it quiet unless somebody forces their hand. If they could have caught him out here, outside the limits they could have whisked him off some place and nobody any the wiser. Kept him bottled up anyway until after the Passover.

'You mean,' said Alpha, 'he can run around in the city and its parts adjacent, spit in their eye, maybe doing a miracle right there on the street.'

'So long as he doesn't go too far,' said the Sicarius. 'That's what they hope—just that he won't go too far. They hope if they play it quiet, he'll play it quiet too. Then people go back home from Passover, go back to work and you have got a new situation.' He paused and studied the movements of the men on the opposite slopes. 'Just give them time to get out of sight and we'll be off to Bethany.'

'Is that where he'll be?' Hop said.

'It's the best guess,' said the Sicarius. 'At the house of the two sisters.'

The Galilean glowered. 'There is no need——' he began. The Sicarius interrupted. 'We have got to bring this man together with him, and bring him quick. He's got to know what's on offer from Mr Jericho. It's the hand of God all right, and Mr Jericho's the knife in God's fist. We have to hurry.'

There was another bit of confused dispute between him and the Galilean, the Galilean seemed to be trying to state all over again the arguments he had used at the inn. The latest events just fixed his unwillingness even to lay Mr Jericho's plan before the Essene. Clearly and simply the hand of God was over the Essene, and the Essene and God should be allowed to do what seemed good to them without interference from outside. The Sicarius shouted or snarled him down. Hop said, 'I have passed my word to contact the Essene.'

'You're just curious to see him,' said the Galilean. 'Just because of that thing he said about you, you told us so yourself. You want to go and gape at him like all the others.'

The Sicarius made a concession. He said that though Hop

had to see the Essene it might not be good for the whole group of them to go across country into Bethany together. Police patrols who might not dare to lay hands on the Essene himself, might think it safe enough to round up these lesser characters. He and the Galilean were known to them as close followers of the Essene and that might make the police hesitate if they saw them just jogging along, just the two of them obviously going to join the Master at Bethany. But if there was a whole band of them, then the police might think they had to act. And if they pulled in the whole lot of them, sooner or later Hop and Alpha would be identified as characters the central authorities were already keeping their eye on. Like the Police Chief had said. He therefore suggested that for security reasons he himself should go immediately to Bethany and join the Essene at the house of the two sisters, that Hop and his two companions follow after an hour or so with the Galilean following them after a similar interval.

To this proposal the Galilean took immediate and violent exception. After first trying to offer other explanations of his objection, he admitted that he found it simply out of the question to allow the Sicarius to be the first to talk with the Essene and naturally put before him the proposition made to Hop by Mr Jericho.

Ever since the physical appearance of the Essene on the track and the subsequent behaviour of the police, the Sicarius had been in nearly boisterous high spirits, what had seemed like a permanent scowl became a kind of grin. This grin he now turned on the Galilean, brandishing it at him so to speak, snapping his powerful fingers.

'Take a look at him,' he said to the others, 'I told you he was scared, scared at what the Master will do when he knows what the score is. He wants to be in there along with me putting in his buts. But this, but that, but the other thing. Well, all right, if you're that worried, it'll make no difference.'

Hop and Alpha watched the pair of them trot off along the path the way they had come, leaving directions as to where they should leave the path which had brought them from the inn and take another forking off from it which would lead them first to the main track, and thus to Bethany itself. Joshua remained seated on the ground without any expression at all, retaining his air of the sleep walker. Alpha said, 'Do you suppose we'll ever see those fellows again? Is this the end of a great friendship? What makes us think the Essene has really gone to Bethany? He may have gone right into the city and those two after him. If you ask me there probably isn't any house of two sisters or whatever he calls it in Bethany, I've been there and I never heard of it.'

'We're trying,' Hop said. 'Bethany.'

'If that's the way you want it,' said Alpha. 'Bethany.'

CHAPTER FOURTEEN

'Shall we really see the dead man walking? Shall we, Pa?'

The small boy tugged at the sleeve of a man beside him sprawled in the shade on the south side of the market place in Bethany.

'So they say, son, so they say.'

'Will he walk and talk just like us, Pa?'

'So they say.'

'Will he have worms growing out of him? Shall we get to see the worms, Pa?'

The father looked sideways at Hop seated near him and smiled and shrugged as though inviting Hop to appreciate the difficulty of answering such a question. He said to the boy: 'I can't guarantee the worms. They say the man who raised him up fixed him up entirely.'

'Doesn't he even stink? Won't he have a great stink on him like dead people do?'

'No stink, no worms, so they say,' said the father.

'There's an awful lot of people,' said the boy. 'Shall we get to see him all right?' He looked anxiously round at the people already lying or squatting on the grass bank beside and behind him and at the groups of twos and threes walking and talking in the market place. From the further side, where the Jerusalem road came in, a new group of half a dozen appeared hurriedly, jostling one another and peering about them like people afraid they have arrived late for a performance at the theatre. 'Have they all come to see the dead man walking?'

'Looks like it. Him and the other one.'

'What other one? I want to see the dead man.'

'The one that raised him up of course.'

'Is he here too?'

Hop was aware of a small jerky movement by Alpha at his side.

'So they say.'

'I want to see the dead man.'

'Don't you want to see the man that made him alive again? The man that did the miracle?' He turned to Hop again and said: 'A very big miracle by all accounts. The whole town's talking.'

The boy said: 'I don't mind if we see him *too*, I don't want to see him *instead*.'

Hop twisted over a little on his hip so that he could talk in a lower voice with his face close to Alpha. There was plenty of noise around to drown his voice even if he had raised it. There were the voices high and low of the crowd, the noise of people coughing and spitting, the slap and shuffle of feet in the dusty square. 'Hear that?' he said. 'Looks as though our two friends have brought us to the right place after all.'

'Can be,' said Alpha, his eyes flitting back and forth across the crowd.

'Better be,' said Hop.

It had been agreed that they were to wait inconspicuously in the market place until they got word from the Sicarius or the Galilean as to the state of affairs, when and how they could contact the Essene himself. So that they sat now in the shade of the south side of the square with the sun beginning to go down, and the people still coming in from the city one way and villages the other to join the crowd already waiting. Joshua sat a little apart, with an air of contemplative resignation.

The sight, noise and smell of the urban crowd seemed to have a tonic effect on Alpha. He appeared as excited as a boy returning after a long trip away from home and happily recognizing the animals of his own familiar farmyard. He pointed out to Hop a known criminal, a strongarm man for one of the gangs who terrorized shop-keepers in a particular city sector. He reported too on the presence among the crowd of several men who, Alpha judged, were detectives from various agencies—the Civil police, the Men in Black, and the Supreme Roman Authority.

The shadows on the market place had lengthened notably, when suddenly there was a change of noise in the place. All at once everyone had stopped chattering and gossiping and said, 'Ah' all together. There was a thick noise too of shuffling feet as the crowd shifted like weeds on a pond under a sudden breeze. Everyone who had been lying or squatting down was standing up. Out of the lane on the west side of the square, a young man came walking alone. Little tussles occurred as the people nearest to the way he was walking tried to push back a little and those behind them jostled for a better view. Beside Hop, the father of the little boy had picked him up and said, 'That's him. That's Lazarus. The one that was dead.'

The little boy stared rigidly and began to kick his feet against his father's stomach. His thin voice was almost a screech of angry protest. 'That's not him,' he said trying to keep his eyes on the walking man and angrily address his father at the same time. The father lowered him in the ground.

'What's the matter?' he said. 'You've seen him, haven't you?'

He turned to Hop and said, 'You can't ever satisfy them, can you.' The boy danced up and down with frustration. 'He doesn't look dead,' he grumbled. 'He looks like everybody else.'

'Of course he does,' said his father. 'That's what he's supposed to do. It's a miracle, don't you understand?'

People all through the crowd were making the same kind of comment as the little boy. 'You couldn't tell to look at him.'

Nor could you. What they were looking at was a young man who looked much like very numerous other young men: clerks in offices, store keepers. The only thing different about this young man was that hundreds of people were staring at him. The fact made him walk stiffly and move his head in an unnatural manner.

He had made things worse by putting on a kind of jauntiness and a small smile which made the effect more unnatural than ever. Then after a few steps it became a genuine smile. He had seen a friend and called out to him, the stiffness went out of his gait as he hurried towards the friend with gestures of greeting. The friend made a vague gesture in return, but instead of stepping forward as expected, stood quite still smiling confusedly; looked anxiously left and right; jerked and edged himself back, leaving two or three strangers between him and the young man, who now halted and stared after him with an expression of wounded bewilderment.

Walking stiffly again he moved forward, the crowd pushing back from his path, so that the whole length of his blue shadow fell on the dust beside him. Seeing another friend he called out to him too, but this time less confidently, with a query in his voice. This second friend had somehow got pushed a little way out in front of the crowd. Without moving forward or trying to move back he answered the young man's greeting with a loud response, but when the young man raised his arms as though to embrace him he kept his own arms casually folded. The other dropped his arms by his side and after that exchanged a few words and moved on.

'Doesn't want to touch him, see?' the father said to Hop. 'Well it's natural, isn't it, I mean to say, four days dead. You'd hardly know what you would feel if you touched him.'

The little boy unable now to see anything past the hips of the people in front of him had started on a new tack. 'He's got worms in his head,' he yelped. 'Worms coming out of his ears. I saw them, I saw them! I saw the worms!' He continued chanting for some time, asserting to himself and all in hearing that that was what he had seen.

After the first awe, the exclamations, chattering and comments broke out all over the crowd. Sightseers who had come from outside Bethany on the news that the man raised from the dead was going to take his first public walk that day, kept assuring and reassuring one another that it was indeed true about the miracle and there was the man walking about. Some of them would stare as he passed, then push their way through the people behind them, run round the back of the crowd, and take up positions further on so as to get a close view again. Some of them had had a long walk in the hot sun and they wanted to make it worth while. Among the natives of Bethany village the consensus was that this young man was certainly Lazarus all of them had known by sight, and most of them had at least exchanged a few words with him from time to time in the past. Or, if it wasn't Lazarus, then it was his spirit miraculously walking about in an exact replica of Lazarus's body. A man behind Hop with a contemptuous voice kept saying, 'Well if it's Lazarus's spirit, then it's Lazarus. It amounts to the same thing.'

To which another contemptuous voice said, 'That's where you're wrong, it's not the same thing at all. If it's Lazarus's spirit walking about in a body that's only an imitation of Lazarus's body, then Lazarus's body is rotting away in that tomb right now, and this Lazarus isn't the same as the other Lazarus.'

To which the first voice said, 'If that's what's worrying you why don't you go inside the tomb and look around? You wouldn't object to doing that, would you?'

He cackled derisively and the other fell silent.

A third voice broke in angrily. 'What are you cutting hairs about, you two? Whichever way it is it's a miracle, isn't it? A miracle right here in our village. You're not denying that are you?'

Meantime the young man continued his lonely walk across the market place, along the far side of it, round it and back towards the lane from which he had come. A dozen people called out to him, and he answered them, and several times two or three would step out from the crowd and stand talking with him. Their expressions smiling or grave were all as unnatural as his. Or it could be said they were expressions natural to people who, though excited to be talking to the results of a miracle, were not certain whether they were talking to a corpse that had been made to act lively, or a living being, or that same Lazarus they had talked to a week before but who had died in the meantime, or something altogether new in the way of a manifestation of powers.

These encounters did not serve to make the young man's promenade appear less lonely.

An observer said, 'It's easy to see that things aren't going to be the same for him from now on.' Several bystanders nodded assent to this statement. After all, they said, it wasn't everyone that was alive one day, then dead the next, and alive again the day after that. For a thing like that to happen to a man was very special indeed. You could wonder what it felt like to be a person and a miracle at the same time.

Then somebody said, Yes, you could wonder about that, and there was no question it was a remarkable thought, but aside from all questions of that kind, the big thing was that it was a miracle, a very great miracle, and this was heartily agreed by all.

With the disappearance of the young man into the lane there was no dispersal of the crowd. On the contrary the place seemed to be more tense, almost thunderous, with expectations than before.

People's faces changed. Faces that had looked like the faces of gaping sightseers now looked more like the faces of pilgrims. Without hearing clearly what anyone was saying, a person standing in the crowd could understand what everyone was saying; that there was a report that the Essene, the Preacher, the Holy Man, the Man who had come riding into Bethany a little while back and done that miracle, had come back to Bethany that day, might be going to come out of the house he was in and say something, and perhaps walk about among the people.

The people at the entrance to the lane at the end of which was this house stood staring down it. Those further off stood at its entrance. It was notable, and Hop did so note, that only a few people entered the lane and even they did not proceed far along it. The crowd, Hop judged, looking about and listening, was restrained by such feelings of shyness, even of reverence, as were naturally produced by the stories about things said and done by the Essene in other places. These stories were going back and forth among the people, sometimes eagerly accepted, other times questioned and derided. There were, too, a good many who took the view that if this Essene could bring to pass one sort of wonderful and unnatural thing, he could bring to pass another sort too, not necessarily of a benign kind. There was for instance the well known story, that same one which the Jericho Police Chief had repeated to Hop when discussing the Essene. It told how as a small child he had beaten two other children to death because they had played some harmless trick on him. Then, when their parents complained he had stricken those same parents blind. Also well known was the story of the schoolmaster who had intended to teach him the alphabet. Not realizing the power in his tiny pupil he nagged him and bothered him. The child had ill-wished him. The imprudent teacher had come out in frightful boils all over his private parts. Such were the powers of the individual now understood to be resting in some room at the house at the end of the lane. Walk down the lane, disturb him, be caught staring at him, and you might, some people thought, get a spell put on you—become suddenly palsied, or, the spell working on another level, find your cattle giving birth to monsters, or your business ruined for no forseeable cause. Best not to run such risks.

For all these reasons the lane remained as empty on this crowded afternoon as a lane in the night-time, and a stranger walking along it would be as conspicuous as one walking through a village by moonlight. The whole crowd would stare and special staring would be done by the branches of all security forces. It seemed to Hop that this little empty stretch of lane separated him from the Essene as completely as though the two of them had been on opposite sides of the country. There was no knowing how long the crowd might simply stand there waiting for something to happen. They had waited for the dead man to walk and he had come. It could be supposed that the next thing they were waiting for would happen too.

Hop suggested to Alpha that they withdraw a little to the bank where they had previously sat and wait events. Either the Essene would appear and they might be able to make some contact with him or, more likely, the Sicarius would send them some message or come out and tell them what was going.

Alpha said, 'You sit and rest them weary bones. This city boy is going to circulate among the rabble.'

Fizzling and sparkling with pleased excitement he danced off into the crowd and could be seen sliding and gliding, walking with walkers talking with talkers, once or twice seeming to encounter an old friend, greeting and putting his head close to the head of some friend or companion of the street for the conduct of what seemed long confidential conversations. Hop could see by the length of the shadows that he had been dozing for some time when Alpha returned.

'Any news?'

There was news and there were rumours. Alpha poured them out together.

The news was that the Essene had been in Bethany, had raised Lazarus from the tomb, had left again secretly, and this very day had returned, openly, riding in with two of his followers. Still later, two other of his followers were believed to have reached Bethany and joined him at the house of the two sisters, who were in fact the sisters of Lazarus himself.

They and their brother were well known in Bethany. But there were all sorts of different stories about their relations with the Essene.

'Well naturally,' said Alpha. 'The younger one, Mary, they say is a very fine girl and supposed to be half out of her wits about the Essene.'

'Never mind about that,' said Hop irritably. 'What about him? What's he doing? Why's he here?'

Some said one thing, Alpha said, and some said another. Whatever the reason, the Essene had for quite a while been a close friend of the family, and lodged at the house of the two sisters when in Bethany. They might be disciples of his teaching or there could be other reasons. But it was a fact that when the brother was taken ill, the sisters had sent messages to the Essene because of his fame as a healer.

They had done that secretly. But then, when he failed to come, and Lazarus died, the elder sister—Martha—had broken down and in her sorrow and disappointment told many close friends that the Essene was a false friend, who had deserted them in their hour of need. Then the younger sister had heard from friends who claimed to know about the situation that in fact the Essene was on the run from the authorities—hiding somewhere up in the Perea district.

'That was what the Knower heard,' said Hop.

So, it was guessed, Mary, who had this mad faith in the Essene, somehow smuggled a message to him in Perea or whatever it was. She said he was their friend and would never desert them if he knew their trouble. And sure enough the next thing anyone knew for certain was that the Essene was back in Bethany. Martha was bitter that he had come too late. But Mary, they said, had said that such a one as the Essene could raise their brother even from the tomb. And that was what had happened. And then the Essene had disappeared again.

'To Ephraim,' said Hop. 'We knew that. But why does he come back? What do they say he's planning to do?'

Alpha's low-voiced chatter became a mutter. For this, he said, was information that came from 'one of the boys' he knew who happened to have some very close connections with 'a certain element' in the secret police. The story was that in making that dash to Bethany to save Lazarus the Essene had taken a huge risk. But he had been and gone so fast that the local police had no time to get instructions: under the general directive to 'seek to avoid commotion' they had not dared to act on their own initiative against an individual such as the Essene, with his local connections, high reputation, etcetera. With the result that the Essene had slipped away. What had happened next was partly guesswork. But it was a fact that the latest orders from on high had been that while great caution must be exercised in the city of Jerusalem, and parts immediately adjacent, the Roman police were to find and seize the Essene anywhere else he might be lurking.

The fugitive might well have had immediate news of that order. He was reported to have secret admirers, followers, believers everywhere—even, according to rumour, high up in the office of the Procurator: Roman officials who were reported to attend secret prayer-meeting with him at night, and listen to his teaching. They could have given him word of an order like that before the Procurator had even signed it.

'So back he comes galloping to Bethany. Just one jump ahead of them.'

'It was a close-run thing,' Hop said. He saw again vividly in his mind's eye that man coiled on his horse, shouting, panting, just a stretch of track ahead of arrest, death. More vaguely he pictured him, weaving back and forth, across the wild country, now here in Bethany: his safety hanging on a thin thread; just the Romans' fear of forces they could not understand or exactly calculate.

He said, 'Time's passing. One of those two should have sent a message by now.'

Alpha said, 'They're crazy, both of them.'

'We still need them.'

Alpha looked at him, with a look of sudden curiosity.

He said, 'What's this about "need them"? I'm nearly home. You're half-way home, anyway. Why wouldn't we cut loose from those crazy men? With this crowd going home, we could get into the city and no questions asked.'

Joshua, as though reality had reached out to him after a long time of hallucination, came out of the dozy trance he had seemed to be in and said, 'The lad's right. That'll be the thing to do, old friend.' 'His voice lost the hopeless tone it had had, and he spoke with warm encouragement.

'This is how it'll be,' he said. 'We get up now, and we go Along with all these people. You and I—we're businessmen I have business in Jerusalem, you in Sachem. We'll just ge home, and when all this blows over, we'll get back to business And I'm sure this young man too will find business in the city.' He paused and considered. 'Probably,' he continued, 'i would be best for you, Hop, not to lodge with me. The two of us together—after Jericho. But I'll arrange for you to lodge with a reliable friend. A businessman like ourselves. Listen now while I tell you just where to find the house.'

Happily, he explained to Hop just how to get to that house how he could wait there, if he so wanted, until everything blew over, and then proceed in good order and decency, home to Sachem.

Hop listened carefully.

The crowd was thinning somewhat in the square. The villagers were going home to supper. Others of the sightseers were crowding into the eating-houses of the place. There was a smell of cooking from everywhere. Some still sat on the bank where Hop, Joshua and Alpha were, eating provisions they had brought with them in bags and baskets.

'Are you listening to me?' said Joshua.

'Sounds like a good idea,' Hop said.

'Well then?'

Hop was aware of Joshua starting to get to his feet, as though the matter were settled, and of Alpha, still squatting his lively eyes dancing with a surprised curiosity. He tried to follow a train of thought, but the thoughts were only pictures He saw Alpha the way he had first seen him on the roadside He saw that guide at Jericho and the smart lieutenant of police. He saw the dark, desperate, thrusting face of Mr Jericho. He saw the Essene, riding. He saw that the mouth of the lane was now deserted except by two men, who stood a little aside from it, watching. He heard himself say, 'I started this.'

Joshua said, 'What?'

'Nothing. Talking to myself.'

Joshua, standing now, shook himself impatiently. 'So we'd better be moving,' he said. 'We need to keep with the crowd.'

Hop remained motionless, looking towards the lane.

In a quick extraordinary gesture, Alpha shot out his hand and gripped Hop's knee.

'Don't do it, uncle,' he said. 'Don't be a crazy man. They're watching there. They'll get you. Come on to the city.'

Hop started upright. He looked in astonishment at the hand on his knee, and then into Alpha's dancing anxious eyes.

'It won't make any difference to you,' he said. 'What's it matter to you what I do?'

'We've done a lot together,' Alpha said.

'Don't worry about me,' Hop said.

Alpha took his hand away and in a little movement got to his feet. He put his hands on his hips and swaggered a little. He said, 'You know me. I don't worry about anyone. You're just the kind of man you are.'

'You said that before,' Hop said.

'How can I remember everything I ever said?'

'What's it matter now, anyway?' He too had got to his feet.

'Not a thing,' Alpha said.

'So,' said Hop, 'you go on into the city while's the going's good. I'm going across there'—he jerked his head towards the darkening, nearly empty square—'to see what happens.'

Joshua spoke with the former resignation in his voice.

'Nothing to be done,' he said. 'If you ever get to the city, you'll find my friends' house, waiting for you. As for me, I'm going home now.'

As he moved off, Hop said to Alpha, 'You'd better get going too.'

Alpha said, 'No hurry, I'll stay around here a little bit. Plenty of life in the wineshops.'

'You can't do anything for me if anything happens,' Hop said.

'Well, just in case,' Alpha said and swaggered off.

Hop looked after him with an amazed expression, shrugged and started across the market place.

He tried to walk like a businessman who is going to an evening appointment on a matter of business. As he reached the beginning of the lane, two of the plain-clothes men, who had been pretending to chat with one another like ordinary citizens, made a break in their chat and were looking at him sharply sideways. He walked on between the houses and there was nobody there. Nobody stopped him or called to him. There were two or three hundred paces to go and he paced along steadily, casually. The businessman paying an evening call. He could hear the noise of the voices in the market place behind him. He thought any moment now there would be a shout or feet hurrying behind him. No shout came and no hurrying feet. He came to the house of the two sisters. There were lights in the upper room, open to the street. There was no noise of people up there, but he thought one of the lights had blinked as though someone had passed quickly in front of it. On the ground floor beside the door there were no windows.

He knocked and while he waited looked back up the lane. It was still empty.

There were footsteps in the upper room and he supposed somebody had come across to the edge of the balcony and was looking down on his head. He was thinking about whether to knock again when there were steps on the stairway. Then there was the sound of bolts being gently drawn, and the door opened and a biggish woman was standing in the entrance holding a small oil lamp at about the level of his head. He gave her time to look him over. He said, 'I have a message,' and then as she still stood there, added, 'It's not something I can explain in the street.'

She hesitated, looking him over again carefully and seeming to play the sound of his voice over in her head as though it might tell her something about the stranger. Then, as she made a motion of her head beckoning him in and still holding the lamp high, closed the door with one hand and shot the bolts again. They were in the narrow passageway of the kind to be expected in a house of that type. She pushed past him and led the way to the end of the passage and through a curtained doorway into a small interior court, out of which a stairway led to the other part of the house. At the bottom of the stairway she stopped and called to someone above.

'Iscar!'

A man came to the top of the stairway just visible in the light of the room behind him. He stood with his hands on the banister looking down and said, 'What is it Martha? who is it?'

Sharing the familiar voice of the Sicarius Hop called out to him and raised his hand in greeting in the darkness. The Sicarius gave a quick exclamation. 'A friend,' he said to Martha and told Hop to come on up. When his head was still only just above the level of the floor, Hop was peering eagerly into the room. He hurried up the last two steps, and went on in. Between him and the balcony looking on to the street there were couches and a long table with bowls and platters on it. There was a heavy smell of scent. From some room at the far end, came the noise of dishes being rattled and the sound of a woman singing in a low voice.

Hop stood still, looking again. The voice of the Sicarius behind him said, 'They've gone. Had to clear out.'

Hop's voice was flat in disappointment. 'Gone where?' he said.

The Sicarius jerked his head over his shoulder. 'To the city,' he said. 'You weren't followed here? Did they stop you, ask any questions?'

He went across to the balcony, looked cautiously into the street and returned. Hop was looking in the direction of the other room. 'It's only Mary,' said the Sicarius, 'the others have gone. Martha, would you bring us some wine? This friend and I need to have a talk.'

Martha said, 'He said he had a message.'

'It was to him,' said Hop sitting down on the couch but still looking about him as though the Essene might be somewhere within call. 'Gone,' he said, half to himself, half to the Sicarius.

'He didn't,' said the Sicarius, 'want to bring trouble on this house. He thought that after dark the crowd could get excited and there'd be a commotion. There's a lot of people coming in from Jerusalem, later on there might have been a demonstration and the police could have moved in and there could have been a big uproar. The house might have been wrecked. Anyway, the women here would have been involved.'

Martha came in with the wine and went away back again to the other room.

'Nobody here but her and the girl Mary,' said the Sicarius. 'And Lazarus is asleep in that other room.'

Hop listened with half his head. The other half was fogged by the news that the Essene had gone, was not there.

'But he was here. You saw him, you talked to him. You told him about Mr Jericho?'

The Sicarius made a big shrug and talked quickly.

He told how he had arrived to find the room full of people including some women followers from Bethany. He and the Galilean had been delayed, taken a long time scouting out the situation and whether it was safe for them to go to the house of the two sisters. No time to tell anything much: and supposing one of the women from outside had been a police spy? All he had time and opportunity to tell the Essene was that there was a man with a message for him that was urgent, terribly urgent. First priority: could affect all future plans: the Essene must see him. Yes, naturally, the Essene would see him.

'Tomorrow?' said Hop.

'Not tomorrow.'

'Why not tomorrow?'

Hop thought he was being calm but when he looked at his hands, saw that they were twisting with impatience. 'Why not tomorrow?'

Because, the Sicarius explained, he himself would probably have no way of contacting the Essene before tomorrow evening. Neither he nor the other close followers knew where the Essene would be at, he said, in Jerusalem tomorrow. He might be resting, or he might be having some secret meeting with the Romans from the Procurator's office, or leaders of street groups from one or other sector of the city, or gang leaders if it came to that. His place of residence in any case unknown.

'But think of the time,' said Hop, 'tomorrow's Passover eve. I have to see him.'

'Do you think I'm in any less of a hurry than you are?' said the Sicarius angrily. 'If I could find a way to take you to him tomorrow, I would. Some time tomorrow, he'll contact all of us, but that'll just be to tell us where we are to meet for the Passover feast. Nine, ten, eleven or twelve of us according as to how many have got into town by tomorrow night.' He paused, glaring at the table and flexing his fingers.

'Listen,' he said. 'You tell me where you'll be, the place our friend Joshua has found for you, and if I can get word to you any time tomorrow, I'll do it. Of course if I could get to the meeting place early before the others show up I might give it to him so urgently, he would just go through the ritual and then quit the feast for a while and meet you.'

Hop remembered sourly the words of Mr Jericho, about changing the history of the world or something to that effect: and here he was, in a village house, with a man who didn't know where his master was, a girl's voice singing, and time going by. Day after tomorrow Passover, and seven days after that, when the great multitudes would be in the city. Still time, but so little of it. Time for the Essene to communicate with Mr Jericho. And of course Mr Jericho with his disciplined force could move fast once he knew when to move. A thought which he had not much considered before, pushed itself into his mind. He said to the Sicarius:

'Are you so absolutely sure he'll agree to the proposition when he hears it?'

He wanted and expected the Sicarius to repeat what he had said earlier at the inn in the argument with the Galilean; that the Essene would grasp this opportunity with both hands. To his surprise the Sicarius said nothing, sat scowling at the floor, got up and walked a couple of paces back and forth, and sat down again, his face not so much scowling as tortured. Watching him, Hop had time to wonder briefly, why he, Hop, should be suddenly dismayed that the Sicarius did not answer at once. Yes, or no, what was it to Hop? What had happened to him? Why did he so much want the answer yes?

Iscar, the Sicarius, said, 'The short answer is, I don't know.' He raised his hand against a possible interruption. 'I know what I said back here at the inn. I believe most of it, and anyway I was trying to get our Galilean friend to see some sense. But even then thinking back on some of the things the Master said from time to time...' he broke off, the muscles of his face twitching. 'Naturally, some of the things may have been just red herrings, false leads to mislead us. Like I said. But this evening...' he pulled at his hand and paced about the room again. 'I tell you I didn't like the atmosphere. I didn't like the mood he was in. Take this row there was about the girl there. Poured all that stuff over his feet and then smashing the bottle. It certainly made me mad. I told her what I thought of her. Even empty, the bottle would have been worth quite a lot—a lot for a poor family. But he seemed to be taking her side. Told me not to trouble her.

'Said something about the poor being always with us; very strange remark for a man in his position.

'I wonder what some of his poor followers would have thought if they'd heard it. And then again, just before he left he said, "Now is the judgment of this world; now the prince of this world shall be cast out." Well you could take it to mean that he was talking about the procurator, the emperor, meaning we were actually going to get action right away. But if you put it together with a lot of those other things he said you could think he meant something quite different. Something to the effect that God would triumph in people's hearts however much they might go on being downtrodden here on earth. He has said things you could take to mean that.'

'So you worry?' said Hop.

'I worry,' said the Sicarius.

Hop sat there silent while the girl out in the kitchen finished one song, and started another. 'So that's it for now,' he said, and getting up added, 'Till tomorrow.'

'Or the day after tomorrow,' said the Sicarius still scowling at the floor.

'Long way off, the day after tomorrow,' said Hop.

He went down the stairs and through the house and out into the lane. It was quiet and empty in the beginning of moonlight. Just before he got to the market place, a man stepped out of the shadow of a house and showed a badge of a Roman policeman. Asked him who he was. Whom had be been visiting? Why?

He was a businessman, said Hop, looking for a business acquaintance.

The detective looked him harshly up and down. It seemed that for two pins he would have reached out and frisked him for a knife. It passed through Hop's mind that when he was just a businessman, going about visiting business acquaintances, this kind of questioning at certain times and certain places had seemed to be natural, a minor inconvenience of life. In present circumstances, he saw the man as an insolent enemy, questioning and probing with the idea of doing him a mischief.

Before, he had never minded that this kind of man had some sort of authority over him.

Now he minded.

Hop's general appearance and tone of voice seemed to have convinced the man that this was just a businessman on business. He looked over his shoulder at the people in the square, and said, talking now as one man to another, 'In a situation like this, you get the jumps. The things people say; here, back in the city. Murder in the air. Tell you, I'll be damned glad when it's over.'

'What's over?'

'The whole thing. Anything can happen,' said the detective.

Hop shrugged, gave him good night and went on across the market square looking for Alpha. Alpha was standing outside a wine shop in close conversation with another young man.

'Time we were moving,' Hop said. Alpha drew him a little aside. 'Listen, uncle,' he said. 'That's an old friend from the city. We thought he and I might just kind of wander into the city together and look up some old pals, see the bright lights. So if I don't show up at your place till morning or thereabouts you'll know I'm just breathing in the myriad sights and sounds of the great city by night. Take care of yourself, uncle. Be seeing you.'

'Tomorrow?'

'Or day after tomorrow.'

CHAPTER FIFTEEN

From that roof in Jerusalem the noise from the street was meaningless, telling nothing. The sound of voices, dozens of them, scores of them, sometimes perhaps hundreds, came humming and buzzing and crackling up to the rooftop without words. What could be seen was as meaningless as what could be heard. Dozens, scores, sometimes probably hundreds of heads bare or covered, just the tops of them visible without faces. Seen from above the dress of these many many people told nothing of what sort of people they were. Nothing explained why the crowd thickened or thinned, why the multitudes passing in each direction went sometimes faster, sometimes slower. The slap and shuffle of all those feet on the road was sometimes heard, more often blotted out by the noise of voices. Hop, the watcher on the roof, his head tingling with thoughts and imaginations of things to come, had the illusion that the crowd was somehow conspiring to keep its thoughts a secret. He kept saying to himself that on what those thoughts were, what they were going to be later today or tomorrow. everything depended. This was the crowd of whose actions and reactions the Romans were so openly afraid; the crowd on whom Mr Jericho relied to assist him and the Essene in changing the history of the world; these were the masses, this was the people of Jerusalem.

Hurt and frustrated by the loud secrecy of this multitude of people going north for no discernible reason, going south with equally obscure purpose or perhaps no purpose at all, Hop tried to shut his mind to the mass and its movement and concentrate on one question only: was or was not the Sicarius to be seen just coming up the street? Would he, his head unrecognizable from above, reveal himself by halting suddenly at the door below and knocking? Screwing up his eyes Hop looked as far as he could down the street to the right, as though, by detecting the Sicarius in the crowd when he was still far off, he might somehow hasten his appearance at the door. He distinguished no one in that direction and when he looked in the other direction could distinguish no one either. Then he had the notion that while he had been looking sideways someone really had stopped suddenly in front of the door and was about to knock. But when he looked down the faceless people were still on the move one way and the other.

He sneered at the senseless crowd, the Sicarius who did not come, and at himself who expected anything different. He went downstairs to the main room of the house. Here there were no windows to the street, only those opening on to the interior courtyard. But a knock at the main door would certainly be heard. So what was the point of getting dizzy with counting and watching on the roof? Joshua had introduced him carefully to the man and woman of the house. He had also explained that what made this house a very safe place for Hop to lie low in was that these people were what Joshua chose to call 'ordinary citizens', were not 'mixed up in politics', not 'interested'. He had intended this description to be reassuring but to Hop when he was brought to the house by Joshua the previous evening, it had seemed simply to put them in some world different from that which he now inhabited. During a night in which his sleep had been broken into irregular patches by imaginary knocks on the door, and his early-morning watch from the roof, he had even forgotten the names of these two people. There seemed no need to think of them otherwise than just as Joshua's Friend and the Friend's Wife. Now the Friend was seated looking out the courtyard and enjoying the cool of the morning. The Friend's Wife was brushing the floor.

Hop sat down and also looked at the courtyard where some small saplings were growing. He said the trees seemed to be doing well. He said he had been on the roof and there were big crowds in the street. The Friend said that was naturally so being the first day of Passover. At normal times there were less people in the street than at times like this. When people came in from the whole countryside and from towns and villages all around there were a great many more people in the streets than you would normally see in Jerusalem. It was more or less the same every year although some years there were rather more people probably and other years rather less.

Hop listened with half his head with the other half straining to hear a knock on the door. Listening to them and remembering what Joshua had said the previous evening, he thought how futile it would be to learn or try to learn these people's opinions of, say, events now and to come. Having decided that it would be futile to try, he immediately found himself unable not to try.

Did they for instance think there were more people coming in from the country this year than normally? They thought it might be so, some people said it was so. On the other hand it was hard to tell as it might not be so after all.

'I mean,' said Hop, 'given the disturbed state of the country one might think that more people might be coming in to the city to—well, to see what's going on.'

Friend said there was no doubt the country was in a disturbed state and that might be a reason for some people to come to the city to see what they could see. On the other hand said Friend's Wife, most people didn't really notice the disturbed state of the country so that probably it made no difference to what they did or didn't do.

Hop said that he had heard some people expected trouble of some kind. He had heard stories about this Essene and Barabbas. Friend's Wife said some people were always expecting trouble, seemed as though they'd nothing better to do than wait for trouble or make trouble. Most people had their jobs of work to do. Friend said as for the Essene and Barabbas there were always people like that. He was fifty-five years of age and he could not remember a time when people like that had not gone about and got themselves talked about. Some of them, there was no question about it, were good men, sincere men, holy men, and others were more or less frauds who lived by preaching about all sorts of matters and setting up as prophets or what not because they were too lazy or otherwise unfitted to do a decent job of work.

Hop told himself that it was nonsensical to continue the discussion and, after a small pause, found himself impelled to continue it. He supposed, he said, that if the Essene or, for that matter, Barabbas had a large following among the people there might be serious trouble if one or other of them chose to lead the people in some kind of subversive action. After all there was always a certain amount of feeling, wasn't there? against the Roman occupation and even against others in authority.

Friend said that seemed to be more or less a political question and he and his wife never mixed in politics, were not at all interested. Live and let live was a good motto said Friend's Wife. In her opinion politics was a waste of time.

Hop heard himself saying as though against his will, 'But if anything happened...'

'Happened?' said Friend.

'I mean you're in the middle of it,' said Hop.

Friend said, 'I don't quite know what you mean by "happened". But I think you'll find that whatever happens most ordinary normal people like us will go on in about the same way without bothering our heads about it too much.'

'Best leave all that sort of thing to the politicians,' said Friend's Wife.

As though feeling that they had perhaps not explained things fully enough to Hop, who was after all a Samaritan, Friend said, 'Of course when we talk about the Essene and Barabbas and so on you mustn't take us as entirely typical. I don't suppose there's one person in a hundred in the city who has ever so much as heard of them.'

'One in a hundred?' said Hop quickly, making—ridiculously he thought—a quick calculation in his head as to what that would mean in terms of total number.

'Just a manner of speaking,' said Friend.

'I'd never heard of this Essene until someone mentioned him,' said Friend's Wife.

'That's what I mean,' said Friend.

Hop sat silently listening for the knock. It occurred to him the trees in the yard must have grown at least an inch or so while they all sat. He got up. Friend and Friend's Wife looked at him apprehensively. Joshua, Hop remembered, had told them that he, Hop, was a highly respectable merchant from Sachem but nevertheless as the result of some legal tangle and agility of business rivals, was in danger of being arrested at the instigation of his creditors if he showed himself in the streets. They had been tolerantly sympathetic. They said they had known cases where perfectly respectable businessmen had been annoyed and harassed in that very manner.

Friend now conveyed to him that they were glad to put up a friend of Joshua's. They naturally took it for granted that he would remain quietly in the house. It would be most embarrassing for them if he were to go out into the street and be pounced upon by the creditors or officers of the law, and some sort of scene were to ensue on their very doorstep. It would make talk among the neighbours.

Hop said he had no idea of going out into the street but would go up to the roof again and take another stroll there. Friend and Friend's Wife had nodded in approval and relief. He strolled.

The strain on his eyes, strain on his mind of looking constantly down at the street and up and down the street waiting and watching for the Sicarius was excessive. He went to and fro from one side of the roof to the other. He would look into the street until his eyes felt dizzy, and then walk away again and look into the empty courtyard. The morning shadows were shortening. In the street the crowds were changing and unchanged. The people moved through it going one way and the other. The crowd looked the same. Perhaps there were more people. Or perhaps that was imagination because it was to be expected that as the first day of Passover went on more and more residents of the city and more and more people from outside would be in the streets celebrating the festival.

So the Sicarius had not come. Unless that man seeming to slow his pace as he came near the house door down below were he. No, it was not he. The faceless man went on with the crowd. So the thing to do is to go over and look at the courtyard and consider the matter coolly.

What good reasons could there be for the Sicarius not coming? Several. First. He had been unable to get the Essene alone to convey to him the full importance of Hop's mission, to mention for the first time Mr Jericho. Possible. Given his apparently intense spy-consciousness, the Essene might have wanted to avoid even seeming in the presence of the others to be conferring secretly with the Sicarius. But that, if one worked it out, would account only for the time up to the final ritual drinking of wine and eating holy bread and the singing of the last Psalm as prescribed. After that, and before the Essene retired to wherever he intended to sleep, surely there would have been an opportunity for the Sicarius to speak privately with him.

Hop remembered suddenly that either the Galilean or possibly the Babylonian had told him at some time that the Sicarius was the unofficial Treasurer of the group. He was in charge of the collection and distribution of funds. Therefore he could easily have made the excuse that he wanted his Master's opinion on some financial matter. In that case he could have talked to the Essene and brought his message to Hop long before daylight.

Second. Perhaps he had got the message but been afraid to come across the city in the dark for fear of being conspicuous. Nonsense. The crowds celebrating in the streets during the night had been greater than in the early morning. Third —Hop turned away from the courtyard and walked slowly across to look down at the street again—the Sicarius had started out with the message but been arrested on the way. Very possible. He was not the Essene and might have been picked up inconspicuously.

Fourth. Hop rocked back and forth on his heels. The outline of the plan had been conveyed to the Essene and he had simply rejected it. But how, Hop heard himself speaking angrily aloud as though questioning and rebuking some figure standing at roof level above the street, could such a person be capable of such a thing? The Sicarius had hinted at the possibility. That had dismayed Hop at the time. Now the mere suggestion, put to himself by himself, angered him. It fell to pieces against the image that had been building in his mind ever since he first heard the story the Essene had made of that thing that happened on the Jericho road.

Although the Sicarius was so close to the Essene and Hop had seen him once only riding hard for his life on the mountain track from Ephraim, perhaps he understood the Essene better than his closest followers.

Nonsense again.

Yet the Essene had seen something about him which he had not known about himself. That implied a kind of bond. Hop could not imagine himself turning down such a plan—Mr Jericho's plan—as the Sicarius might have outlined without insisting on seeing the man who had brought it to Jerusalem. Nor would the Essene turn it down in that off-hand way. And so?

His head was swimming partly with his thoughts, partly with the movement of the crowd. He said to himself wearily that the crowd was behaving just as before: and no sooner had he said and thought this, and angrily considered it, than he noticed that all at once it was not behaving just as before.

Something had changed. He screwed up his eyes trying to figure out what that was. Then he saw that at the furthest point at which he could see the street to his right, a group of half a dozen men, one a little ahead of the others, was moving faster than the people around and in front of it. The leader was pushing and thrusting. The others were close behind him in a small group. They came forward in a wedge looking as though they were trying to run, but not running because the crowd was too thick. The leader was shouting something. Now his voice was loud and vehement enough to throw words right up to the level of the roof. What he was shouting was the same thing over and over again, urgently calling on people to get out of the way, to let him through.

He and his wedge of men came down the centre of the street and passed the door of Friend's house and were almost directly below Hop, already a little way to his left, when they came up against a section of the crowd more dense than it had been further back.

People seemed to be refusing to make way or be hurried.

They could be seen turning over their shoulders and yelling at the leader of the wedge; then several turned, standing their ground and gesticulating indignantly. The leader's voice rose in a harsh scream ordering them with curses to get out of the way. Not budging, they shouted back at him.

Then with a gesture so fast and violent that it had happened before Hop grasped that it was beginning to happen, the leader had a knife out from under his cloak and lunged with it, and every man of the men in the wedge had a knife out too, and had moved up beside him. The noise from both ends of the street went on as before but just below where Hop stood there was a sudden silence as though the bottom had fallen out of the street.

For a moment the men with knives did nothing and the people who had been standing against them did nothing. Then with a scrambling movement they turned their backs on the line of armed men and some pushed and jostled their way out of the centre of the street to squeeze themselves against the houses, and others began to run and started to shout as they went to those in front of them who had still seen nothing. Again the leader went ahead, the wedge re-formed and went forward much faster than before, the crowd splitting and running before it. The men who had first tried to bar the way came out into the centre of the street again and started hurrying and running in the opposite direction, shouting and making signals to the people ahead of them who had been standing still, bewildered.

Then like a pipe the water is draining out of, the street was nearly empty. Hop looked down dazedly at the few people who still stood about turning their heads this way and that, seemingly dazed too. Without knowing what he was going to do he made for the stairhead. He stumbled down a couple of steps.

Then he heard a heavy knocking at the street door of the house.

As he came into the big main room he saw Friend's Wife standing rigid with her fists up to her mouth. Friend was already going down the stairs to the street floor. Hop stood still and waited. He heard Friend fumbling with the bolts then pulling them. There was the noise of the door being opened, of somebody seeming to jump across the threshold, and the door slamming again and the bolts being shot. There was a murmuring or loud whispering at the foot of the stairs. Stiff with tension Hop moved a step or two and called out.

'Iscar!'

'It's me, Joshua,' said Joshua's breathless voice from below and there Joshua was coming up the stair and standing at the top of it just inside the room breathing hoarsely and trembling all over.

Hop continued staring at him in a stupor of disappointment. 'I thought you were Iscar, the Sicarius,' he said flatly. Joshua, shaking badly, was being helped across the room to a couch by Friend. Friend's Wife moved quickly to a cupboard for a pitcher of wine. Talking partly to himself and partly to Hop, Joshua kept repeating: 'Nothing to be surprised at. I said all along nothing good would come. I said that. You remember my saying that.'

Hop came out of his stupor and said: 'Yes, yes, yes, but what's happened? What goes on?' And then as Joshua continued to puff shakily and turn to reach in a hurry for the wine Friend's Wife was pouring: 'What was all that in the street? What were those men with the knives?'

'With knives? In our street?' Friend and Friend's Wife spoke almost together; startled but sounding reproachful too, as though Joshua had been responsible for bringing such people there.

Hop waited while Joshua took a big gulp of wine. It was dismaying to see a man ordinarily so grave and composed, or else seeming wrapped in some interior meditation, thrown into such disarray. Joshua drank and took a deep breath. 'I'm not,' he said, speaking more calmly, 'used to this sort of thing. Not cut out for it.' He smiled very briefly. 'Like you said, I've got a big belly. Been running and pushing and dodging through the crowds the last half-hour. You've heard nothing?'

'We've heard nothing, nothing at all,' said Friend and Friend's Wife.

'I saw the men with knives,' said Hop. 'What is it?'

Joshua spread his hands. 'It may be a rumour, you understand. That's all I heard. Rumours everywhere. People get so excited.' He paused to get his breath under control again and took another drink of wine.

'The word is,' said Joshua, 'they've arrested the Essene.'

Hop sat down carefully, staring at him and waiting. Before Joshua could say anything Friend said: 'And so? And so? What's about it? What's it to do with you, us? Or your friend here?' He looked at Hop with repugnance. 'You told us he was simply, I mean to say, you said, a businessman, certain difficulties. Where does the Essene come into it?'

Joshua disregarded him and spoke directly to Hop. He knew, he said very little. An hour ago he had gone out to visit an acquaintance. And suddenly there was a commotion at a street corner and a man rushed past shouting something, something about an arrest, or 'They've got him!' or something of that kind. And then shouts and rumours flew up and down the street and Joshua found himself with a group of men talking at a corner. Some of the rumours flying from all directions seemed to have settled on them. From them Joshua heard for the first time that the Essene was supposed to have been arrested.

It had happened in Bethany, one of them said.

The way he had heard it was that they had arrested the young man Lazarus too, the one that was supposed to have been raised from the dead. The Romans were going to charge him with perpetrating a fraud, not having been dead at all. It had been part of a plot, the man said, to raise the popular admiration of the Essene who was plotting revolt against the Romans.

Another man said that that was a typical Roman smear story. They would do anything to discredit the Essene. Everyone knew Lazarus had been dead for four days and then raised from the grave. Then a third interrupted to say that in any case the arrest hadn't taken place in Bethany at all but what had happened was that the Essene had been celebrating the eve of Passover supper with his friends when the Roman police, brutally disregarding the ritual and sacred character of the feast, had broken in, charged them all with conspiracy and arrested the Essene.

Knowing Hop's special interest in the Essene, Joshua had moved on, stopping to join a group here and there, hoping to find out which of the stories was true, if any. It had not been easy, he said, because most people either had not heard the rumours or were uninterested. Many of them were greeting old friends they had not seen since they were all up for the Passover from different parts of the country last year. But the few who had heard the rumours and were interested were excitedly and passionately interested. Hearing two strangers discussing the arrest, a third would join in as a matter of course as though their common concern had made them intimates at once.

'It was as though,' Joshua said, 'the news made them all members of a secret society. Not an enormous number of them considering the number of people in the streets, but still a lot.'

The most reliable news, Joshua thought, he had got from a farmer who had a small place out beyond the Bethany gate, just at the foot of the Mount of Olives. As he came into the city in the early morning he heard from local people stories of strange doings in the area during the night.

Nobody, it seemed, wanted to admit having actually seen anything but it was generally agreed that sometime early in the night a strong force of Roman police had arrived in the neighbourhood and taken up positions in a grove of olive trees.

An event like that could mean trouble.

From a distance the Romans must have been watched by a number of anxious, suspicious and generally hostile persons from the farms round about, and from the near-by village of Bethphage. But when the farmer asked this man or that whether he had been among the watchers he was told no, but the man had talked with an unknown man who had seen everything. The police had been there a long time waiting for something to happen which they obviously expected to happen.

Then a party of men, a dozen or so, had come out from the direction of the Bethany gate, headed towards Bethphage village. One man who, although he denied it, seemed evidently to have watched the scene himself, had said that this group had halted beside a sort of cave in the hillside which was used for the local olive press. That would be 200 or 300 paces from the trees where the police were concealed.

The moonlight had been very bright by then and one man could be seen to be making some sort of address or giving instructions to the others and someone or other from the village had said that this man was certainly the Essene who had raised Lazarus from the dead; he had seen him in Bethany several times and couldn't possibly be mistaken. But the police had gone on waiting, doing nothing.

This peculiar behaviour put the villagers in a great state of anxiety. They watched all the more keenly to see what would come next. What came next was that the Essene, supposing that it really was the Essene, and three others left the rest of the party and went walking into a patch of land near the olive press which for some reason was called the Garden of the Olive Press. One of the nameless watchers had evidently been close enough to observe the doings of these four. With the police ambushed there in that unexplained and menacing fashion it was necessary to keep a sharp eye on everything that people did. They might for some strange reason be going into the village and get up to something which would bring the police after them.

But that was not what happened.

Before they had gone very far the four stopped and it looked, from his gestures in the moonlight, as though the Essene were telling the other three to stay where they were while he went a bit further by himself. From the way they stood there looking all about them it seemed that they had been told to keep a look out. The Essene went right on into the garden and was out of sight of the three but not of the village watchers. They saw him suddenly stop and go down on his knees and then throw himself full length on the ground. One man, whether truly or just because he wanted to show that he had seen or observed more than other people, said that he had heard the prostrate figure groaning painfully and seen it shudder all over like a man in a fit. No one could say just how long this went on but it was a long time because when he came back to the other three they had apparently got tired of standing and sat down and were dozing.

The Essene came up quietly and stood over them and it was easy to guess that he was asking them what the hell they thought they were doing, half asleep when they ought to be on the look out. It could be judged from that that he was suspicious of something, perhaps thought that one of the city gangs was laying for him. Clouds had come across the moon so that no one could agree exactly on what happened next or what caused it to happen suddenly when it did.

One minute the police were squatting down without sound or movement and the next they were going fast across towards the olive press and they were up there by the cave in a half-circle so that the Essene and his friends could hardly be seen. From what they thought a safe distance the villagers could not hear anything that was said, only that a loud dispute was going on, with the commander of the police squad shouting orders and shouts of protest coming from the group round the Essene. Then there was a mixed up kind of scuffle and the next thing to be seen was the Essene being pulled along by himself by a couple of policemen, and other police chasing his followers, who had to run for it as best they could.

The farmer had no information about anything that took place after that because naturally the villagers, once the police had cleared off, went home to bed. There was no way of knowing where the Essene had been taken; maybe out to some police post in the country or back to the city.

'If it really was the Essene,' Joshua said again. Hop sat staring at the floor, and Friend and Friend's Wife regarded him with aversion. He might have been doing sums in his head or putting a puzzle together.

Friend had been pursuing a line of thought. He said to Joshua: 'You said your friend here had a special interest in the Essene? In that case I must say I don't think it friendly of you to have told us that story about him being just a business-man. I'd be justified in saying you brought him into this house under false pretences.'

'False pretences, that's what it is,' said Friend's Wife.

They seemed to be waiting for an apology but Joshua looked at them as though he were seeing them from a distance.

'You don't,' he said, 'understand all the things that have happened since this man brought another man to my inn in Jericho. A concatenation of circumstances. A series of events planned by God. All part of the evil times we live in.'

Talking to himself Hop said: 'All this was hours ago. They'll have taken him to the Praetorium, to the Procurator's headquarters.' Joshua turned away from Friend and Friend's Wife and said: 'Some people were saying in the street that they took him to the other side of the city, to Caiphas's palace. To the High Priest.'

'Why should they do that? What would Roman police be doing taking a prisoner to the Men in Black? If he's charged with sedition, subversion or whatever it is that would be a matter entirely for the Romans. Their jurisdiction.'

'But,' said Joshua, 'they might want to involve our high priest and our church organization in some way. After all, everyone knows the top people of the Men in Black as you call them are hostile to the Essene. The Romans might think it a fine plan to get them compromised. They could hope it would divide public feeling.'

There was such a noise in the street that it came through the walls of the house into the room: not the vague hum of voices but sharp barking shouts and even the pound and hammer of feet running. Friend and Friend's Wife looked towards their room's wall, from beyond which the sounds came, with alarm and disgust. Hop made for the stair to the roof and Joshua rose and followed him. Friend called to him to stay where he was, but he shook his head and followed, going heavily but steady now on his feet. From the roof they saw two wedges of men almost exactly like the one Hop had seen a little while before, only one or two of them with knives drawn, but all pounding along hard.

'Who are they? What is it?' asked Hop.

Joshua watched the men pass and disappear and said: 'I understand now. I can tell you. A man was telling me about it earlier. He said that all over the city the subversives or whatever you want to call them have little street groups made up of maybe just a few in each street: the real hard core, the enthusiasts, and they have to be able-bodied fighters too. They call them all sorts of names—People's Guards and such.

'Sometimes when the Romans decide to raid a house or shop or drinking place, looking for men on the run and such like, these fellows can turn out in a flash and defend the whole street. Some streets the Romans have to leave to themselves whatever they may know about things going on there. Naturally these fellows get a lot of respect from the people, even people who aren't political at all.'

Hop looked down into the street. 'But there are no police here. They're not defending the street against anyone.'

There was a long silence. Then Joshua said: 'Suppose this time they're not defending anything. Suppose this time they're attacking instead. Suppose they're going to rescue the Essene?'

'You think so?'

'Why not think so? Some time there will be a revolt. It has been foretold by the prophets. Revolt and blood and destruction. The abomination of desolation which the prophet Daniel wrote of. Perhaps not for years and years. Or perhaps it is beginning now, today.'

'Then,' said Hop, and stopped. He was staring across the roofs in the direction of the hill where the Praetorium stood, and listening to many sounds from the city.

He turned away from the street and paced slowly across the roof to look down into the courtyard. As he came pacing slowly back Joshua said to him, 'I know what you've decided to do.'

'How do you know? What am I going to do?'

'I know because I know the kind of man you are.' He smiled. 'You're going to risk your stupid neck going out of this house into the streets and trying to get out of the city and make contact with your Mr Jericho.'

'You're a clever old thing, Joshua.'

'If I were you I wouldn't do it for all the money in the treasury. You'll be killed by one lot or another before you get anywhere near him. And anyway, how do you know one of his contact men isn't on his way to him already with the news?'

'Probably. Not certain. They may not know enough about Mr Jericho's plans to understand the urgency. They may be hanging around waiting for more certain news. You can't rely on anyone else doing what they're supposed to do. But there's another thing. Mr Jericho thinks I am a confidential agent of the Essene. If I tell him the Essene had the plan from me before he was arrested, and already gave instructions to his groups in the city, he'll believe it, and so he'll act.'

Hop was suddenly aware that until he spoke those words to Joshua, he had not consciously thought of playing that trick on Mr Jericho. Yet now it seemed the essential thing to do, the thing that could make all the troubles of his recent time worth while.

Joshua said, 'D'you suppose he'll believe you?'

Hop said, 'I can try. Like that I'll be really doing something.'

'Doing?'

'Being—how can I say it?—being a little bit in charge of things. Not just being used.'

'You feel that way about the Essene? Or is it about the Romans, or the people, or the revolt? Strange to me that you should feel that way.'

'Strange to me too,' Hop said.

'It's the will of God. You'll need a mule. As a businessman you'd look suspicious travelling that distance on foot. Have you enough money to buy a mule?'

'Yes, I took some from my partner.'

'It may be difficult to get one. The holiday, the disturbances. You can't wander the streets looking for a mule-trader. The garrison probably has detectives out looking for you. Where's your young friend, Alpha?'

'He was out on the town last night. Hasn't come back yet.'

'He looked like the kind of fellow who'd be good at finding a mule in an emergency.'

'He's probably sleeping it off somewhere.'

'My friends below have a mule. It's stabled somewhere behind the house.'

'Could you persuade them to sell it to me?'

'I can try. But as you see, they have somewhat lost faith in me.'

The argument about the mule with Friend and Friend's Wife was long and bitter. Friend's Wife, her eyes wet with furious vexation, announced a pre-vision of things to come.

'So this man, friend of the Essene—and why you, our old friend, should bring such a man to our house under false pretences I don't know—buys our mule and what happens? He wants to ride into the country, I suppose, to round up more villagers with pikes and scythes and send them into the city to join their filthy friends in commotion and riot. He rides about among them pouring out money lavishly. The police catch him at it. They arrest him and drag him and our mule to the police station.

'There are,' she cried, 'plenty of villagers to testify that he has been riding about throwing silver right and left and preaching revolution and blood and yelling for the murder of the procurator and the high priests and the solid businessmen and solid householders who work for what they've got, and everybody who isn't one of the scum of the streets.

'And where, ask the police, did you get that mule? And pretty soon some man from the city, maybe one of our neighbours, recognizes this mule as they drag it and the man here through the streets. It's a very big mule and it's got very special markings that anyone who'd seen it would remember. And quick as a flash they know it's our mule and they'll be at the door here breaking in and asking questions and arresting us and charging us as accessories to whatever.'

'So you'd rather he stayed in the house?' said Joshua.

'Stay?' said Friend.

'Until maybe his friends come for him or of course the police may trace him here.'

Raging, they agreed to sell Hop the animal. They put a huge price on it 'on account of the risk they were running'.

Joshua forced them to reduce it by pointing out the risk they ran with Hop holed up in their house was greater still.

Friend was not permitted by his wife to go across the yard with Hop, show him the stable, and prepare the distinctive mule for the journey.

She said that Joshua knew quite well where the animal was, and the harness. In her tone as she said this, and in other comments that she made, it became clear that she was already in a manner of speaking drawing in the hem of her garment from contact with Joshua. In the short time since he came knocking at the door with the news of the arrest of the Essene Joshua had suffered a transformation in her sight and one very much for the worse. This steady old friend of the family with his pot belly and his sound business in Jericho had somehow—and she indicated that it was a dark mystery to her how such a thing could have come to pass—been drawn into a nasty area, an area which she and her husband had spent their lives shunning and skirting.

God knew what diseases, possibly fatal, to security a man might pick up there, even a man like Joshua. From the way she said goodbye to him it was evident that it would suit her very well if he, after assisting Hop with the mule, were to continue on into the lane behind the stable rather than return through their house. Friend managed a smile but she looked impatient even as Joshua said: 'Goodbye friends, till we meet again,' and paced in a dignified manner with Hop across the yard.

They found a bag of the best and most expensive fodder and busied themselves giving the animal water and an invigorating meal. They stood watching it eat for what seemed a long time. Through the flimsy walls of the stable the sounds of the city came loudly but not clearly. Mostly they seemed the same meaningless hum and murmur that Hop had been listening to from the roof before the men with the knives had come rushing into the street. Once in a while could be heard, or a person listening specially for it could imagine he heard, a fiercer more purposeful shouting. That would be coming, it could be imagined, from the direction of the Praetorium on the Antonia Hill. Hop cocked his head listening for it while Joshua watched the mule as though that were his only business and interest. Once, from out of this seeming absorption, he said angrily: 'You think I should say something? Make comment on events? Just because there's time to say something before this animal ends feeding so I should say it? Useless.'

Hop nodded at him and smiled, and resumed listening to the city. When the mule was ready at last Joshua started to unfasten the stable door. He said: 'I'll shut it after you've gone. It'll be safer for me to go out through the house. Looks more natural. My dear old friends won't like it, even that small little thing. They'll think it could compromise them. But that's what they'll have to pay for our dear old friendship.'

He got the door open, looked cautiously up and down the lane, signalled to Hop that all was clear, gestured goodbye to him as he went out leading the mule.

CHAPTER SIXTEEN

Mounted and moving out of the lane into a larger thoroughfare, Hop found his attention being dragged painfully three ways. He needed to attend to the immediate and urgent business of watching out for possible danger and impediment to his own safe passage through the city to the gate from which he had decided he would make his attempt to leave. He must keep thinking too of what he must do and say when he got to the gate and after he had passed it, supposing he ever did pass it.

And, as though it were more important even than these other two problems, he needed to attend to what could be seen and heard of things happening in the city, wanting to peer about him and stop and listen and turn this way and that through streets and lanes, investigating as though the big mule with the peculiar markings were walking observantly about the city with an invisible man on its back.

He thought that if he were a resident of Jerusalem, or if Alpha were with him, he would have been able to distinguish between what was special this day and what was normal in the streets and in the movement of the people. Even without such knowledge he could reach certain conclusions.

For instance, in the street he was passing along there were certainly less people than would have been there on an ordinary day and far less considering that this was the first day of Passover. Also the people seemed to be moving faster and more purposefully than those he had watched from the roof earlier. Those earlier crowds had been strolling aimlessly. These people looked to him like people who have suddenly decided that there is going to be a storm soon, and all at once have stopped strolling and are hurrying homewards. Also like people expecting a storm were those he saw standing or sitting just inside doors or open frontages, expecting the breaking of a storm out of the clear sky, and would stay where they were until they knew just what was going to happen or not happen.

But a little further on he came to a small square which had the air, he thought, that it must surely always have on the very first day of Passover: very numerous people going leisurely about, talking, as the mule moved slowly through them, in the accents of country people from at least two quite faraway districts. Probably this was a quarter of the city where inns and lodging houses catered particularly for people from those districts. And probably these visitors if they heard as they must have heard of commotions and excitements taking place, say, in the direction of the Praetorium, thought these were part of the ordinary goings on in the big city.

Hop thought that if elephants paraded suddenly the country people would marvel, but take it for granted that this event too was part of normal city life, or at least of city life on this high day and holiday.

And then, pacing sedately, carrying a businessman appreciating his quiet holiday, the mule had left the square, passed through a short mean street, where people were running like leaves in a sharp gust, and in a moment Hop, halting the mule just inside the mean street, saw why. A detachment of Roman cavalry was coming up the street at a very fast trot. It could be seen that they would simply run down anyone who remained in their way. But it was not a raid; not a raid certainly on that street. The soldiers rode straight ahead, looked straight ahead, not giving any attention at all to people crowding into doorways or rushing up side streets.

Waiting for them to pass, and until a man riding down that street on a mule would no longer be conspicuous, Hop brooded on what he had seen and found it significant. The soldiery were coming from the direction of the gate towards which he was making. At all main gates, so far as he knew, there were, in addition to the police, army posts manned by soldiers from the garrison. The men he had seen trotting so urgently past would amount in numbers to about the total personnel of such a post.

So they were being withdrawn in a hurry.

To reinforce the garrison at the Praetorium? Or to join a force being assembled somewhere to charge a crowd the police had lost control of? Whatever way you looked at it it meant, must mean, Hop told himself, that the Romans were hard pressed; that this thing was serious. Thinking that, he became impatient waiting for the street to become normal again. It was not now a long ride to the gate but it would be a dangerous one for a lone rider coming along a deserted roadway on that peculiar and memorable mule.

It seemed to take a long time for the scattered leaves to come back again. But he would make no move until there were other mule riders passing this way and that in front of him. At length he said: 'Jog' and the mule was jogging gently on the road that would lead presently to the gate. For questioners at the gate he had his story ready and there was time to think a little ahead. Now that it was too late to change his plan he began to wonder whether he had been right in choosing to leave the city by this gate instead of the gate leading to the Jericho road.

This way he would have to get a safe distance from the city, and then make a long circuit over rough country before getting into an area where he would have the chance of falling in with the advance scouts of Mr Jericho.

It would take time.

And the sight of those troopers trotting so fast had made the thought of time passing actually painful to him. On the other hand it had seemed stupid to leave Jerusalem by the direct exit to the Jericho road. That was the way he had intended to go when he made his decision on the roof of Friend's house. It was the way by which he had left before. But there could be some guard on the gate who might remember, or more likely there would be one of the spies whom the Romans were known to move in as innocent householders or shopkeepers into houses just this side of the gates. If such a person had been given a description of him by the garrison authorities as a suspected agent of the Essene, and had seen him recently, he might get a double jog to his memory on seeing him again today. Recently? But that had surely been a long time ago when he started out on his journey to Jericho. He compelled himself to realize that it had not been a long time ago at all; really a very small number of days. The chance, he had decided, was too big to take.

And now for good or ill he had come to this gate instead.

It could be seen at once that the civil police on duty there were on special alert. Surprisingly, it seemed to him, there had apparently been no general order to stop people coming into the city. Instead they were being stopped and questioned and he saw one man, riding a mule like himself, forced to open his saddlebag while it was searched for arms.

There were a lot of country folk coming in. These would be people who had held their eve of Passover feast at home rather than with friends or relatives in the city. Hop could see them crowding beyond the gate, some of them waiting patiently, others gesticulating in protest at the delay. He had reckoned that by this time there would be many people leaving the city, hurrying home to the country before the breaking of the expected storm, like those he had seen earlier hurrying home in the streets. To his dismay it was not so.

There seemed to be two or three people on foot going his way and pushing past those who were coming in. But he was the only rider. And it seemed to him his tall, exceptional mule must catch the eye of every policeman and spy in sight, causing them to give its rider a second and unwelcome look. He felt himself the target of such looks as he was forced to wait while the police corporal who ought to have been dealing with him finished his examination of the saddlebags of the other man on the mule.

That other man sat there calm, resigned, without apprehension. His whole attitude and expression betokened innocence in a convincing manner. Hop told himself that he must imitate that man's air and manner. What he could do Hop could do. But after all it was easy for this other man—he really did not have any weapons in his saddlebags. Before Hop had time dangerously to reflect on the kind of weapon he had in his own head the corporal came over to him.

Where was he going? He named a place half a day's ride away on the road to Joppa. He himself, he explained, was a native of Joppa. He had come up to the city for the Passover but almost immediately on arrival had received news from a later traveller that his married sister in the village named, who had been in poor health when he passed through on his way up to the city, had taken a turn for the worse and he was returning to be at what he feared might be her death bed.

For a moment, while the corporal seemed to be considering this story, Hop was so sharply aware of his own real purposes that the story seemed absurd to himself.

Also he had the idea that perhaps the corporal was not really considering his answers at all, but had received a signal from some other policeman or spy who had recognized Hop by an official description, and was simply waiting for a sergeant or some other superior to come and make an arrest. This possibility became so real to him that the immediate future blazed up at him in a ghastly mirage. He saw his arrest, his imprisonment in the guard house, the seizure of his mule, cross-questioning by some high-up police official in the city, and time passing, slipping away, lost for ever with nothing accomplished.

Now he saw the corporal glaring at him angrily and making a sharp gesture. The mirage had been so vivid that for a stupid moment Hop thought that this was the arrest and that he was being told to dismount. Then with astonishment he grasped that the corporal was simply signalling him to move on, and glaring because he was slow to obey.

Then the corporal, nervous on account of the general alert, was shouting: 'Get on with it! Get going!' As the large beast walked forward Hop controlled a crazy spasm of laughter, hearing the policeman telling him again, to get going, to get on with his business. 'You see,' he muttered wildly to the mule, 'we are under police orders. They are instructing us to do what we have set out to do.'

He jogged the mule into a quick walk. Up to now he had thought of the exceptional build of the creature as a liability. Now feeling its strength under him and the length of its stride he regarded it with love and admiration such as he would have for a good boat on a sea that could turn stormy. He looked at the sun and at the shadows of trees and shrubs still growing shorter. For a long while yet he would have to go further from the city and further from Jericho or wherever it was on the Jericho road that Mr Jericho had established his headquarters and was waiting.

In the sharp sunlight he could hear quite distinctly that last word that had floated to him through the darkness as Mr Jericho left the barn. 'Hurry!'

He wondered again if he had not made a mistake in avoiding the direct route. The passage through the gate had been so simple, so harmlessly easy. It could have been the same at the other gate. The thought gave him a pang of guilt. It was as though by taking this particular decision, unnecessarily as it seemed now, he had wasted time and by so doing betrayed something or other. The stab of guilt was so sharp that he made to push the mule into a trot. Then he controlled himself. To start trotting now would appear suspicious to the police at the gate if they were watching. If he had made a mistake he had made it. The danger of a mistake was that having made it, the realization that it had been a mistake frightened you into making another. He let the mule keep on walking.

He arranged the problem in his head in a geometrical manner. It was a question of moving north-west on his present course, far enough to be clear of the city not only on this route, but later when he turned eastwards. But no further than that. Every unnecessary step to the north-west was a waste of time. The steepness, sometimes extreme, of the road's ups and downs made it difficult to calculate accurately how long it would take to go how far. Years ago he had once travelled this road and he figured that about two hours' riding at the fast walking pace of the mule would get him to the point where he could turn east. He thought, but was not sure that he remembered rightly, that at the place he was thinking of there was some kind of track running across country eastwards. Having settled on that immediate objective, he became daunted by the thought of the next two hours. Danger could jump on him at any time. There could be a Civil Police patrol or a patrol of the Roman mounted police, such as he had seen the previous day, or possibly—his imagination painting things black—a village or even big farm where people had been made suspicious and hostile to strangers by rumours of trouble in the city, of miscreants such as Friend's Wife had envisaged prowling the land.

The dangers were bad, and worse was that there was nothing he could do to prepare against them. He jogged uphill and downhill, thinking of nothing but the pace and distance and the time of day told him by his informative shadow, rippling out slantways from a point between his own right knee and the large right ear of the mule.

The shadow had considerably shrunk and shrivelled when, topping a ridge, and looking down the slope ahead, he saw that there was a fair track leading from his road away to the east.

He was sure that he was still some way from the point at which he had it in mind to turn, but suddenly his impatience to be at least headed towards the Jericho road became urgent. So urgent that instead of proceeding along the road to the point where the track left it, he abruptly pulled the mule to the right and urged it forward across the rough and stony scrubland, so as to join the track where it dipped out of sight without following the two sides of the triangle made by the road and the track. An experienced rider, co-operating fully with the mule, he found it a relief to have his attention concentrated on negotiating at the best pace reasonable this pathless patch of scrubby territory. Or, he had just time to think before he reached the track, perhaps his ears were making long distance signals to him without him being entirely aware of it.

For at that moment with a sharp stab of alarm he heard the irregular fall of hoofs coming fast up the far slope of the ridge he had just breasted. He kicked the mule into a trot, reached the point where the track dipped, looked back quickly once to make sure that he must now be invisible from the road itself, and sat as rigid to look at as Lot's wife, but a great deal more lively. Questions with no answers vibrated in his head. Go forward quickly and put more ground between him and whoever was on the road? That might be the thing to do, for the pace he had heard them moving at assured him that these were no casual travellers. They were people chasing something. But he had no idea of the lie of the land. A sudden rise might bring him into view of those chasers.

Or dismount, and lie low?

The size of the mule under him, and its great head before him, made that hazardous. So stay here, rigidly still, waiting for the huntsmen to pass—or not pass—the turn-off point of the track from the road. Now they were coming down the slope, three or four of them he judged, and the rhythm of their hoofs telling that they were no rabble of riders, but men riding in formation. Now it seemed they must have reached the turn-off point and gone on past it, but perhaps his hopeful ears were misleading him. He waited and there was no check in the pound of the hoofs, the sound of them was getting less. Perhaps they had sighted him far back and been so close that they were sure that if he had turned off he would have been still in sight. And so he would have been if he had followed the two sides of the triangle.

He shivered and began to sweat.

So the description of him had reached that gate and the corporal had remembered him and the hunters been sent on his tracks. The moment of shivering fright passed and his spirits lifted. Now he was a fox running on its own, unmistakably a wild verminous thing. There were no more stories to invent. What respectable businessman would be trekking all by himself across this great empty tract on a path probably used only by shepherds? From now on at any threat of interference or chase it would be run, hide or fight, no other choice. In the meantime the essential was to get the top speed out of the mule that he could without risking a laming stumble or fall. The track being alternately dangerous going and smoothly even gave the mule an opportunity to demonstrate that it was not merely a physical showpiece but of an intelligence as remarkable as its size. A unique mule for Hop who had known many mules. A gift from God.

Once or twice as he rode, with the huntsmen somewhere out there looking for him, he remembered the sight of the Essene tearing down from Ephraim to Bethany. Now he was in the Praetorium. But Hop had never been there and his thoughts could not follow him or picture what things would be like. His imagination drew for him a grotesque scene of the Essene still on his horse—for that was the only way he could picture him—before a half-circle of huge-headed Romans, all of them having the head of Caesar on the coins.

He thought of the questioning and answering that had taken place when he was first brought before Mr Jericho, police chief of that city. But Mr Jericho was certainly no Roman. Hop had never been questioned by that class of Roman. He could not begin to imagine what they would be saying just now to the Essene, or what the Essene would be answering to them. He had no notion either of how long such proceedings might go on. He knew very little of Roman law except insofar as it concerned a peaceable businessman and his commercial dealings. He knew in a crude general way that the end point of crimes such as the Essene now presumably stood accused of was flogging followed by crucifixion. But how long did there have to be between the stage things might be supposed to be at now and that point?

He said out loud, 'Hurry!' and the mule was hurrying.

Wiping out the picture of the Essene and these Roman heads came a recollection of an old story. A fussy, impatient traveller hires a mule and says to it, 'How long will you take to get me to Heborn?', or Beer-Sheba, or wherever it might be. And the mule says, 'Taking it fast four hours; taking it gently, three.'

Around mid-day he began to think about water for the creature. Certainly it could go on for hours yet without any, but it would be the fresher for a drink. And suppose there were more than just two or three hours to go before there was any hope of getting in touch with Mr Jericho's men? It was half an hour before the mule made it known by movements of its head and snorting of its nostrils that it had smelled water, unless it had smelled people.

It was water.

The mule drank from a small hill stream and Hop drank wine from his flask. He walked about a little to ease his riding muscles and munched on a hunk of bread. Gently, gently because of the story, hurrying, hurrying because of the need, they went on while the sun sank half-way to the horizon behind them and threw the shadow of Hop's head on the road in front between the shadows of the mule's ears. Sometime in that late afternoon Hop thought he began to recognize the contours of the country lying a little to the north of the Jerusalem–Jericho road.

In the last few miles the track had almost disappeared and the safe pace had been desperately slow. Now they would have to go slowly anyway, not on account of the ground underfoot, but to give Hop a chance to scan the landscape: looking out for the hostile figures perhaps fanning out from the road or, even as soon as this, for Mr Jericho's advance scouts. In the slanting light of the sun behind him he could see a long way. He saw nothing moving. He pressed on, following what there was of the track, but careful to watch that it did not bring him out suddenly within sight of the road somewhere to the south.

There were others about more experienced than he. Two

dark-faced men had jumped from nowhere. They came out of brushwood beside the track, one coming from each side of it, and now each of them had a hold of the mule's bridle and the one who was holding it with his left hand had a sword in his right. The mule made an angry protest with his head and violently jolted Hop in the saddle as it lashed out with its hind legs. The two men held on, keeping their eyes on Hop. One of them spoke soothingly to the mule in muleteer's lingo. It calmed itself. The staring inspection by the man with the sword was different from the glare of the corporal at the gate. Inspecting in his turn, Hop recognized the familiar badges of the Jericho police. And the swordsman said, 'Are you the man they call Hop?'

At the words, and during the short exchange that followed, Hop felt as though an almost unbelievable magic carpet had appeared and was already about to carry him with miraculous speed towards his objective. They were going to take him to Mr Jericho. While the swordsman stood beside him, still holding the bridle of the mule, the other policeman disappeared into the thickets, and after no long time came back with two horses which had been concealed as expertly as their riders. They moved off in single file, Hop and the mule between the two horsemen.

The swordsman said there was no danger from the Garrison patrols. This territory was clear of them. Sometime in the late morning they had taken themselves off, heading, other scouts had reported, for the city. Hop made calculations in his head. So whatever was happening there to alarm the Romans and make them send for reinforcements was still happening, or had been until a quite short time ago. His sense of urgency became truly painful. Something in the shape of the landscape made him suddenly call out to the policeman ahead of him. 'Where are we going?' The policeman seemed not to hear, and rode on saying nothing until they came to a place where the path broadened so that he could let his horse drop back until he was alongside Hop's mule. Then he said, 'You want to know where we're going? We're going to the place they call the Inn of the Knower. Funny name. Seems the boss man there is one of those sects or whatever it is they call the Knowers.'

Hop looked surprised enough for the man to add, 'The

Chief's kind of taken it over. Nice place for a headquarters. That is if we've got to be near the big city.'

'He's there? The Chief?'

'In and out and round about,' said the policeman. 'Mostly in. Has his couple of aides there, gets messages, reports and whatever.'

Hop cursed himself. If he had known that, he could have taken a chance on coming out by the nearest gate and would have been at the inn hours ago. With such a short distance to cover it would have been worth the risk perhaps. Instead of which he had gone circling round trying to reach the Jericho road at the place Mr Jericho had said he would be at that night in the barn.

He cursed Mr Jericho too.

Then, he reflected, the situation was changing all the time and what way could there have been for Mr Jericho to send word to him about the change of plan? But the thought of all those hours spent on the road hurt him like a stomach ache. He wanted to question the policemen. But he had no idea of how much Mr Jericho's men knew of his plans even at this late hour. He was afraid that any question of his might give something away. He jogged on silently and they were on the path to the inn and at the gate of the wall, waiting while one of the policemen pushed it open and shut it again and then moving across the field towards the untidy little buildings at the back of the inn itself.

Creating the illusion that nothing had happened since the night when Hop had come with Alpha and Simon of Sachem and Joshua on their flight from Jericho, the Babylonian wobbled bearishly to meet them exactly as he had then. He led the way along the passages to the big room where the music and the dancing had been. When Hop had last seen it it had been a room full of the disorder and smell of a room just vacated by very numerous people. Now it was in order, but seemed utterly empty as though even the couches and cushions and low tables might soon be carried out and the place finally abandoned. The two policemen went on across the room and out, leaving Hop alone with the Babylonian who said:

'As you see, we are now under the high protection of the Jericho police. They are thieves of course. All policemen are. Not more so by instinct than other people but their low pay forces them to steal, plunder and extort. I have nothing for them or against them; I would say they are opportunists. They certainly are not here to make my inn flourish.'

'But perhaps they make it safer?'

'Safe? Safer? What words to use at this time. Or, if you understand life the way it is, at any time. I never asked to be put under the protection of the man from Jericho any more than I asked to be thrown into this life, this world. In the prison of this world one cell is like another, one situation like another. To deceive and bemuse us, the Archons by their artifice and guile try to pretend that one thing in this world is better than another, one thing worse than another. In prison when you're moved from one cell to another you are at first delighted because the new cell has a window and the other had none. But just as you are thinking how you have bettered yourself and are staring with admiration at the window you find you are up to your ankles in water, whereas the previous cell had a dry floor. There are particular differences but no general differences.'

Oppressed by the emptiness of the room Hop said, 'And your woman, Helena? She is gone?' for he had the sense that the whole place must be empty.

'I have her locked away in a part of the inn where the police will not think of looking for her. You will think perhaps it should be her role to offer herself to them, to submit to them. But just at the present time and in their present mood I apprehend that if she is going to lay her frame down for them, they will start fighting over her among themselves before her role is accomplished; they would kill each other and there would be a lot of senseless trouble. They might even kill her and I do not think that is her proper fate.'

The Babylonian's florid talk in the emptiness of the room afflicted Hop with the sensation of having been dropped through some hole in reality into a void; far, far away from events roaring and grinding to some conclusion in the fury and pain of the city. Exasperated and restless he said, 'And Mr Jericho? Where the hell is he?'

The Babylonian spread his arms wide and counselled patience in a maddening flow of words. The police who had brought Hop in would have gone no doubt to find the Chief who could not be far away, seeing perhaps to the dispositions of his forces, he would be here soon to get the news.

'He has had only one message from the city. The messenger reported that the first man who had tried to make his way here was killed within a few yards of the city walls. Then they closed the gates, I don't know just how that man got out.'

'Damn how he got out,' said Hop, 'what did he say, what news did he bring?'

'Only that the Essene had been arrested and brought, the man thought, before some Roman court specially got together to deal with this case. He said all indications were that the Romans are in a state of very great nervousness and alarm.'

'I know that. But what about what's causing the alarm? What about the people? What did he say of the rising?'

The Babylonian shrugged. He said, 'Perhaps Mr Jericho with his great military and political experience can evaluate what the man said. To me it was all confusion. Though whether the confusion was in the man's mind or was there in the streets I can't say.'

Hop walked furiously about the room, took a long drink from a pitcher of strong liquor offered him by the Babylonian and started towards the interior doorway saying he would go and look for the messenger and cross-question him himself.

'No need,' said the Babylonian. 'I can hear him coming, Mr Jericho I mean. I should know his step by now.'

Walking elegantly with his head in the air, Mr Jericho stepped into the room. Hop strode quickly, almost running, to meet him, shouting out a greeting and questions altogether, his depression and loneliness blown away in the wind of his excitement as though now real life were starting again and going to move fast. Talking as elegantly as he walked, Mr Jericho seated himself on a couch and signalled to Hop to sit down beside him. At the same moment the Babylonian got to his feet, arranged the jug of liquor and drinking mugs on a table before the couch, and went rolling out of the room. Mr Jericho looked after him for a moment and then down at his own thigh which had suddenly been gripped just above the knee by Hop's big hand with the sinews standing out on it. He looked at it as though his attention had suddenly been drawn to somebody else's leg that had been gripped by an impetuous big hand. Then he turned towards Hop's face thrust forward on a neck straining with eagerness, the eyes blazing excitedly, the lips moving wordlessly to control the torrent of words behind them. Mr Jericho smiled at the other man as though he was smiling at a boy who had rushed up to him, bubbling uncontrollably with some boyish piece of news.

As he told the Police Chief how he had seen the Essene, talked with him and laid before him the plan; how the Essene had at once caught fire, had instructed him to go immediately to Mr Jericho and inform him that if he moved at once, there would be fullest co-ordination with the rising in the city; as he poured out all this, Hop had no sense of acting a part, of inventing anything. He vehemently and hallucinatedly believed that this was what had happened, just as it ought to have happened.

As he went on to tell of the things he really had seen—the great holiday crowds aimless in the streets, the sudden coming of the knife men, the withdrawal of the Romans from the gates, the general aspects of these streets and squares, his words came faster and faster.

'And all that time,' he said, forgetting that he only imagined this without the possibility of knowing it at all exactly, 'there was the Essene at the Praetorium, before the Roman court. All those Romans, like the face on the coins, you know.'

Mr Jericho listened, looking straight ahead of him.

'So you see,' Hop concluded, excitedly gripping that thin thigh as though confirming a promise. Like a boy waiting with his mouth half open for what the other would say, he sat gripping the thigh and waited, the muscles on his neck strained and tense.

Still not looking directly at him, Mr Jericho said, 'For how long were you in the city after the beginning of these,' he paused, hesitating for a word, 'disturbances?'

Hop told him.

'And approximately how long do you reckon, roughly speaking, that it is since you left the city to come here?'

Hop told him, explaining why it had taken so long.

'I see,' said Mr Jericho, and fell silent again, playing with the loose end of his girdle.

CHAPTER SEVENTEEN

This 'I see' seemed to hang in the empty air for a moment. Then Hop said:

'So you can see that with the masses of the people rising in the city, led by these organized groups of knife-men, your men, properly trained, as well armed as the Romans, when they go into action will be decisive. The Romans can't stand against those two forces working together.'

Mr Jericho said, 'Thank you. I recognize the quotation from myself.'

His quiet aloof tone, as though there were time to chat quietly, moved Hop to say roughly, 'So in my opinion there's no time to lose. That's obvious, isn't it?' He was breathing now into Mr Jericho's face. He put his hand on the man's shoulder, as though he were going to take a grip on him and lift him off the couch. The police chief made a small, shrug, releasing his shoulder, and inclined his head, resting it gracefully on his hand. Hop leaned back a little himself, and watched and listened.

Mr Jericho said that it was, of course, unfortunate that only one of his own men—and he not among the best informed—had until now reported on the state of the affairs in the city. The others seemed stupidly to have been taken by surprise when the Romans ordered the closing of the gates. Presumably they had quite under-estimated the extent of the Roman panic.

But they were able and experienced men. They could be relied on to find early ways and means to circumvent the impediments placed in the way of communication between them and himself. Up-to-date reports would come. It was self-evident that to act without benefit of such reports would be frivolous; could even mean disaster for, Mr Jericho said, 'our common cause'. But let Hop be in no doubt that such reports, providing a reliable basis for action, would surely come. He did not for one moment under-estimate the value of Hop's very, very vivid and colourful account of events. But clearly it was not, inevitably could not be an account of the situation as it had developed in the long period between Hop's departure from the city and the present time.

'You will understand,' said Mr Jericho, 'that in the circumstances it would be not merely rash but criminal on my part to risk the life of even a single one of the men under my command in a random plunge into unplumbed waters.'

Hop's mouth twisted in a sharp grimace.

'You said what?' he said unpleasantly.

'I was trying to explain that I, as their commander, enjoying as I do the unquestioning loyalty of my men, can certainly not honourably take the responsibility of leading them recklessly into a situation of which I have had no opportunity to inform myself sufficiently. I should never,' he concluded, resting his head on his hand and speaking with solemnity, 'forgive myself.'

Hop made a dry, spitting noise with his lips. He said:

'I didn't hear so much about your responsibilities to the rank-and-file the other night there in the barn. I tell you those people are on the move. Now's the time, and the hell with waiting for more reports.'

After a little pause, Mr Jericho, speaking as though he had heard almost nothing of what Hop had been shouting, said:

'Tell me, what does this Essene really look like? I never saw him so to speak face to face, as you did. How does he talk when he's not preaching to the multitudes?'

What disgusting police instinct, Hop asked himself, had enabled the man even to suspect that Hop had never had that interview just before the Essene was arrested? Had never had the chance to put the plan to him? He pretended to ponder on the best way of summing up the appearance and manner of the Essene in private conversation. All the time his thoughts were muddled by the flashing recollection of the only view he had ever had of the Essene: the figure riding furiously on the road from Ephraim.

He said lamely, 'Nothing so very special about him. Talks like dozens of other people of the same sort.'

Mr Jericho said, 'Curious. I had heard otherwise.'

He sat, thinking ostentatiously. 'Well,' he said, as though

business had now been satisfactorily concluded, 'so you see there's nothing we can do but wait. Always so hard,' he added as he went across the room, 'for active men like ourselves.'

Night had fallen before the next messenger came. The Babylonian announced the fact to Hop. 'He is with that Chief now,' said the Babylonian. 'Seems he couldn't get through till after dark.'

'So the Romans must still be in control of the gates.'

'It would take more than a mob to drive them out of there,' said the Babylonian. 'It would need a proper assault force.'

'So the news can't be good.'

'We shall know soon.'

'He'll lie to me.'

'Probably. But you'll know all the same. D'you think I, proprietor of this famous inn and hostelry, would allow plottings and machinations to be devised under its roof without taking steps to apprise myself of them, by cunning, artifice and guile? He has chosen to take over this place as his Headquarters. I have chosen to arrange for him to be secretly overheard. Helena is skilled in concealments and stratagems. She will hear it all.'

'So that business of hiding her from the police? This was the real reason.'

'What I told you could have been true, too. Every knife can be given a double edge.'

'Has the messenger been here long?'

'No. We have to wait.'

'Wait, wait, wait,' said Hop.

'I'll bring lamps. It may be a long wait. Other messengers may come.'

They did. Three in all, at intervals of an hour or more. Helena, said the Babylonian, could not leave her listening-post. He waddled in and out with this information, disappearing, perhaps to listen too. 'You should sleep,' the Babylonian told him. 'You may yet have need of great activity.'

'Sleep?'

'Sleep can be an indispensable factor in survival.'

'But...'

'So what else can you do for your Essene or whatever?'

Hop growled at him, stretched out and slept a little, came awake by fits and starts, and slept a little again.

The night was turning pale when the Babylonian woke him.

Here was the news: as of some time between midnight and dawn. The Roman court, after some hours' recess, had convened again at the Praetorium. At one point one of the High Priests—Caiaphas, the messenger thought, but was uncertain, being a stranger to Jerusalem—had apparently been summoned in a hurry to give evidence. It was supposed, Mr Jericho's informant said, that the Romans would want to mobilize support from that quarter.

In the city there had been sporadic rioting at intervals throughout the day. Minor clashes with the police, with casualties, some fatal, on both sides. By early afternoon a very large crowd, headed by organized bands of armed men, had converged on the neighbourhood of the Praetorium. After prolonged tussles with the soldiery, culminating in what amounted to a pitched battle in which an unknown number were killed and many more badly hurt, the crowd moved across town to the prison where Barabbas was held. They tried to storm the jail, demanding Barabbas's release. But the assault on the jail had been defeated, at least for the time being.

So far as could be judged, the rebellious elements were in more or less effective control of extensive areas of the city, and it was impossible for police or military to penetrate those areas. On the other hand in many sections the mass of the populace appeared almost indifferent to the latest events. The disturbance of the traditional Passover holiday was widely resented. After the first repulse of the main attacks on the Praetorium and the jail, it was not as yet clear whether the leaders of the militant elements were adopting strictly defensive positions, or were organizing some renewed major attack.

The usual rumours were circulating to the effect that outside help from unspecified sources was on its way. Some, at least, of these rumours had been spread by one of the Essene's most active followers who had actually been overheard proclaiming to one group of militants after another that 'armed forces from Jericho' were on their way. The very latest reports, necessarily speculative and to be treated with caution, were that the Romans were going to rush the court proceedings to a conclusion before morning, and have the sentence carried out that very afternoon.

Hop said, 'Where is he? The police Chief?'

'I'll find out.'

Hop raged about the room. He found himself listening alertly, as though expecting at any moment to hear a sound here or there that would mean something. The Babylonian returned followed by a servant bringing bread and wine.

'What is he doing?' Hop snapped at him. 'What's he saying?'

'His aides are coming and going. I think, my friend, that unless within a short time, a few hours at most, he hears of some big movement of the people in the city, our guest will leave us for the place whence he came. That is the impression gained from his confabulations with his aides.'

Quite late in that long day the news came suddenly. The Babylonian reported that the Chief of Police had given orders for his men to be ready to move off, withdrawing towards Jericho within the hour.

'They'll obey, of course,' said Hop stupidly.

'Of course. I don't think they've any idea why they were brought up here in the first place. Of course they know that the first patrols were sent to chase you and your friends. But I understand they believe now that the reason the main force was brought up here was to be at hand to go into the city and give support to the Roman garrison if needed.'

'They believe that?'

'Some of them may have guessed the truth. What does it matter to us what they believe?'

Hop put his head in his hands and sat with his shoulders sagging. The Babylonian spoke to him sharply.

'No time for that,' he said. 'Suppose he thinks you know too much to be left alive—or at any rate to be left here? More likely, of course, that he, in his guileful mentality and ratiocination will consider it best not to make talk among his men by having you killed or kidnapped. He will calculatingly estimate that the Romans would never believe your story anyhow. Even if they did, they would not know anything they didn't suspect already. They may act against the police chief, or they may deem it cleverest to keep him there, subject to blackmail. But these speculations are too flimsy to risk your life on. You must disappear.'

'And you?'

'On this occasion, the inn-keeper, too, will be absent from the door speeding the parting guest. In the meantime, you must be buried. In the secret bowels of this inn.'

Hop, lying on a couch in the silent underground room, to which the Babylonian had brought him, had no means of telling how much time was passing. Despite the lamp on the floor beside him, he felt blind as well as deaf. He said aloud to himself, 'I might as well be in my grave.'

He said, 'But this is no grave. I'm alive. I have to think of what has to be done next.'

As though otherwise he might have evaded it, smudged it, distorted it in his mind, he continued putting the situation into words muttered to himself. No doubt, no doubt at all, the revolt had failed. Probably the Essene was already condemned. Might already be on his way to execution. And Mr Jericho was on his way back to Jericho. So he, Hop, was a link from nowhere to nowhere. A man on his own. A man on his own and on the run. The Romans looking for him. Not safe here, or in Sachem, or anywhere in this country. Must cross the border. To Egypt. If only Alpha were here he would know how such a crossing was best made. They would be after Alpha too. Perhaps he had already started by some secret route to Egypt.

From Egypt Hop must get word to Sarah in Sachem. He must consult the Babylonian. Where was he? He waited in a long fury of impatience.

When at last he came to the underground place, and told that the place was clear of police, and led the way up a passageway which opened into a piece of waste land, Hop was dazed by darkness. It was already night, and there were thick clouds over the moon.

'One of your friends is here,' said the Babylonian.

'Alpha?' Hop said eagerly.

'No. Not him. I think something happened to him. This is the one we called the Galilean. He's in poor shape. It seems he has witnessed the demise of his Master.'

'The Essene is dead?'

The Babylonian nodded and walked on towards one of the outbuildings. Against a wall, the Galilean was standing looking as rigid and lifeless as a pole hung with loose clothing. He seemed to be mouthing words. For a time Hop could understand nothing of what he was trying to say. When they had got him across to a bench and made him drink, he kept being shaken by shudders, and his usually puzzled eyes looked not just puzzled but nearly crazy.

'Now you must tell. It's your duty to tell,' said the Babylonian in a tone of stern authority.

The Galilean began to talk, or rather to mumble and ramble and from time to time break down with shudders.

'There were big crowds. But they did nothing. Too many soldiers.' 'Soldiers where?' 'On the way to where they crucified him and around the crosses.'

He stopped and looked dazedly about him. He suffered a convulsion of his face and body. The Babylonian hit him sharply on the cheek with the flat of his hand.

'And so? You saw him crucified?'

'Not being raised on the cross. But a little afterwards. Three of them together.'

He looked suddenly at Hop as though aware of him for the first time.

'Your friend was there too.'

'Friend? The Sicarius?'

'Not him. The other. The one you called Alpha.'

Hop moved his hand back and forth across his face.

'How?' he asked dully. 'Why? What for?'

'They caught him thieving. He had a knife. Armed robbery. He had a lot of previous convictions the men in that crowd said. They said he was the sort that was born to be hanged.' He stopped and looked furiously at Hop. 'Why do you ask about him? What about him? The Master is dead.'

The Babylonian sat thoughtfully and said, 'There was no disturbance? No trouble with the soldiers?'

'None. No one did anything.'

His convulsion came again. The Babylonian said, 'You understand what it means? The Romans have won all along the line. Very soon, my friend, they will be here. We must none of us be here when they come.'

'Not you, either? And Helena?'

'Not either of us. After the things that have happened in this inn the Romans would...'

He broke off and moved away in a strangely businesslike manner. On his return he said:

'I have made necessary arrangements for you to start on your journey. Southwards, I venture to imagine. A man from the stables who must get away too will guide you on the way. He understands such things. If you are willing, if he is fit to move, you can take that Galilean with you.'

'And you?' Hop asked again. 'And Helena?'

The Babylonian seemed to swell before his eyes as he had seen him swell before, like a great frog. His voice rose into something more like a chant than ordinary speech.

'We shall not stay for the torturers. We shall show them a miracle. When they come, we shall be upon the topmost roof-beam of the house. They will think us surrounded, but we shall not be surrounded. There will be one way out that they cannot block or bar. The way upwards. Outwards. For ever.'

'What way is that?'

'The way of fire. Unknown to them, before going up on to the topmost beam of the house, I shall have already set fire to the house, using all my artifice and cunning so that the flames will reach us, will enfold us, will bear us away before any soldier can move. They will have to stand there, and look on at the escape of the Knowers.'

Hop stood silent.

Just before the man from the stable appeared to guide him and the Galilean on the first steps of their journey, he said, the thought just striking him:

'What about that first messenger that came? The one that was blinded.'

'He died here two days ago,' said the Babylonian. 'Now it is time for you to go.'

The Galilean seemed not to understand. They had trouble getting him to his feet, and explaining to him he had to walk a long way to the place where mules would be ready.

They were still urging him, when there came from beyond the inn on the city side a great barking of dogs.

'Go,' shouted the Babylonian. 'They are coming.... Drag him or leave him.' He was gone.

Pulling the Galilean between them, Hop and the stable-man made their way hurried and stumbling across the dark field. The mules, said their guide, were tethered down in the glen. They started down, forced to go slowly, stumbling and slithering. They reached the bottom at last. While they were still busy about the mules the stableman seemed suddenly to see or hear something behind them. He pointed back, up the hillside. There was a quick faint movement of light in the darkness. Then the light grew steadier and brighter.

The stableman stared in a kind of ecstasy. He said, 'She will be singing now. They are standing there on the rim of the world.'

Hop stood staring with him. They thought they could see not only light, but even the tips of flames. Then the stableman said there was no time to be lost. They must be on the move at once. They had a long way to go.

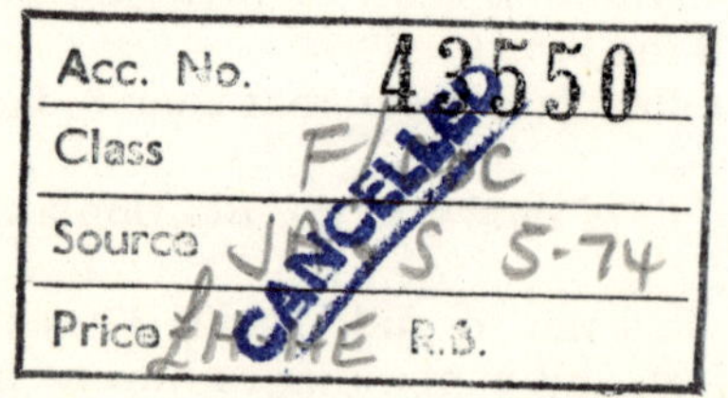